To C

Best Wishes
Enjoy this Rat
Whitey Bulger

WHITEY BULGER: THE BIGGEST RAT

By
Joe Bruno

Joe Bruno

Copyright © 2013 Joe Bruno. All rights reserved. No part of this book may be used or reproduced in any manner whatsoever without written permission except in the case of brief quotations embodied in critical articles and reviews.

Published by: Knickerbocker Publishing Co.

Editor: Lawrence Venturato

Cover By: Alchemy Covers

Formatting by Anessa Books

ISBN-10:1492901199
ISBN-13:9781492901198

"RATS ARE NOT MADE; PEOPLE ARE BORN RATS."

- Mathew J. Mari, New York City Criminal Attorney for 36 years

Chapter One
"You know who I am. I'm Whitey Bulger."

The first time aspiring musician Joshua Bond met "America's Most Wanted Fugitive," Whitey Bulger, Bond knew the spry 77-year-old retiree as plain old Charlie Gasko.

In 2007, the 26-year-old Bond had just moved to Santa Monica, California with plans of getting involved in the in the Hollywood film business or music business, whichever came first. Bond played guitar in a band called the Kings. Since work was hard to come by, he needed a way to pay the rent and keep food on the table while he pursued his dreams. As a result, Bond took a job as co-manager of the Princess Eugenia Apartments where he received free living quarters in apartment 304, as one of the perks that came with the job. His next-door neighbor, living in apartment 303, was Charlie Gasko and his wife Carol (real name Catherine Greig).

Bond liked to play the guitar in his apartment, sometimes loud enough to be heard clearly through the walls into apartment 303. One day, after playing a particularly stirring riff, Bond heard a knock on his apartment door. This was the first time this phenomenon had occurred, and Bond figured he was about to get a neighborly complaint about the noise. When Bond opened the door, he came face to face with the man he knew as "Charlie" from next door. Bond recoiled, waiting to receive a string of obscenities. Instead, he received a gift.

While Bond stood there quivering, Whitey told Bond

he was fond of his music, which was a cross between country western and the blues. That said, Whitey handed Bond a black wool Stetson hat, sporting a leather band sprinkled with silver buttons.

"I don't wear this hat anymore," Whitey told Bond. "I think maybe you could use it."

Bond, tickled pink at the lack of a reprimand, eagerly accepted the hat, and then he bid Whitey goodbye.

But it was not goodbye for long.

Whitey developed the habit of knocking on Bond's door at least twice a week, supposedly to make small talk. The truth is, Bulger, on the run for more than a decade, didn't trust anybody, and he wanted to know all he could about everything connected to the Princess Eugenia Apartments. To Whitey, being pals with the co-manager was simply good business acumen.

Whitey, being Whitey, found it difficult not to intrude on his young friend without bearing gifts, whether Bond needed them or not. Whitey gave Bond a beard trimmer; a subtle hint maybe Bond was looking a little too scruffy, and Whitey didn't like scruffy.

Whitey was a fitness buff, and he thought Bond was a little out of shape for a man fifty years his junior. So, Whitey dipped into his retirement savings and bought Bond a weight set, complete with a bench and a stomach-crunching thingamajig.

Over the years, Whitey was diligent about taking good care of the assistant manager of the Princess Eugenia Apartments. During the Christmas holidays, instead of cash, Whitey one year bequeathed Bond a spiffy decorative plate, another year he gave Bond an Elvis Presley coffee table (no musician should ever be without one).

However, Whitey was a bit gruff. He insisted on proper decorum when it came to Bond recognizing his benevolence. One holiday season, Whitey left a bag full of

Christmas presents at Bond's door. Later, when Whitey and Bonds crossed paths in the underground garage, Bond nary mentioned a word about the gifts. This pissed off Whitey, leading him to reprimand Bond for his lack of respect, even going as far as to "suggest" Bond jot him and Carol a sincere thank-you note. Bond duly complied, kissing off the incident off as nothing more than an old man asking for his due.

During the period from 2007 to 2011, Bond and Whitey maintained a friendly relationship. An uncle/nephew type of rapport developed between the two, where Whitey dispensed advice and Bond made believe he took it. Whitey seemed like a nice elderly man, but Bond was only interested in his music career. Putting up with Whitey was part of the job of being co-manager of the Princess Eugenia Apartments. Bond humored Whitey, and Whitey ate up what seemed to be the young man's deference to Whitey's superior intellect and lifelong experiences.

Bond knew of only one instance where old Charlie Gasko indicated he was capable of violence, and this was because Whitey told Bond about the incident himself.

The Ocean View Manor, a state-licensed residential facility for the mentally disabled, was located a few doors down from Princess Eugenia Apartments. Mentally ill people sometimes do strange things. One resident in particular got his jollies by hiding in the bushes near the facility, and then springing out at an unsuspecting passerby to scare him out of his skin.

One night, as was his wont, Whitey took his moll, Catherine Greig, on a late-night fitness stroll. Suddenly, the eccentric from the Ocean View Manor bounded from the bushes, intending to scare Whitey and Greig.

But Whitey doesn't scare easily.

Whitey told Bond, when the lunatic rushed at him and his wife, Whitey, who always kept a big knife strapped to his ankle, grabbed the man by the neck, pulled out his knife, waved it in the man's face, and said, "If you ever do that to me again, I will cut you to pieces."

Fast-forward to June 22, 2011.

Bond had plans to go to a concert in Hollywood that evening with his pal, Neal Marsh, to see the band, My Morning Jacket. The other co-manager of the Princess Eugenia Apartments, Birgitta Farinelli, had gone on vacation. So, Bond told his assistant, Thea, to substitute for him at the manager's desk, located in the hotel across the street from Princess Eugenia Apartments, while Bond sawed a few afternoon Z's on his apartment couch.

At about 3:30 p.m., Bond's phone rang, rousing him from a deep sleep. Thea was on the line and told him F.B.I. agents were in his office. The feds said they needed to speak to Bond immediately about one of the tenants.

This unwelcome intrusion into his afternoon nap did not please Bond. He planned to motor off to Hollywood in a few hours and didn't appreciate any unnecessary distractions.

Thea handed the phone to F.B.I. agent, Scott Garriola, who told Bond that it was imperative that he come to the office immediately, if not sooner.

"Can't this wait until tomorrow?" Bond asked.

"No, it can't," Garriola said. "I need you here now!"

Knowing you don't argue with the feds, Bond dragged himself off his couch, splashed a little water on his face, and then exited his apartment. When he reached the manager's office, Bond met Garriola and another federal agent. The agents showed Bond a string of photos of the couple Bond knew as Charlie and Carol Gasko. The Feds asked Bond if he could confirm their identities and he did so.

"Yes, I know them," Bond told Garriola. "That's Charlie and Carol from apartment 303."

"Are you absolutely sure?" Garriola asked.

I'm Whitey Bulger

"Definitely; that's them," Bond said.

Garriola told Bond who his neighbors really were, including the information that Whitey was alleged to be a serial murderer. Garriola wanted to arrest Whitey outside his apartment because Whitey's M.O. indicated he kept an arsenal of guns nearby at all times. To facilitate the arrest, Garriola asked Bond if he would be so kind as to go up to apartment 303 and knock on the door.

Bond was not brave. He also was not stupid. Bond didn't mind knocking on apartment 303's door to talk to old Charlie. But confronting a lunatic like Whitey Bulger was not high on Bond's list of things to do.

So, Garriola came up with a plan that would not put Bond in any danger.

Garriola ran down to Whitey's storage locker, located in the garage of the Princess Eugenia Apartments. Using a pair of bolt cutters, Garriola chopped Whitey's lock to pieces, giving the impression petty thieves had stolen Whitey's possessions.

After rushing back to the manager's office, Garriola ordered Bond to phone apartment 303 and tell Whitey his locker had been broken into. By this time, Bond had done a little Googling of Whitey on the office computer. What he saw did not calm his nerves.

Bond later told CBS News, "I went to his (Whitey's) Wikipedia page, and I'm kinda, like, scrolling through, and it's like, murder and extortion, and all this stuff."

Nonetheless, Bond summoned up the courage and phoned apartment 303.

No answer.

Then he tried the cellphone number Carol (Catherine Greig) had given him as a backup.

Still no answer.

Garriola checked with a fellow agent, who confirmed that surveillance definitely showed a man and a woman were present in apartment 303. Garriola tried again to convince Bond to knock on the door of apartment 303.

Bond again refused and who could blame him? He wasn't being paid by the Princess Eugenia Apartments to put his life on the line.

Before Garriola could decide what to do, the phone rang in the manager's office. It was Catherine Greig inquiring if Bond had just called her cell phone. Bond admitted he had, and then told Greig Garriola's malarkey about their storage locker having been broken into.

Grieg hesitated, and then after conferring with Whitey, she said her husband would meet Bond in the garage.

In the underground garage, Whitey didn't get close to his locker. Before he knew what was happening, more than 40 F.B.I. agents in full riot gear, with their guns and rifles pointed his way, surrounded Whitey.

Garriola barked at Whitey, "Get down on your knees!"

Whitey was dressed in white clothes with a white summer hat on his head. (Whitey was a noted Howard Hughes-type neat freak, fearful of the slightest grime.)

"Fuck you!" Whitey said. "There's oil on the floor!"

Garriola told Whitey to move a few steps to his right, and then get down on his knees.

Whitey cursed some more.

Finally, Whitey found a clean spot and got down on his knees, where the agents cuffed Whitey's hands behind his back.

"Please identify yourself," Garriola said.

"I'm Charlie Gasko," Whitey replied.

"You're not Charlie Gasko," Garriola said. "How about we go upstairs and ask your girlfriend to identify you as Charlie Gasko? She's in enough trouble already."

Whitey grunted.

"Okay. You know who I am," Whitey said. "I'm Whitey Bulger."

The 16-year manhunt for the "Most Wanted" criminal in America had finally ended.

Chapter Two
Making Your Bones

James Joseph Bulger Jr. was born on September 3, 1929 in the town of Everett, Mass., an industrial hamlet just north of Boston. Before Bulger was born, his father, James Sr., had lost his left arm at the elbow after getting it caught between two freight cars while working in the local rail yards. Bulger Sr., who had had an unsuccessful marriage while he was in his twenties, became smitten with Jean McCarthy, who was 22 years his junior. They married and had a daughter; also named Jean, the year before the junior Bulger was born. James Jr. had piercing blue eyes and a light complexion, as well as straw colored hair. Because of his striking looks, his childhood friends called him "Whitey," a nickname Bulger never liked. Whitey preferred to be called "Jimmy."

When he was six years old, the Bulger family moved from Everett to Dorchester in Boston and became parishioners of St. Mark's Church. Whitey didn't distinguish himself in the St. Mark's elementary school. He was too fidgety, barely able to sit still. The following year the Bulgers moved into a triple-decker house on Crescent Avenue, which was located in the St. Margaret Parish.

The locale changed, but Whitey's attitude in the classroom remained the same.

Whitey's younger brother, William "Billy" Bulger, wrote in his autobiography *While the Music Lasts: My Life in Politics*, "My brother Jimmy found school boring. His teachers, like my mother, often discovered that Jimmy was suddenly missing."

In 1938, the Bulger family moved again; this time to the newly built Old Harbor Village projects: a government-funded housing development containing 1016 apartments. Through a lottery, the Bulgers were able to obtain a three-bedroom apartment, on the top (third) floor at 41 Logan Way, which was part of a three-section Boston neighborhood called Southie. Southie was predominantly Irish with a few Italians sprinkled in for flavor. The new digs came in handy for the Bulgers, since the Bulger brood had grown to five children by this time. Besides Jean, James, and William Bulger, there was also Carol and an infant named John, whom everyone called Jack.

While some things change, other things remain the same.

Whitey was no better a student at Thomas N. Hart Public Grammar School than he had been at St. Mark's and St. Margaret's. Whitey was ostensibly a student at Thomas N. Hart from the fifth to the eighth grade, but his marks were an embarrassment to the Bulger family.

A federal probation officer wrote in Whitey's 1956 presentence investigation report: "His scholastic record was poor. He failed in all of his subjects, receiving poor marks in conduct and effort. The school report shows that he was surly, lazy, and had no interest in school work."

When he was 13-years-old, Whitey was arrested for the first time on a charge of school delinquency and larceny, but he was quickly let go. Back on the streets, Whitey joined a local gang called the Shamrocks, and his early life of crime quickly escalated. Whitey spent some time in a juvenile reformatory, which only increased Whitey's knowledge of how to operate successfully in the underworld.

Over the next three years, Whitey was arrested six more times. His crimes became more violent, including charges for assault and battery. Since political influences throughout Southie favored the Irish, Whitey never spent a night in the big boy's slammer.

When he was seventeen, Whitey enlisted as a roustabout (circus laborer) in the traveling Ringling Brothers and Barnum and Bailey Circus.

In an interview with the *Boston Globe*, Whitey's brother Billy explained Whitey's actions this way: "I think Jimmy had a more adventuresome spirit than some. It didn't always involve doing something wrong. The circus came to town; he went off with the circus. Something like that looked like adventures, so off he went."

Circus work was hard and the pay wasn't that great. Whitey's job entailed putting up circus tents and tearing them down. He scooped up dung left behind by the circus animals, most of them huge creatures, known to eat large quantities of chow. Predictably, shoveling mammoth piles of crap was not what Whitey had in mind as a vocation, so he quit after one year.

Free from circus constraints, Whitey returned to the streets of Southie, without a high school diploma and without any visible means of support. Despite these drawbacks, Whitey was able to drive a new car, which piqued the interest of the local police. Police intelligence pegged Whitey as a "tailgater," or a thief who made his living selling goods that had fallen off the tailgates of parked trucks making deliveries in the neighborhood. In this line of work, an arrest was usually imminent. But Whitey was quick and efficient, and the law was always two steps behind.

Whitey's brother Billy said he saw his brother's outlook on life change when Whitey was still a teenager.

"I saw Jim change from a blithe spirit to a rebel whose cause I could never discern," Billy said. "He was in a constant state of revolt against - I'm not sure what. He was as restless as a claustrophobic in a dark closet."

When he was eighteen, Whitey was arrested; not for tailgating, but once more for assault and battery. Irish political contacts in Southie once again pulled strings for the neighborhood Irish lad, and Whitey escaped jail time after paying a measly fine of fifty bucks.

Yet, his brother Billy did not think what Whitey was doing as a teenager was that far out of line.

"Jim's scrapes were small in those growing up years," Billy said. "But in time there were enough of them to make him known to the police. That was a dangerous situation. Some policemen used their billy clubs more than their brains. And Jim was defiant and wouldn't give an inch. His speech was bold. He was often beaten, sometimes savagely. For a while I thought that all police were vicious."

Figuring he was destined for the clink if he remained in the streets of Southie, Whitey finally did the right thing - the patriotic thing - he enlisted in the United States Air Force while the war was raging in Korea. After enduring basic training, Whitey was stationed at the Smokey Hill Air Force base in Salina, Kansas. Later, he was transferred to the Mountain Home Air Force Base in Idaho.

Yet, Whitey's pent up anger repeatedly got the best of him. Whitey was locked in the stockade several times for assault. As a result, he was not considered by his superiors as a prime candidate to fight the war in Korea. This suited Whitey just fine. Instead, he enjoyed a military career stateside, frequently going absent without leave.

His brother Billy wrote, "It was clear he was enjoying himself. The Air Force apparently had more rules than planes, and he delighted in breaking or circumventing a great number of them. It appeared from his letters that he contrived a new system each week for being absent without leave, and he did so with impunity. His conduct was not from lack of patriotism. He was just being Jim. I believed then, and I believe now, that he would have performed well in combat."

Younger brother Billy may have been right, but the odds are certainly against it. It's hard to envision Whitey could have prevented himself from stealing whatever he could get his hands on, and then selling the pilfered goods on the Korean black market. Creeps like Whitey talk patriotism but, in their mental make-up, patriotism takes a backseat to crooked capitalism. The truth is most criminals would rather make an illegal dime than a legal dollar. It's just the way they're wired.

Despite the fact that Whitey, by any measure, was a dreadful United States airman, he somehow managed to get an honorable discharge from the military. Apparently, the "Luck of the Irish" extended to Whitey in the Armed Forces too; either that or he had a Southie connection pulling strings for him inside the military.

Although there is no proof, the latter is more likely.

*****

In mid-1952, Whitey was back on the streets of Southie doing what he had done before: stealing from trucks and pulling off an occasional armed robbery. But Whitey had his sights on something bigger: the banks.

Whitey's bank-robbing rabbi was Carl Smith, an Indianan who used Boston as one of his recruiting sites for accomplices. Other individuals in Smith's bank-robbing crew included Ronnie Dermody, Richard Barchard, and Billy O'Brien. The gang robbed banks in Pawtucket, R.I., Hammond, Ind., and Melrose, Mass., a suburb north of Boston. Not all the gang members were participants in the same bank robberies; most robberies were a two-man job.

One bank robber, usually Whitey, blasted into the bank with two revolvers pointed in front of him like Yosemite Sam, screaming, "This is a robbery! Everybody down on the floor!"

After all of the customers and bank employees had hit the deck, the second bank robber would jump behind the teller's cage and scoop up all cash.

During one robbery, Whitey barked at the terrified bank customers and employees, "We aren't going to hurt anybody. We have to make a living. Dillinger did."

When he was on bank-robbing expeditions with his pals, Whitey sometimes took his girlfriend, Jacquie McAuliffe, who looked like a cross between Marilyn Monroe and Jayne Mansfield, which meant she was built, but probably not too bright. Sometimes, Jacquie sat in a car outside the bank as a lookout. Basically Jacquie was eye candy Whitey liked to flaunt from Boston all the way down to Florida and sometimes as far as the West Coast.

It was the Hammond bank job that was Whitey's undoing. Smith was collared first. As soon as the prison doors closed behind him, Smith, as easy as a kid eating candy, gave up Whitey as one of his accomplices. When Whitey discovered the Indiana police had a warrant out for his arrest, he scooped up Jacquie, and they began a madcap tour of the United States that included stops in Reno, San Francisco, Salt Lake City, and the windy city of Chicago.

However, Jacquie had a six-year-old daughter in Southie, and she missed her like the dickens. Not thinking with the head on his shoulders, Whitey drove Jacquie back to Boston, where they hid out in an array of boarding houses and hotels.

Whitey became so paranoid about his appearance that he dyed his hair jet-black and wore goofy black, horned-rimmed, Buddy Holly-type glasses. To avoid detection, Whitey and Jacquie rarely ventured outside the walls of whatever dive they inhabited. And when Whitey did dare to slither around town, he stuck a big stogie in his mouth, thinking it somehow altered his facial appearance. On that account, Whitey was just as bright as Jacquie.

Cops don't exactly operate like Sherlock Holmes, so it's usually a rat who causes a criminal's house-of-cards of freedom to collapse.

An F.B.I. informant recognized Whitey at a club in Revere, and he dropped a dime to the feds. Whitey was arrested and brought to the federal clink, where he met, for the first time, a notoriously crooked F.B.I. agent named Paul Rico. Rico convinced Whitey to become a rat too. Whitey figured it was an acceptable thing to do, since Carl Smith had snitched on him in the first place.

But Smith had already given up Whitey. Cops and robbers know the first person to turn state's evidence gets the best deal. Whitey understood he had to give the feds something they didn't already have in order to trade that something for a better sentence.

Without hesitation, Whitey told the feds Richard Barchard had participated in the Hammond bank robbery, and that Billy O'Brien was his sole accomplice when they heisted a bank in Melrose, Mass. After they were arrested, both Barchard and O'Brien soon pled guilty. Because he had a record as long as a giraffe's neck, Barchard got a 20-year sentence. O'Brien had no previous criminal record, so he only got eight years in the can.

While in jail, Barchard tried to stick it to Whitey for ratting on him. Barchard filed a false report with the F.B.I, claiming Whitey had killed a man in Indiana. But after a year's investigation, the feds concluded Barchard's accusation was nothing more than a simple act of revenge. Although cleared of all charges, Whitey had a few sleepless nights in the slammer.

Whitey convinced his girlfriend Jacquie to eat cheese too. At Whitey's request, Jacquie verified what Whitey told the feds about who had participated in which bank robbery. Since Jacquie corroborated what Whitey had already told them, the feds gave Jacquie a free get-out-of-jail card.

Jacquie repaid Whitey a few years later by writing him a "Dear John" letter while he was still incarcerated.

Chalk up Jacquie McAuliffe as another rat deserting a sinking ship.

Chapter Three
In the Can

Becoming a rat didn't stop Whitey from doing hard time in prison. Instead of being treated with kid gloves, as the law had done with him in the past, Whitey ran up against one tough hombre in Judge George Sweeney. Judge Sweeney was swayed by the presentencing report, which said Whitey had an I.Q of 113 and was intelligent enough to know better than to embark on a life of crime.

The report also said, "The prognosis for his future behavior in society is poor."

Sweeney stared at the report, and then he stared at Whitey. Without blinking, Judge Sweeney gave Whitey 20 years. Whitey was lucky Judge Sweeny didn't listen to the prosecutor, who had asked for 25 years as the proper sentence for Whitey's actions.

Whitey began his stretch as an inmate at the Federal Penitentiary in Atlanta. Right off the bat, Whitey started doing everything right for a change, so that he could be paroled at the earliest possible date, which was estimated to be in mid-1963.

In 1961, Whitey's younger brother, Billy, graduated from Boston College Law School. Using some of the usual Southie pull, William "Billy" Bulger was soon elected to the Massachusetts House of Representatives. Billy nudged some of his friends in Congress, hoping to get his brother Whitey preferential treatment in prison and, if possible, moved to a federal lockup closer to the family home in Boston. But the wheels of Boston's local politics had little bearing on federal prison procedures, so Whitey stewed in prison. Whitey made sure not to break any prison rules, so the good time he accumulated in the can would earn him an earlier release date than the 20-year term imposed on him by Judge Sweeney.

While still in the Atlanta lockup, Whitey Bulger got a buggy idea.

After being assigned to the prison hospital, Whitey heard through prison scuttlebutt that inmates who agreed to participate in a program geared to studying schizophrenia would receive a few extra bucks a month in their prison account, and be given extra good time; thereby, enabling them to cut short their sentences. The only hitch was these inmates would have to be injected with the psychedelic drug LSD (Lysergic acid diethylamide), which was virtually unknown to the public at the time.

The stated purpose of the program turned out to be a lie. It was later revealed that the Central Intelligence Agency was behind the program. The C.I.A wanted to study the effects of LSD on mind control, which the C.I.A. could put to great use in many ways.

Injecting LSD into men would allow the C.I.A. to order the men to do things they normally wouldn't do without the aid of the drug. Consider the possibilities if LSD tricked a man into telling the truth when telling a lie would be in his best interest. This would be of great use to the C.I.A. during enhanced interrogations of the enemy, or of Americans whom the C.I.A. believed to be spies.

Despite the fact he was going to be used as a human lab rat, Whitey signed up for the program, which resulted in him being injected with LSD once a month for fifteen months. For his contribution to the cause, Whitey received a paltry three bucks a month extra and a mere fifty-four days knocked off his sentence, hardly proper payment for having one's brains scrambled.

Richard Sunday was a fellow inmate of Whitey's in

In the Can

Atlanta. Sunday has remained in contact with Whitey throughout the years, even after Bulger's arrest in 2011. At the age of 19, while a member of the United States Army, Sunday was convicted of raping a woman in Korea and sentenced to life, which was later reduced to 25 years.

Sunday witnessed first-hand the effects of LSD on Whitey. Sunday said after Whitey had been injected with the drug, Whitey screamed like a mad man, wilding waving his hands as if he was striking out at an invisible object. Sunday said Whitey's drug-induced conversations rambled without any obvious intent or meaning.

"He was one crazy individual when he was on those drugs," Sunday said. "He was a lunåtic."

In the mid-1980's, when Whitey ran Boston with an iron fist, he told his chief underling, Kevin Weeks, that the LSD injections haunted him for the rest of his life.

After turning state's evidence to reduce his prison term, Weeks said, "Jimmy told me that for 15 months he was either injected with LSD, or given it as a liquid. Jimmy said it made him crazy and unable to stand the thought of a needle ever piercing his skin again. It was also the reason he never got a good night's sleep. He still woke up screaming in the middle of the night and frequently suffered hallucinations."

It was later revealed that 18 prisoners took part in the Atlanta Federal Prison LSD Program. Some of them lost their minds completely, while others committed suicide. As for Whitey, he was screwed up mentally before he went to prison. He continued stalking the streets of Boston with the same twisted mindset after he was released from prison. Except for a few sleepless nights and occasional pink elephant sightings, it's uncertain if the drug had any lasting effect on Whitey whatsoever. He was a nut job before he dropped LSD in prison and remained a nut job after he was released from prison.

Despite efforts by his brother Billy to get Whitey

transferred to a prison closer to home (Billy was a law school student at the time, but still had Southie's political pull at his disposal), on November 2, 1959, Whitey was transferred to the Alcatraz Federal Penitentiary. Situated on a rocky island in San Francisco Bay, it was affectionately called "The Rock."

*****

The main prison at Alcatraz was built from 1910-1912. At first, it was used strictly as a United States Army Military Prison. It also provided housing for the Bureau of Prisons staff and their families. In 1934, the island became a part of the Federal Bureau of Prisons. At this time, the prison was modernized to meet the requirements of a top-notch security prison.

Despite its reputation as the last stop for incorrigible convicts, the living conditions at Alcatraz were better than most federal prisons. Inmates had their own private cells, which made them less vulnerable to attacks from other inmates. Plus, the food at Alcatraz was considered as good as it got in the prison system, and inmates were allowed to eat as much as they desired. Although Alcatraz wasn't a vacationer's paradise, compared to other prisons, the conditions were such that many inmates asked to be transferred to the "The Rock."

Without crowding the prisoners in too tight, Alcatraz was able to house 1576 of America's most notorious criminals. Outlaws like Al Capone, Robert Franklin Stroud ("The Birdman of Alcatraz"), George "Machine Gun" Kelly, Arthur "Doc" Barker, and Alvin "Creepy" Karpis, at one time or another, received their mail at Alcatraz. (Karpis served more time at Alcatraz than any other inmate.) Because of the cold waters and strong currents of San Francisco Bay, Alcatraz was reputed to be America's toughest prison. It was deemed to be inescapable.

But that didn't stop convicts from trying.

A total of 36 prisoners made 14 escape attempts during

In the Can

the 29 years of the prison's existence. The bloodiest incident was the 1946 "Battle of Alcatraz", which lasted the better part of three days.

On May 2, 1946, at around 2 p.m., Bernard Coy and Marvin Hubbard (who had once escaped from a prison in Atlanta) overpowered Alcatraz guard William Miller outside C Block. With the keys to the cells now in their possession, Coy and Hubbard entered C-Block and released prisoners, Joseph Cretzer and Clarence Carnes, from their cells.

C-Block had a caged elevated gun gallery, which was periodically patrolled by an armed guard. But the cons had timed their attack on Miller to coincide with the guard, Bert Burch, temporarily leaving the gun gallery. Fortunately, for the hopeful escapees, Burch had also left his rifle in the gallery.

Coy, who had starved himself for weeks, climbed up to the gun gallery cage and used a wrench to spread the bars apart. This allowed him to squeeze through the bars and into the gallery, where he confiscated Burch's Springfield rifle. When Burch returned, Coy overpowered him and took him as a hostage. Coy then grabbed Burch's M1911 pistol and lowered it on a rope to his buddies below. Next, Coy collected a number of clubs and gas grenades, which he also lowered to his pals.

With Burch as a hostage, Coy continued along the gallery until he reached D-Block. There, he forced guard Cecil Corwin to open the door to C-Block; thereby releasing a dozen inmates into D-Bloc, including Sam Shockley and Miran Thompson.

However, ten of the inmates, including Clarence Carnes, got cold feet and willingly returned to their cells in C-Block. That left Coy, Hubbard, Shockley, Cretzer, and Thompson as the only inmates still attempting the escape. These convicts locked up the three guards in a C-Block cell.

Their plan was to get into the kitchen and use a key taken from one of the guards to open the kitchen door, which led to the prison yard. From there they would make their way to the prison dock, where they would seize the prison boat, and direct it to the docks of San Francisco and freedom.

Then their luck changed.

For some unknown reason, the lock on the door leading from the kitchen to the prison yard jammed. No matter how hard they tried to unjam the lock, the escapees could not get the door open.

Coy, Hubbard, Cretzer, Shockley, and Thompson rushed back to C-Block. As new guards rushed inside C-Block to see what had happened to the hostages, they were also overpowered and thrown into cells. Soon, the convicts had nine guards locked up in two separate cells, but they still had no way of escaping.

But Coy would not give up without a fight.

Using a guard's rifle, Coy fired at the guards who were standing watch in neighboring towers. Not being the greatest shooter, Coy missed all of his targets.

Assistant Warden, Ed Miller, rushed to C-Block to investigate the commotion. He was armed only with a billy club and a gas grenade. Coy spotted Miller and fired at him. But Coy missed again. Miller ran back to D-Block and sounded the escape alarm.

Coy, Hubbard, Shockley, Cretzer, and Thompson were spooked by the sound of the alarm. At this point, they realized their escape attempt was doomed. Shockley and Thompson convinced Cretzer to kill the hostage guards so they could not later testify against them.

Cretzer did as he was told. He opened fire, wounding five guards, including Miller, who later died from his wounds.

Carnes, Shockley and Thompson then decided to play dumb. They returned to their cells as if nothing had happened. Coy, Hubbard, and Cretzer, however, decided to

In the Can

fight until death. In the confusion, one of the wounded guards discreetly wrote down the names of the convicts involved in the escape attempt, circling the names of the ringleaders.

Hours passed, but nothing happened.

At exactly 6 p.m., a squad of about 20 armed guards entered the elevated gun gallery. A gun battle ensued, as the convicts and guards exchanged fire. The guards were sitting ducks; while the position of convicts kept them out of range of the guards' bullets. One of the guards, Harold Stiles, was shot to death; five others were wounded. None of the convicts got as much as a scratch on them.

At least not yet.

Prison officials decided to cut off the electricity and wait until there was total darkness.

Prison Warden, James A. Johnson, called in two platoons of United States Marines, under the command of General "Vinegar" Joe Stilwell, to join the battle. But the Marines found themselves at a disadvantage because a standing rule at Alcatraz prohibited guns inside the cell blocks, lest one of the inmates disarm one of the guards and turned the gun on the guards. Remember, Coy and Hubbard overpowered guard Miller *outside* C-Block.

At 7 p.m., when the prison was in total darkness, two squads of unarmed guards rushed into C-Block in an attempt to rescue their colleagues. They succeeded in doing so, but one of the guards was wounded by the convicts.

The renegade convicts, however, were still inside C-Block; armed and dangerous.

This is where the prison officials started using their brains.

The Marines drilled holes in the prison roof and dropped grenades into the areas where they believed the convicts were hiding. Their plan was to gradually maneuver the convicts into a utility corridor, where the guards could trap them. This worked for a while, but the convicts would not take the bait right away.

This is where the trapped convicts began using their brains.

As the clock struck midnight moving the calendar into May 3rd, the convicts phoned Warden Johnson and tried to work out a deal. Johnson cut them off at the knees. He told the convicts he would only accept total surrender without any terms whatsoever.

The warden's tactic of maneuvering the armed convicts in a narrow corridor eventually worked, but it took some time.

At 9 p.m. on May 3rd, Johnson ordered his guards and the Marines to fire volley after volley into a narrow corridor of C-Block, where he assumed the convicts were now holed up and out of ammunition. The firing continued periodically throughout the night and into the next morning.

Finally, at 9:40 a.m. on May 4th, the guards and the Marines bum-rushed the narrow corridor, ready to fire on the trapped convicts. But they didn't have to.

They found the dead bodies of Cretzer, Coy and Hubbard. Miran Thompson and Sam Shockley surrendered, saying the three dead convicts had coerced them into this predicament. But that didn't wash since their names had already been written on a piece of paper by one of the wounded guards before he was rescued.

For their efforts, on December 3, 1948, Thompson and Shockley were both put to death in San Quentin's gas chamber. Clarence Carnes, who had originally been released from his cell by Coy, but did not take part in any of the festivities, was given an extended sentence. Carnes was released from prison in 1973.

There was only one successful escape attempt in the history of Alcatraz, but the F.B.I. was unable to ascertain if the three men survived or had drowned in the icy waters of

In the Can

San Francisco Bay.

Bank robber brothers, John and Clarence Anglin, were arrested and convicted in 1956 and hit with 15-to-20-year sentences. They were sent to the federal penitentiary in Atlanta, where they met armed robber Frank Lee Morris and car thief Allen Clayton West. While they were in Atlanta, the Anglin brothers made several escape attempts, but they were unsuccessful every time. By September 1961, all four men had been transferred to Alcatraz, where they set out to do something that had never done before.

It took months of planning until June 11th, 1962, when the four men carried out their plan. For several months, the men had been digging holes in their cell walls using spoons. On the night of June 11th, the men placed dummy heads, which they had constructed with a mixture of soap, toilet paper and real hair, in their bunks to fool the prison guards, who made periodic night-time visual inspections of the cells. Then John and Clarence Anglin, along with Frank Lee Morris, crawled through the holes in the walls of their cells into an unused service corridor.

Allen Clayton West tried to do the same in his cell, but was unable to do so. He had not actually gone all the way through the hole in his cell wall before the night of the jailbreak. When he tried to punch through the remaining section of the hole on the big night, he found himself impeded by an iron bar. West had no choice but to remain in his cell, while the other three men continued with their escape attempt.

From the service corridor, the Anglin brothers and Morris climbed into a ventilation shaft that led them to the roof. Then they climbed down the other side of the roof and scaled the prison fence. A few feet from the water's edge, they assembled a raft, fashioned from standard-issue prison raincoats and contact cement. At around 10 p.m., they flung the raft into the water, jumped into the raft, and began paddling with their hands.

They were never seen or heard from again.

The next morning after the escape was discovered, Allen Clayton West started singing to save his own skin. West told the F.B.I. the details of the plot, which led the feds to the spot where the three men had constructed the raft. There the feds found remnants of the raft, paddles, and a bag containing personal items belonging to the Anglin brothers, which verified West's story.

West also told the feds, once they had reached land, the escapees planned to steal clothes and a car. But after a thorough investigation of the surrounding area, there were no reports of clothes or a car being stolen. As a result, the F.B.I. concluded the Anglin brothers and Morris had drowned in the cold waters of San Francisco Bay.

For his cooperation, West was never charged in the escape attempt.

The story doesn't end there.

The F.B.I. may have made a gigantic blunder in this case by trying to save face and their occasionally unearned reputation as an elite crime-fighting force. It's possible the feds tailored their investigation, and its results, to put themselves and the prison staff at Alcatraz in the best possible light.

In 2003, in the first season of the TV program *Mythbusters*, the producers of the show did a test to see if it was feasible to construct a raft from standard-issue prison raincoats and contact cement, and then determine if such a raft could navigate the waters of the San Francisco Bay until it made landfall.

The test was conducted, and such a plan was confirmed to be possible.

Then in 2011, the *National Geographic Channel* ran a story of the escape plot. According to independent investigators, the raft was found on the mainland, and footprints were seen leading away from the raft. The investigators also discovered there had been a report of a blue Chevrolet stolen from a home that night in the area where the raft had been found.

Despite the tale peddled by the Alcatraz Federal Prison system and the F.B.I., it's quite possible that the Anglin brothers and Morris did indeed escape from the inescapable Rock.

But we will never know for sure.

*****

In late 1959, when Whitey Bulger arrived at Alcatraz Prison, escape was the last thing on his mind.

In Alcatraz, unlike in Atlanta, every convict had his own five-foot by nine-foot cell. The inmates were required to do a full day's work from Monday to Friday, with weekends off, unless they had been dispatched to the hole (solitary confinement) for a disciplinary infraction. The trick for Whitey was to weasel his way into a plum assignment, where the work wasn't too hard and the environment was as pleasant as possible.

The prison guard who passed out the job assignments was a crabby old soul with hands like meat hooks. His name was Maurice Ordway. He was an institution at Alcatraz, having been a "screw" there longer than anyone else. Ordway's nickname was "Double Tough" because he constantly told inmates who had an attitude, "You think you're tough? Well I'm double-tough."

But Whitey was the ultimate schemer. After Ordway told Whitey that breaking his hump in a sweltering kitchen would be his new gig, Whitey shot Ordway his best poker face, and said, "I heard they have meat cleavers and big knives in the kitchen."

Ordway thought it over for a moment, and he decided having a nut like Whitey loose in a room with potential murder weapons was not exactly the smartest thing to do. So, Ordway assigned Whitey a plum job working in the prison clothing room, handing out prison-issued duds to his fellow inmates.

Whitey proved once more that he was diabolical when it came to getting what he wanted.

Soon after Whitey arrived at Alcatraz, he was joined by his old Atlanta prison buddy Richard Sunday, who had been banished from Atlanta and sent to Alcatraz for cracking the head of a fellow inmate.

After his release from prison, Sunday told the *Boston Globe*, "At Alcatraz you had to watch your back and you had to have someone watch your back. Jimmy watched my back and I watched his."

At Alcatraz, Whitey became pals with the aforementioned Clarence Carnes, a native American known as "The Choctaw Kid." At the age of 16, Carnes was sentenced to life in prison for the Oklahoma murder of a garage attendant during a botched robbery. In the 1946 book "Escape from Alcatraz," Carnes had originally been released from his cell, but when he decided the plot was doomed to failure, he willingly went back into his cell. Because two prison officers died during the botched escape attempt, Carnes was tried for murder, along with Sam Shockley and Miran Thompson. All three men were found guilty. Although Shockley and Thompson were executed for their crimes, Carnes was given a 99-year sentence, which included the possibility of parole.

By the time Whitey had arrived at Alcatraz, Carnes was an Alcatraz legend. He had the coveted job of delivering library books to inmates in their cells. At Alcatraz, Whitey took up reading as a way to pass the time. Carnes always gave Whitey books he believed would increase Whitey's knowledge of America; especially books that dealt with the plight of the Native American Indian. Carnes told Whitey that when Carnes died he wanted to be buried on Choctaw land in Oklahoma, where he had been born.

In 1988, unbeknownst to Whitey, Carnes passed away

in a Missouri prison. Because Carnes had no next of kin, the prison officials buried him in a pauper's grave. When Whitey found out the fate of his Alcatraz buddy in early 1989, Whitey paid for Carnes's exhumation, and had Carnes's body transported to Oklahoma to be buried on Choctaw ground.

Even bad men occasionally do good things.

*****

With pressure from Billy Bulger and House Majority Leader John McCormack (the second in line to succeed the President of the United States in case of a national catastrophe), the Department of Corrections began looking at Whitey in a different light. With a little prodding from the two politicians (Speaker of the House McCormack obviously had more pull than little Billy Bulger), James Bennett, the Director of the Bureau of Prisons, ordered his staff at Alcatraz to do a complete review of Whitey's prison behavior. Knowing he was close to getting a new lease on life, Whitey began telling anyone who would listen how he had become a changed man in prison. Whitey said he had disgraced his family. As soon as he was a free man, he swore he would go on the straight and narrow.

Influenced by Whitey's pronouncements (and with pressure from their superiors), prison officials started to view Whitey as a man who had nearly completed his personal reclamation project. In an annual review of Whitey's case file by prison officials, Whitey was said to be "extremely nervous and jumpy" and "on guard at all times." However, in the same report it said Whitey maintained he would go to school as soon as he was released from prison, in order to "redeem himself in the eyes of his family and friends."

The kicker in this report was the conclusion: "James Bulger seems entirely sincere in this regard."

Then, in an unusual turn of events, James Bennett, the Director of the Bureau of Prisons, traveled to Alcatraz to interview Whitey. The fix for Whitey was in. After Bennett's visit, a prison report said, "Since his interview with Mr. Bennett, his (Whitey's) attitude has been excellent." The reports also said Whitey had "an ebullient personality."

After the proper strings had been pulled by his brother Billy's political pals, in April of 1962, Whitey was transferred to the penitentiary in Leavenworth, Kansas. James Bennett himself signed the order for this transfer.

While Whitey was a resident at Leavenworth, he was assigned to "rat and pest control," which was a subsidiary of the Leavenworth Sanitation Department. This was not the last time Whitey's concentrated his efforts on getting rid of rats.

While Leavenworth was a lot closer visit for Whitey's family than Alcatraz, it was still far enough from Southie to prevent the Bulger clan from frequent visits. Consequently, House Majority Leader John McCormack started another letter-writing campaign on Whitey's behalf. In September of 1963, as a result of McCormack's intervention, Whitey was transferred to a prison closer to home: the federal penitentiary in Lewisburg, PA.

Billy Bulger said he thought the prison guards at Lewisburg did not play fair with his brother Whitey.

"When my brother was transferred to Lewisburg, I bought a stripped-down Chevrolet and drove my father there," Billy said. "Some guards, knowing Jim lifted weights, had thrown his weights in the ice and snow to punish him. Jim's hands were sore and his palms were covered with open red sores where they had frozen to the iron. I was angered, but Jim thought it was a huge joke that the guards could think he'd be stopped by a little pain. He told me, 'You have to score very high on the stupidity test to be a guard in this place.'"

When Billy asked Whitey if any of the prisoners at Lewisburg had given him trouble, Whitey replied, "Nothing I couldn't handle."

In the Can

When he was transferred to Lewisburg, Whitey had been rejected for parole two times, which is not unusual for a man who was hit with a twenty-year rap. But Billy Bulger and John McCormack continued applying pressure to the higher-ups in the Federal Bureau of Prisons. As a result, when Whitey appeared before the parole board for the third time, the outcome was rigged in Whitey's favor.

Prison hat in hand, Whitey told the parole board he had a legitimate job waiting for him outside prison walls. This bogus work was supposed to be at Farnsworth Press in Boston, where Whitey would allegedly operate the printing presses. Whitey's future pay at Farnsworth Press was said to be a measly $1.50 an hour, but certainly higher remuneration than he was presently receiving in Club Fed.

The parole board swallowed Whitey's pablum, and on March 1, 1965, after serving only nine years of a 20-year term, Whitey exited Lewisburg prison with a smile on his face and $64.27 in his pocket.

Whitey's lack of funds did not last for long.

Chapter Four
Up the Totem Pole

Whitey was thirty-five-years-old when he hit the streets of Boston again. By this time, his brother Billy was a three-term state representative. Billy used his massive influence, much greater on the streets of Boston than it has been with the Federal Prison System, to get Whitey a job, ostensibly as a janitor at the local courthouse. This pleased Whitey's parole officer. But Whitey basically showed up at work to collect his $76-a-week paycheck. Pity the courthouse supervisor who asked Whitey to scrub the toilets.

After a few months of much needed rest and relaxation, Whitey took up with the mighty Killeen gang as a street collector and as an enforcer. While in prison, Whitey read up on the best criminal minds known to man, especially Niccolo Machiavelli, the 16th century Italian philosopher and realist, who taught precepts like, "The end justifies the means," and "It's much better to be feared than loved."

The Southie-based Killeens were led by three brothers: Donald, Kenneth, and Edward. The Killeens were constantly fighting with the notorious Mullin Gang from Winter Hill in Somerville, led by Buddy McLean. Add to the mixture the murderous McLaughlin brothers from nearby Charlestown and South Boston's Mullin Gang, and by the time Whitey was released from prison, there was a Celtic War of sorts taking place almost every day in and around Boston.

Of course, there was also the New England Italian La

Up the Totem Pole

Cosa Nostra (the feds call it the Mafia, but, in fact, the Mafia exists only in Sicily), which also had a huge presence in Boston. But in the mostly Irish Southie section of town, the Italians took their cuts from whomever was in power, while staying clear of the street battles for control of the Irish rackets.

While riding shotgun for the Killeens, Whitey became fast pals with an Italian-American named Steve Flemmi, a murderous thug who constantly resisted offers to be inducted into the La Cosa Nostra. The fact that Flemmi repelled proposals to be "made" should have sent strong signals to the Italian mob that Flemmi might be untrustworthy (men were occasionally killed when they refused their "button"). Letting Flemmi slide was a big mistake for the Italian mob. They would later pay dearly for this oversight. Many of them would lose their freedom.

In 1934, Flemmi, the oldest of three sons, was born to Italian immigrants Giovanni and Irene Flemmi. He was raised in an Orchard Park tenement in Roxbury, Mass. Flemmi's father was a bricklayer, and his mother was a full-time stay-at-home mom. Flemmi was described by a former mistress as "mild mannered and personable."

However, two of Flemmi's heartthrobs would beg to differ with this assessment, since Flemmi was involved in their murders. He even pulled out his erstwhile girlfriends' teeth with pliers after they were dead so they couldn't be identified.

After being a terror on the streets as a teenager (he was arrested at 14 for "sexual misbehavior"), Flemmi decided to join the United States Army. Flemmi was only 17-years-old at the time and too young to enlist, so he borrowed the identity of a high school buddy who had reached the age for qualification into the armed services. At the time, the Korean War was in full blast. Flemmi was a sharpshooter with an army-issued rifle. As a member of the 187th Airborne, Flemmi reportedly killed five Chinese soldiers the first time he went into battle. As a result of his prowess on the battlefield, Flemmi acquired the nickname "The Rifleman," which later became the name of Flemmi's autobiography.

Flemmi's army career ended in 1955. Back on the streets of Boston, he got into the loansharking business with Edward "Wimpy" Barrett, who was a key member of the McLaughlin gang. Backed by the McLaughlins, Flemmi moved up the underworld ladder quickly. By 1958, he had his sticky fingers in many illegal activities, including robbing banks. Flemmi's base of operations was a convenience store in Roxbury, where he planned various schemes and scores.

Soon, Flemmi came across the F.B.I.'s radar. In 1958, Paul Rico, the same agent who busted Whitey in 1955, paid a visit to Flemmi's convenience store hangout. Rico was on a rampage to bust up the Italian mob, and he knew that Flemmi, though ostensibly with the McLaughlins, was friendly with enough Italian mobsters to be able to provide Rico with inside information on the La Cosa Nostra's illegal activities.

For weeks, Rico and his partner, Dennis Condon, did a tag-team-routine on Flemmi, and soon Flemmi realized he had nothing to lose and much to gain by playing ball with the feds. Rico convinced Flemmi to leave the McLaughlins, and change sides to the Winter Hill Mob. When Flemmi met with Winter Hill's boss, Buddy McLean, he was shocked to discover McLean was also in bed with the feds.

Over the next seven years, Flemmi played both sides of the fence, giving Rico the dirt on La Cosa Nostra, while protecting his cronies in the Winter Hill Mob. In 1965, Flemmi made it official. He became a paid government informant, on the record, with the codename "Jack from Boston."

The Killeen gang, which ruled Southie, was originally run by four brothers: George, Eddie, Donnie, and Kenny. George was blasted from the scene in 1950, and Eddie was gunned down in 1968. Donnie and Kenny ran their gambling and loansharking business from the Transit Café, a rundown dive on West Broadway. By 1968, Whitey was one of the Killeen's top enforcers. He was mentored by the Killeen's most feared hitman, Billy O'Sullivan, better known as "Billy-O".

By this time, the Winter Hill Mob had decimated the McLaughlin Gang, and the Mullin gang, named after an old neighborhood war hero, was engaged in daily battles with the Killeens over control of Southie's rackets. Because the Mullins had a mere 20 men in their gang, the Killeens' main strategy was to pick off the Mullins one by one until the Mullins ceased to exist.

Two of the key Mullins were Irish-born Pat Nee and Boston's own Paulie McGonagle. One night, Whitey and Billy-O were cruising the streets of Boston in Billy-O's car, when they spotted who they thought to be Paulie McGonagle driving on East 7th Street in City Point. They followed McGonagle to his home, and before McGonagle could get out of his car, Whitey pulled alongside and shot McGonagle in the face.

The only problem was, it was not Paulie McGonagle. Instead, Whitey had just killed Paulie's brother, Donnie McGonagle, a hard-working stiff and a civilian in the Irish gang wars. This was a terrible mistake on Whitey's part.

But it didn't seem to bother Whitey that much. Less than an hour later, he and Billy-O chowed down several pork chops rustled up in Billy-O's apartment just a few miles from the scene of the wrong-man hit.

In early 1969, Pat Nee dropped into a Boston bar called the Mad Hatter, which was a hangout for members of all the local Irish gangs. It was a place where it was understood nobody was going to get hurt because of gangland differences. Sitting at the bar was Whitey, whom Nee knew only as an ex-bank robber named Jimmy. Nee also knew Whitey was with the Killeens. He suspected

Whitey might have been involved in the Donnie McGonagle shooting as well as several others shootings of the quickly dwindling Mullin gang.

Still, the Mad Hatter was a neutral place, where a bloke could have a drink without getting his brains splattered all over the sawdust-covered floor. So Nee and Bulger sat at the bar and engaged in small talk about growing up in Southie and the plight of the Boston Red Sox, who had not won a World Series since 1912.

While Whitey and Nee were shooting the spit, a Mullin gang member named Mickey Dwyer rushed into the bar. Dwyer was an ex-boxer with a beat-up face to start with. But Nee was shocked when he saw Dwyer was now missing his entire nose and was bleeding profusely from a hole in the middle of his face all over the Mad Hatter's floor. Dwyer had also been shot in the arm.

Dwyer rushed into Nee's arms, and he told Nee he had been in the Killeen's Transit Café where he had gotten into an argument with Kenny Killeen.

Dwyer said, "That bastard Killeen shot me in the arm, and then he bit my nose off!"

As a couple of Mullin gangsters rushed Dwyer to the hospital before he bled to death, Nee yelled at the other Mullins in attendance, "Fuck the Killeens. Let's go get them!"

At this point, Whitey, the only Killeen in the joint, started having uneasy thoughts he might be taken out, Mad Hatter or no Mad Hatter.

Instead, Nee turned to Whitey and asked, "Do you have a car?"

After Whitey answered in the affirmative, Nee said, "Okay, let's get over to the Transit."

Several Mullins, including Nee, piled into Whitey's car, and with Whitey at the wheel, they hustled over to the Transit Café, where Whitey's crew hung out. When they got there, the Killeens had already vacated the premises.

Nee and Whitey shook hands and bid their goodbyes, both realizing the war was escalating and they were fighting on opposite sides.

Sure enough, a few weeks later, Nee was sitting in the passenger seat of a Mullin car as it passed the Mad Hatter. Low and behold, Nee spotted Whitey just as he was about to enter the gang-neutral bar. Since Whitey was technically not inside the Mad Hatter, but just outside the front door, Nee split hairs and decided "The Mad Hatter Truce" was not in effect.

Nee ordered the driver to stop the car. Then, he screamed at Whitey, "Hey Whitey, this is for you!"

Nee pointed a .38 caliber pistol at Whitey, and he commenced firing. Whitey dove to the pavement and hid behind a parked car. As Nee fired several more rounds, Whitey pulled a pistol from an ankle holster and returned fire. It was like a Blind Man's Shootout at the O.K. Corral. Neither man was able to wound the other, and if Nee hadn't yelled first, Whitey would have been toast, and I wouldn't be writing this book.

Another time, Nee hid in the bushes in front of Whitey's mother's house waiting for Whitey to make his exit. When Whitey finally did show his face outside the front door, Nee again fired wildly; as Whitey skedaddled back into the arms of his loving mother.

Things got so hot for Whitey on the streets of Boston, he sometime hid out at his Mom's house for weeks at a time.

Nee got sidetracked for a while by the barroom killing of his brother Peter. Nee tried to avenge his brother's murder by taking out the known perpetrator, a drunken chap by the name of Kevin Daley. Although Nee ambushed Daly near Daly's house, shot him five times, kicked him in the face and ribs, and spat on him, Daly somehow survived. Daly told the cops who had done him wrong, and Nee was arrested for Daly's assault.

However, when it was time for Daly to testify against Nee in court, Daly, hunched in a wheelchair, told the judge his sworn statement saying Nee was his shooter was incorrect.

Nee took a deep breath and was set loose back on the dangerous streets of Boston.

While Nee was in prison awaiting trial, Whitey figured his problem with Nee was over. But with Nee back in the game, Whitey knew it was time he did some of the ambushing and shooting himself.

Whitey discovered Nee had abandoned his home in Southie and was hiding out in his girlfriend's apartment in the Bunker Hill projects in nearby Charlestown. Even though he never left the abode, Nee always had a gun within arm's reach, just in case.

As was said in the book *Whitey Bulger* by Kevin Cullen and Shelley Murphy, Nee was watching television in his girlfriend's ground-floor apartment with his girlfriend's young daughter. Just in case, Nee had a gun hidden under a dish towel on the coffee table.

Nee said, "The light from the TV lit up the window of the apartment, and I could see a rifle barrel pointed at the window. Actually, at me. I saw Whitey's face. I knew it was him and he had the drop on me."

As Nee rushed for his gun, the little girl jumped up.

"She was right in the line of fire," Nee said. "She was between me and the window. I looked right over at Whitey. He lowered his gun and smiled at me. And then he just disappeared."

Whitey had obeyed a gangland rule you never shoot with little kids in the line of fire.

Nee ran outside the apartment pointing his gun, but Whitey had already jumped into a waiting car. There were several people between Nee and Whitey's car, so Nee lowered his gun. Whitey's getaway car burned rubber as it sped away.

"I never regretted not shooting Whitey, because I could have hit anybody, even though I was pretty sure I would have gotten Whitey," Nee said. "And if I had, a lot of other people would still be alive."

Chapter Five
King of the Hill

By 1972, Whitey figured it was time to make an upwardly mobile move in the rackets. That meant getting rid of the Killeens so he could take over their operations. Whitey figured Donnie Killeen was the toughest and the boss, so he would have to go first. But Whitey discovered something was in the wind, and he may not have to get his hands dirty.

On May 13, 1972, Donnie Killeen was hosting a birthday party for his young daughter at his home in Framingham when the phone rang. Donnie answered the call. It must have been important because Donnie kissed his wife and daughter, and told them he'd be back after he took care of some business.

A few seconds later, the partying people inside the house heard loud noises, like exploding firecrackers. Donnie's wife, Donna, ran outside, and she found her husband slumped dead behind the wheel; with more holes in him than ten pounds of Swiss cheese.

The murder weapon was an old gangland staple: the Thompson submachine gun, which was also called the "Tommy Gun," "The Chicago Organ Grinder," and "The Chopper." The Thompson submachine gun fires .45 APC cartridges, with a magazine that holds as many as 30 rounds. And by the looks of Donnie Killeen's body, all 30 rounds found their mark.

With Donnie Killeen six feet under, presumably done in by the Mullin gang who wanted to take over the Killeens' rackets, Donnie's brother Kenny finally decided that retiring from the underworld was the smart thing to do. Kenny's decision was facilitated by a little incident that occurred just days after his brother Donnie had bought the ranch.

Kenny Killeen emerged onto the patio of his South Boston apartment on Marine Avenue to pick up his morning newspaper. As luck would have it, just as Kenny bent down to pick up the tabloid, a sniper fired a bullet that missed its mark, but destroyed the wrought-iron railing around the patio (remember, Steve Flemmi was called "The Rifleman" because of his expertise in these sorts of things). Kenny darted back inside his apartment before he got the same medicine as the wrought-iron railing.

A week later, Kenny Killeen was strolling along City Point when a car pulled up next to him. Whitey leaned out the passenger window; holding a pistol.

Whitey yelled at Killeen, "Hey, Kenny. It's over! You're out of business! No future warnings!"

That said, Whitey's car sped away.

Kenny Killeen got the message. He meekly resigned his position as head of the Killeens, effective immediately.

With both Killeens gone, Whitey was now the top-ranking member of the Killeen gang, which was like being a captain in the Swiss navy. So, Whitey figured a meeting with the Mullin Gang might work in his favor. Whitey decided to invite Howie Winter, head of the Winter Hill Mob, to act as a mediator, so at the meeting's end, everyone would know who was who and what was what. Whitey figured he'd emerge from that meeting either quite dead, or in a better position than he presently occupied.

The meeting was set for Chandler's Restaurant in the South End of Boston. Chandler's was a well-known Irish mob hangout, where numerous meetings had taken place in the past to determine specific territories for the myriad Irish gangs. It was owned by John Martorano and his brother, Jimmy.

Representing the Mullins was Pat Nee, Paulie McGonagle (still very much alive), and degenerate-killer, Tommy King. Representing himself was Whitey. Whitey's capable hitman, Billy O'Sullivan, had been taken out by the Mullins in 1973, so as far as the Killeen gang was concerned, Whitey was the boss and the only member of note.

Howie Winter was considered the top Irish mob boss in Boston, so he sat at the head of the table. To his right was Mafioso Joe Russo, from the North End, who was there to make sure the right decisions were made as far as the Italians were concerned. But it was Howie Winter who ran the show.

Knowing Whitey's cunning, it's hard to believe Whitey did not know he had become, throughout the years, one of Howie Winter's favorite Irish gangsters. Winter knew the Killeens were extinct, so he offered Whitey a position as head of the Southie faction of the Winter Hill Mob. Winter was so enamored with Whitey's leadership skills, he even offered to bankroll a bookie operation in Southie, where he and Whitey would split the profits.

This basically put the Mullins, who would soon lose that gang name, under Whitey's leadership. This didn't sit well with Nee, McGonagle, or King. However, since Winter was the big Irish boss backed by the Italians, there was nothing they could do but accept the arrangement.

Whitey gladly took the bargain, but he knew he would have to deal with the disgruntled ex-Mullins in the not-too-distant future.

With Paulie McGonagle and Tommy King technically in Whitey's crew, Whitey convinced King that McGonagle had to go for the betterment of the gang. Figuring Whitey was his boss and it's a bad thing to go against the boss, in 1974 King agreed to take part in the McGonagle hit.

After Whitey enticed McGonagle into his car, Tommy King, sitting in the back seat, put two bullets in the back of McGonagle's head. They buried McGonagle's body at

King of the Hill

Tenan Beach, which had a great view of Downtown Boston. But not for Paulie McGonagle anymore.

A few days later, McGonagle's car was found near the docks in Charlestown. To throw the law off the scent, Whitey conveniently left McGonagle's wallet floating near the location where McGonagle was whacked, but far from where McGonagle's body was actually buried. McGonagle's remains were discovered in 2000 when Whitey's underling, Kevin Weeks, started singing to the law about who was buried and where.

Whitey never liked any loose ends and Tommy King was a loose end.

King and Whitey had once gotten into a bar-room brawl. King was cleaning the floor with Whitey when another gang member pulled King off the bloodied Whitey. This incident was the impetus for Whitey to endorse King's death warrant in blood.

In 1975, Whitey signed up as a full-fledged government informant. The only stipulation was that he not kill anybody. Whitey, who had his fingers crossed when he made the deal with the F.B.I., decided to take care of the Tommy King situation. To handle the problem, Whitey enlisted killers John Martorano and Steve Flemmi, who, by this time, were spending a lot of time with Whitey.

Whitey called King and said he needed him for the hit of a Boston hoodlum who had to go. Whitey picked up King at a neighborhood bar and ushered King into the front passenger seat (known as the death seat for good reason). John Martorano sat in the back seat, and Flemmi drove a back-up car close behind.

While Whitey and King were making small talk, Martorano shot King several times in the back of the head. Whitey and his boys then buried King's body in the marshes near the Neponset River in Quincy. In 2000, Kevin Weeks led the police to King's body. On the same night Whitey killed King, he also killed King's friend Buddy Leonard. The

Leonard killing was a red herring to throw the law off the track.

King was a hothead who hated cops. And he frequently let the cops know he hated cops. Before he was whacked, King had told a Boston police detective, who was giving him grief, that if the bull didn't lay off, he would kill him as easily as he had killed numerous mobsters. The detective knew that King wasn't too bright, but he also knew King had a reputation for killing people who pissed him off. So, the detective took King's threats seriously, as well he should. Consequently, the detective approached Whitey and pleaded his case. The detective knew Whitey was smart enough to understand killing an officer of the law was bad for business.

Whitey told the detective not to worry. He would take care of the King situation. What Whitey didn't tell the detective was that King was already dead and buried.

A short time later, Whitey contacted the same detective and told him King would no longer be a problem. By doing it this way, Whitey figured he had at least one Boston detective who owed him a serious favor, in addition to the F.B.I. who were already eating pablum out of Whitey's hands.

Chapter Six
In Bed With The Feds

From the time Howie Winter inserted Whitey as head of the Southie crew, Whitey started raking in cash. Because he was on the Massachusetts state police's radar, Whitey struck up an alliance with an old acquaintance from Southie who just happened to be an F.B.I. agent. In 1975, this lawman was given the task of turning informants, with the expressed purpose of decimating the Italian mob in Boston, especially the Angiulo brothers. The eldest brother, Gennaro (Jerry), was the Underboss of the Providence-based Patriarca Crime Family.

This agent's name was John Connolly, who would go on to make crooked F.B.I. agent Paul Rico look like a choirboy.

The first time Connolly met Whitey he was eight-years-old and Whitey was already a neighborhood big shot. Whitey bought Connolly an ice cream cone, which made Connolly feel like he had just met Ted Williams. That incident did not bode well for future developments in Boston.

Connolly was born on August 1, 1940, in the same Old Harbor Village projects that housed the Bulger clan. Connolly's father was a popular Irish immigrant, who was known by his pals as "Galway John."

When Connolly was 12-years-old, his family moved to the City Point neighborhood in South Boston. Connolly had no contact with Whitey after the "ice cream incident." Instead, Connolly, who was an altar boy at St. Monica's and a good baseball player, became close with Billy Bulger, who also had been an altar boy and a fine baseball player himself. It was rumored that Billy gave young Connolly the nickname "Elvis" because of the way Connolly combed his wavy black hair in an Elvis-style ducktail. In fact, Connolly didn't get the nickname Elvis until he was in his twenties and already an F.B.I. agent.

Billy Bulger became a mentor to Connolly and was possibly the biggest positive influence in Connolly's life. After Connolly graduated from high school, Billy convinced him to attend Billy's alma mater, Boston College. After graduating from B.C., Connolly entertained the thought of becoming a lawyer like Billy. Connolly briefly attended Suffolk University Law School, but then realized being a lawyer was not the vocation he desired.

Again, Connolly went to his mentor, Billy Bulger, now a state representative, and asked Billy if he thought Connolly would be suited for a career in law enforcement. Billy answered in the affirmative. Billy then encouraged House Speaker McCormack, the same pal who had helped Billy's brother Whitey in jail, to write a nice letter on Connolly's behalf to J. Edgar Hoover, the head of the F.B.I.

The letter started with "Dear Edgar, it had come to my attention that the son of a lifelong friend has applied to become a special agent of the Federal Bureau of Investigation..."

In October of 1968, despite the fact that he had a bad hip, which could prevent him from performing strenuous duties, John Connolly became an enforcement agent for the F.B.I.

Connolly was first sent to the F.B.I. office in Baltimore, and then to San Francisco. In an upwardly mobile move, Connolly was transferred to New York City, where he was involved in a successful effort to break up a child pornography ring.

Then Connolly caught a break, which involved

In Bed With The Feds

Whitey's pal, Steve Flemmi.

In 1969, Flemmi and an Italian mob crony, Frank "Cadillac" Salemme, bombed the car of a lawyer who was causing grief for the local La Cosa Nostra (LCN). The lawyer lived, but he was minus one leg.

Flemmi was tipped off by his old F.B.I. handler, Paul Rico, that they were about to be arrested. Taking the cue, Flemmi and Salemme split up and went on the lam: Flemmi to Montreal, Canada and Salemme to New York City. Flemmi, who took a job as a printer in Montreal, kept in close contact with Rico and Rico's partner, Dennis Condon. In 1971, both feds tried to flip Whitey to become an informant, but to no avail.

In early 1972, Rico contacted Flemmi and told him, if he would drop a dime on Salemme's whereabouts, Rico would arrange for Flemmi's safe passage back to Boston. Flemmi knew exactly where Salemme was staying in New York City. And Flemmi, being the rat he always had been, relayed Salemme's location to Rico. Rico, in turn, immediately contacted Connolly in New York City with the information. Salemme was whistling a happy tune while strolling down a Third Avenue sidewalk, when Connolly emerged from the crowd and slapped the cuffs on him.

Salemme went on trial in Boston for bombing the lawyer's car, and then Rico worked his magic again. Rico convinced the chief witness to say, under oath, that it was Salemme alone, who had bombed the lawyer's car. Salemme was convicted and nailed with a 30-year sentence, while Flemmi got the green light from Rico to come back to Beantown.

Soon, Flemmi was working with the Winter Hill Mob and becoming very close to Whitey. No one in the Winter Hill Mob knew Flemmi was an F.B.I. snitch with close ties to agents Rico and Condon. Flemmi saw no problem with being a rat since the F.B.I. had its sights set on the LCN. They could care less about the crimes the Winter Hill Mob were perpetrating in Boston.

After he busted Frank Salemme, Connolly knew it would help his career if he could get transferred to Boston, where he had friends in high and in low places. Connolly also knew Rico and Condon were near retirement and that they would like to groom Connolly as their replacement in the F.B.I.'s Boston office, whose mission was to wipe out the LCN.

In 1975, Connolly petitioned his bosses for a transfer to Boston. Part of the reason Connelly gave was so he could be close to his sick father, Galway John, who managed to live for another 10 years. With House Speaker John McCormack again pulling the strings, Connolly got his wish. He was assigned a desk at One Center Plaza in Government Center in Boston.

The F.B.I. in Boston would never be the same.

Connolly took little time putting his Whitey Bulger plan into motion. But things had to be settled with Steve Flemmi first.

Flemmi met Condon and Rico for lunch, where the two rogue agents introduced Flemmi to John Connolly, the same lad Whitey had bought vanilla ice cream so many years before. It's not certain who set up Connolly's meeting with Whitey, but it's safe to assume Rico and Condon, along with a little prodding from Flemmi, were instrumental in arranging things. There is no proof Billy Bulger knew about Connolly's plans for his brother or whether Billy put in a good word for Connolly with Whitey. However, both scenarios are plausible and consistent with Billy Bulger's relationship with both men.

However, this is what we do know:

On a starry night in mid-1975, John Connolly parked his government-issued Plymouth in a parking lot alongside Wollaston Beach in Quincy, Mass. Wollaston Beach is located on Quincy Bay, which is part of Boston Harbor. By this time, Dennis Condon had already tried to recruit

In Bed With The Feds

Whitey, but all he got from him was a little information on the gang wars of the early 1970's; i.e., who was who after the dust cleared and why. Whitey had refused to do anything else with the F.B.I., leading Condon to cease his efforts to turn Whitey into a rat. Because Connolly grew up in the same Old Harbor Village projects with Whitey and because Connolly was still friendly with Billy Bulger, the Boston F.B.I. office thought he had a chance to get Whitey to flip.

Connolly did not see Whitey approaching his car. In fact, he was somewhat startled when Whitey appeared out of nowhere, opened the front passenger door, and jumped in beside Connolly.

"What did you do, parachute in?" Connolly asked.

"Nah, I just parked on a side street and walked over to the beach," Whitey said.

"Do you know who I am?" Connolly asked.

"Yeah, you're a friend of my brother Billy," Whitey said. "That's why I'm here."

That broke the ice, and after some small talk about the old neighborhood, Connolly made his pitch.

"You should think about using your friends in law enforcement," Connolly said.

Connolly explained to Whitey why playing ball with the feds was a great idea and why it could benefit both of them.

By the mid-1970's, the mostly-Irish Winter Hill Mob was having problems with the Italian mob over the rights to install lucrative cigarette machines and juke boxes throughout the Boston area. Jerry Angiulo, who had a reputation of having close contacts in the Boston Police Department, led the local LCN. It was speculated that Angiulo used these contacts to have men arrested whom Angiulo thought were a threat to his operation. Whitey and his boys were in constant fear of Angiulo setting them up for a pinch.

As was reported in *Black Mass*, by Dick Lehr and

Gerard O'Neil, at his first meeting with Connolly, Whitey voiced his anxieties about Angiulo and his methods.

"What if three cops stop me at night and say there was a machine gun in my car?" Whitey said. "Who is the judge going to believe? Me or the three cops?"

"That's why you should use your friends," Connolly said.

"Who?" Whitey asked. "You?"

"That's right," Connolly said. "Me."

Connolly suggested, if Whitey played his cards right, he could turn the tables on Angiulo and the Italian mob. All Whitey had to do was tell the F.B.I., though Connolly, what the LCN was doing illegally and, if possible, when and where illegal acts were set to take place.

Connolly said, "If we are chewing on the Mafia, it's going to be very difficult for them to be chewing on you."

Whitey was intrigued by Connolly's proposition. Whitey hated the Italians. He despised their puffed-up sense of importance, flashy suits, pinkie rings, and stinking cologne. Whitey could see no possible downside in cooperating with Connolly and the F.B.I. Still, Whitey had misgivings about joining Team America."

Connolly sensed Whitey's concerns. He told Whitey, "Just hear me out. I hear Jerry is feeding information to law enforcement to get you pinched."

Then, Connolly added, "The Mafia has all the contacts, you know that."

Then there was the problem of LCN gang member, Larry Zannino, who had been threatening to go to war with the Winter Hill Mob over the placement of vending machines in South Boston.

Connolly told Whitey, "I'm aware that you are aware that Zannino and his outfit are going to make a move on you."

"Why, you don't think we can win that war?" Whitey said.

Connolly told Whitey he thought Whitey and Flemmi were tougher and smarter than Angiulo and Zannino, but that wasn't the issue. Connolly told Whitey it made more sense to do things intelligently and with the F.B.I.'s help.

"I have a proposal," Connolly said. "Why don't you do to them what they are doing to you? Fight fire with fire. You help take out the Mafia and you'll be the talk of the country."

Whitey told Connolly he'd think about it, and he exited Connolly's car without committing either way.

Whitey immediately ran to his best bud, Steve Flemmi. Whitey told Flemmi about Connolly's proposal. But Whitey told no one else in the Winter Hill Mob, not even John Martorano, one of the Winter Hill Mob's most feared killers and a man becoming increasingly close to Whitey.

Flemmi had a dilemma. Flemmi had been an F.B.I. snitch, working with Rico and Condon for many years. By Whitey approaching him about the Connolly deal, did it mean Whitey knew Flemmi was already cooperating with the feds? And did it really matter?

After thinking it over carefully, Flemmi told Whitey, "Yeah, I think it's a good idea. Go talk with him and set up a deal. I'm in."

Two weeks later, Whitey met Connolly in Connolly's car, again at Wollaston Beach.

Whitey told Connolly a little white lie, the first of many.

"My crew went for it," he told Connolly.

Whitey attached his own addendums to the deal. Whitey told Connolly he was not going to be an informant (a rat). Instead, he wanted to be considered and called a "liaison" between the Winter Hill Mob and the F.B.I. Whitey said he would inform only on the Italians, whom he considered the enemy - not on other Irish mobsters.

Connolly bit his tongue to conceal his glee.

Connolly told Whitey, "Sure, why not? Have it your way."

Connolly added, "We won't bother you in any of your activities. But just don't clip (kill) anyone. Okay?"

Whitey said, "Yeah, sure. Whatever you say."

The two former residents of the Old Harbor Village projects shook hands, cementing the deal.

Before Whitey left, he told Connolly, "My brother Billy is to know nothing about our arrangement."

Now it was Connolly's turn to say, "Yeah sure, whatever you say."

The Devil's pact, now signed in blood, was a fait accompli.

Less than a month later, Whitey, ignoring Connolly's addendum to their deal, whacked Tommy King and many others after King. The Boston F.B.I. would be none the wiser, if they even cared.

*****

Soon after he made his deal with Connolly, and knowing Flemmi had been talking with Rico and Condon for years, Whitey suggested to Flemmi maybe Flemmi should meet with Connolly again, just to set the record straight. Rico had already retired and Dennis Condon was ready to pack it in too. The plan was for Condon to hand off Flemmi to Connolly, who would become Flemmi's new contact with the F.B.I.

Later, when Condon and Connolly met Flemmi at a Boston suburb diner, it became clear to Flemmi he had no choice but to go along with the program. If Flemmi told Condon and Connolly to take a walk, the feds could leak word to the rest of the Winter Hill Mob and the Italian LCN as well, that Flemmi had been singing like a canary for years. If that happened, Flemmi wouldn't last a day in the streets of Boston.

In Bed With The Feds

When Flemmi said to count him in, Connolly and Condon exploded with joy. Both feds knew the Italian mob had little use for Whitey; he was Irish, for Pete's sake. However, an Italian like Flemmi, whom the LCN had tried to recruit for years, was golden. The Italians would say things to Flemmi they would never say to Whitey. All Connolly had to do was convince his bosses that the bulk of the LCN information was coming from Whitey instead of Flemmi; making Whitey untouchable on the streets of Boston and the surrounding area.

This was a case of a Southie Irishman taking care of another Southie Irishman, and vice versa; let the Italian mob be damned.

To make both Flemmi and Whitey feel better about themselves, Connolly reinforced the notion in both their minds they were not rats, but rather smart businessmen who were playing the angles in their own favor. Surely, Connolly had to know both Whitey and Flemmi killed first and asked questions later. Only a moron would believe they were no longer going to whack any more enemies, just because Whitey and Flemmi said so.

The problem for Connolly was to keep both Whitey and Flemmi out of trouble. If they did get into trouble, Connolly was going to use the full force of the F.B.I. to keep Whitey and Flemmi on the streets and singing.

Thing were fine and dandy until 1977, when Connolly learned Whitey, along with other Winter Hill Mob buddies, including Howie Winter, was set to be indicted in a long-standing horse racing scheme. This was just after the F.B.I. had promoted John Morris as Connolly's supervisor.

The quiet, but ambitious Morris, was the exact opposite of the loud, backslapping Connolly. Yet, Morris somehow got sucked into the Whitey myth. Morris went along with Connolly's scheme to insulate Connolly's Southie pal, Whitey Bulger, from any possible indictments.

For years, Howie Winter had been partners with

Anthony "Fat Tony" Ciulla, a man who had a pervasive presence at the racetracks throughout the East Coast. Ciulla, a leg-breaking 6-foot-4 inches and 250 pounds, had his fangs into many jockeys. For a few hundred bucks, these jockeys would hold back their horses, so the horses the Winter Hill Mob bet on would win the race.

One day in 1974, a New Jersey jockey took Ciulla's cash and rode his horse to victory anyway. Ciulla, Winter, and the rest of Winter's mob, including Whitey, were incensed. Winter's goons beat the crap out of the tiny jockey, warning him if that ever happened again he'd be horsemeat himself. Instead of taking this advice to heart, the jockey ran to the New Jersey State police and he told them his story. Consequently, Ciulla was arrested, tried, and convicted of extortion and horse race fixing. He was sentenced to a four-to-six year term in a New Jersey state pen.

Mobsters know state prison is not a picnic like federal prisons. Ciulla, ostensibly a tough guy, grew tired of the bad food and dangerous surroundings. In 1976, Ciulla had enough of his situation and he decided to rat on Winter and the Winter Hill Mob, including John Martorano, Whitey and Flemmi. For some reason, the New Jersey State Police brought in the F.B.I., and Connolly soon learned that Winter, Whitey, and Flemmi were in danger of going to prison. Connolly didn't care much what happened to Winter. In fact, getting Winter off the streets might work to the advantage of Whitey, Flemmi, and certainly Connolly.

Instead of keeping a low profile like most rats, Ciulla relished the role of being a big-time mob stoolie. Ciulla was the subject of a cover story in a November 6, 1978 Sports Illustrated issue, for which he was paid $10,000. This article detailed the innermost workings of the horse race-fixing scheme, identifying Ciulla as the "master race fixer."

Ciulla took the stand in the trial against several jockeys who accepted the Winter Hill Mob's bribery money. He proudly announced his four partners were Howie Winter, John Martorano, Steve Flemmi, and Whitey Bulger, all mobsters from Boston.

In early 1979, with the spit about to hit the fan, Connolly and his boss John Morris asked for an audience with Whitey at Whitey's South Boston apartment. Things were dire at this point, so the feds ignored the possibility of being spotted entering Whitey's apartment, which would have meant curtains for Whitey and the feds' chances for a big LCN bust.

At this meeting, Whitey did what he did best. He lied. Whitey told the feds Ciulla's statement that Whitey and Flemmi were involved in the horse race-fixing scheme was categorically false. Even though Connolly and Morris had to know Whitey was not telling the truth, his denials put them at ease.

The feds told Whitey to tell Flemmi not to worry about anything. They had an ace in the hole, which would insulate Whitey and Flemmi from the upcoming indictments.

Then, Morris and Connolly, for the first time, officially went over to the dark side.

Connolly and Morris were committed to keeping Whitey and Flemmi on the streets and informing on the Italian mob, even if it meant they would have to lie and break the law themselves. Connolly and Morris convinced themselves that the end justifies the means.

May justice be damned.

Without permission from F.B.I. headquarters, Connolly and Morris made a secret visit to the chief federal prosecutor in the horse race-fixing case, Jeremiah T. O'Sullivan – a fine Irish lad if there ever was one. O'Sullivan had one thing in common with Connolly and Morris: he had an intense dislike for the Italian LCN, and would do anything in his power to take the Italians down. The only problem for Connolly and Morris was O'Sullivan, after a two-year investigation, had already written up the indictments in the case and the defendants included both Whitey and Flemmi.

Since Connolly and Morris knew about O'Sullivan's LCN quest, they made him an offer O'Sullivan could not refuse. They told O'Sullivan both Whitey and Flemmi were F.B.I. informants, who were helping the feds bring an airtight case against the most hated LCN member in the Boston area: Gennaro (Jerry) Angiulo. This was music to O'Sullivan's ears. He could care less about imprisoning gangsters like Whitey and Flemmi, when the big fish – Angiulo – was dangling out there to be taken.

O'Sullivan rushed to tell Ciulla the bad news. Howie Winter and a few of his boys were still going to be prosecuted, but Whitey and Flemmi had been severed from the indictment. The reason O'Sullivan gave Ciulla for the startling turn of events was that Ciulla's testimony against Winter could be independently corroborated with things like telephone records, and restaurant and hotel receipts. But O'Sullivan had no such corroborating evidence on Whitey and Flemmi.

This made Ciulla's teeth hurt. Ciulla insisted that Whitey and Flemmi were just as guilty in the horse race-fixing scheme as were Howie Winter and the others. Furthermore, Ciulla knew the more men he betrayed who were left out on the streets; the better chance he would get whacked, even while he was ensconced in the Witness Protection Program. Ciulla understood there were crooked F.B.I. agents and crooked Boston cops. It was not beyond the realm of possibility that someone in law enforcement would give up his location so he could be killed by Whitey and his boys.

Ciulla would not be the first man under police protection to be eliminated by his enemies.

In 1941, Jewish killer and major canary, Abe "Kid Twist" Reles, a top hitman for Murder Incorporated, went flying, without a parachute, out the fourth-floor window of the Half Moon Hotel in Coney Island, N.Y. This occurred after Reles had testified in several mob trials and was set to squeal in several more, including those of Benjamin "Bugsy" Siegel and Albert "The Mad Hatter" Anastasia. The rumor was several New York City policemen, who were supposed to stand 24-hour guard over Reles, had flung Reles out the window. Another rumor had it that mobster Frank Costello paid a $50,000 bribe to those same cops for an early-morning garbage disposal.

O'Sullivan's decision to sever Whitey and Flemmi from the horse race-fixing indictments did not please Ciulla. And he told O'Sullivan so in no uncertain terms.

This presented O'Sullivan with a delicate dilemma. If he put Ciulla on the stand to testify against Howie Winter and several of Winter Hill Mob members, there was no way O'Sullivan could stop Ciulla from blurting out the names of Whitey Bulger and Steve Flemmi, while under oath.

Finally, with Ciulla begging and crying, O'Sullivan told him the truth: Whitey and Flemmi were F.B.I. confidential informants, who were helping the F.B.I. take down LCN's top bosses. They would be of no use to the F.B.I. if they were locked up in jail.

Ciulla chewed on this for a while, and it didn't taste like chicken.

Ciulla knew O'Sullivan was steadfast in removing Whitey and Flemmi from the indictment. But he also knew he had some leverage in this case, since one thing prosecutors like O'Sullivan couldn't stomach was an unpredictable key witness in court.

So Ciulla made a deal. He'd forget the names Whitey Bulger and Steve Flemmi, if O'Sullivan extracted a promise from Whitey and Flemmi they would not use their contacts in law enforcement to locate and kill Ciulla. Why Ciulla would believe anything Whitey and Flemmi promised is problematical. But he insisted on the deal anyway.

Whitey and Flemmi were never indicted in the horse

race-fixing scheme. But before the arrests came down, Whitey warned John Martorano that Martorano was going to be named in the indictments. Quickly, Martorano went into the wind before the feds could slap the cuffs on him. Martorano remained on the lam in the state of Florida for the rest of his criminal career.

Howie Winter was convicted, and he got a ten-year sentence, which made Whitey the top dog of the Winter Hill Mob in Boston. Ciulla did his time in prison, and then he disappeared into the Witness Protection Program.

There is no proof Ciulla was ever hunted down and whacked by Whitey's crew.

There's also no proof that he wasn't.

When Howie Winter ran the Winter Hill Mob, his base of operations was a dilapidated garage he owned on Marshall Street. Whitey's first action as the boss was to move his headquarters from Marshall Street to another garage on Lancaster Street, which Whitey called the Lancaster Foreign Car Service. Whitey made this move chiefly because Winter told Whitey he was selling the property because he needed the cash. The garage was only a short walk from Jerry Angiulo's North End headquarters, which made it quite easy for Whitey and Flemmi to keep tabs on the their favorite Italian enemies.

In short order, the Massachusetts State Police located Whitey's new headquarters, where they got a court order to install a bug so they could keep abreast of Whitey's activities. The state cops even rented a room across from the garage (above a gay bar), so they could film the comings and goings of every person who entered the premises.

But before they could get a significant sound bite, Whitey stopped talking business in the garage. Although every crook in town – Irish and Italian – stopped in for a visit, not one word concerning illegal activities was ever recorded over a three-month period. So, it was obvious to the state police the bug had been compromised and they were right. But it wasn't the F.B.I. who had tipped off Whitey about the bug; instead, it was a crooked state police officer whom Whitey had been paying off for years.

However, Jack O'Donovan, a state detective whose specialty was organized crime, incorrectly blamed the F.B.I., with whom he had battled several times over jurisdictional matters, for telling Whitey about the bug. O'Donovan called for a meeting with Morris and Connolly to discuss the situation. At this meeting, O'Donovan told Connolly and Morris what he thought about their cozy relationship with Whitey. The feds giggled at O'Donovan's rant about the bug. But the next thing O'Donovan said gave Connolly and Morris agita.

O'Donovan told the two feds, "We know for a fact both Whitey and Flemmi are F.B.I. informants."

O'Donovan later repeated his statement to the new man in charge of the F.B.I.'s Boston office: Larry Sarhatt. Sarhatt called Connolly and Morris on the carpet, and he told them the one thing they did not want to hear: "Close the F.B.I. files on Whitey Bulger and Steve Flemmi. We don't want them as informants any longer."

Dejected, Connolly and Morris visited Whitey and Flemmi. The feds told the two gangsters the bad news: they were no longer wanted or needed by the F.B.I.

Brushing a tear from his eye, Connolly said, "We won't be able to meet with you anymore."

It's not certain whose idea it was – Connolly's or Whitey's – but someone came up with a last-ditch plan to save Whitey and Flemmi from being severed from the F.B.I.'s informant list. Connolly and Morris had to prove to their boss, Larry Sarhatt, both Whitey and Flemmi were essential to bringing down the Boston branch of the LCN.

So they came up with a plan.

Knowing their F.B.I. lives depended on a good performance, Whitey and Flemmi paid a visit to 98 Prince

Street, the headquarters for the F.B.I.'s main target – Jerry Angiulo. Flemmi was a frequent visitor to Angiulo's lair, but Whitey hardly ever entered the premises. This should have tipped off Angiulo that maybe something wasn't right. But it didn't, and Angiulo would live to regret his lack of perspicacity.

The actual reason for the visit was for Whitey and Flemmi to draw up a detailed layout of the joint, so the F.B.I., who had already obtained a warrant to bug Angiulo's headquarters, would know exactly where to plant the bug to garner the most information.

Mission accomplished, Whitey and Flemmi presented the setup to Connolly, who gave it to Sarhatt. This reinforced the perception of their importance in helping the feds bring down the Italian mob.

But before he signed off on keeping Whitey and Flemmi in the fold, Sarhatt insisted on meeting Whitey Bulger himself. For some reason - probably because Connolly pushed Whitey as being more important to the cause than Flemmi - Flemmi was not invited to this meeting.

When he met Sarhatt at a hotel near Logan Airport, Whitey, who had the gift of gab, turned on the bullshit full blast. He convinced Sarhatt he was long-time pals with Connolly, and before him, Paul Rico. Whitey said he was committed to taking down the LCN as much the F.B.I. was.

When Sarhatt brought up the fact the state police knew Whitey was an informant, and could leak it to the underworld, Whitey smirked, and said "So what? No one would believe them. It would be too incredible."

Amazingly, Sarhatt bought Whitey's blather. He re-installed Whitey, and his partner Steve Flemmi, as Boston's top F.B.I. informants.

Gullible is not strong enough a word for Larry Sarhatt.

*****

John Connolly's supervisor, John Morris, may have been

a lot of things, but being discreet was not one of them.

After he conned Sarhatt into reinstating Whitey and Flemmi, Morris thought it would be a dandy idea to throw a party for the two gangsters at Morris's own home. Connolly told Whitey Morris was a wine fanatic, so Whitey made sure to bring a case of the finest grape to Morris's home. Because of Morris's fondness for wine, Whitey gave Morris the codename "Vino."

Whitey and Flemmi continued to give Morris cases of wine on every special occasion, and occasionally when there wasn't any special occasion. Once, Whitey was brazen enough to send a case of wine to Morris at his F.B.I. office using John Connolly as the delivery boy.

That day, Connolly strolled into the office and told Morris he has a present for him in the F.B.I. underground garage. Morris accompanied Connolly to the garage, and when Connolly opened the trunk of his car, he presently Morris with a case of wine, compliments of Whitey and Flemmi. Without batting an eye, Morris pulled his car next to Connolly's car and transferred the case into the trunk of his car. Whitey and Flemmi knew Morris's weakness for wine and figured, if they could keep him loaded as long as possible, the F.B.I. would become their own little fiefdom.

With the bug firmly in place at 98 Price Street, the F.B.I. was getting some tidy tidbits about the LCN's operations. Morris was so giddy about the results of the wiretap that he imprudently called for a celebration at the Colonnade Hotel in Boston. The guest list was short. It consisted of John Morris, John Connolly, Whitey Bulger, Steve Flemmi, and a case of Morris's favorite vino.

Morris drank hardily, and Connolly guzzled a few glasses. But Whitey and Flemmi, wanting to stay in complete control, only took a few sips here and there.

After Morris knocked down a couple of bottles of red wine, he was brazen and stupid enough to play one of the tapes the feds had recorded from the F.B.I. bug at 98 Prince

Street. Whitey and Flemmi were all ears, as they heard Jerry Angiulo and an associate, Larry Zannino, blab about participating in several illegal activities, including the beating of a woman who had talked too much for her own good.

When the party ended, Morris was dead drunk. Whitey, driving Morris's own car, took the supervisor of Boston's Organized Crime Division back home. Flemmi followed Whitey in his own car. After Whitey deposited a shitfaced Morris at his home's doorstep, Whitey jumped into Flemmi's car.

It was at this point that the two gangsters realized the tape containing confidential F.B.I. information had been left in the hotel room at The Colonnade. Flemmi dropped Whitey off at Whitey's home, and then rushed back to the hotel to retrieve the tape. Flemmi didn't have the key to the room, so he conned the desk clerk with a few bucks to let him in the room only for a minute, which is all Flemmi needed to slip the telltale tape into his pocket. Flemmi kept this tape as a souvenir, just in case he needed it down the road.

By early 1981, it was clear to Whitey and Flemmi that they controlled the F.B.I. and not the other way around. The inmates were now running the asylum known as the F.B.I. in Boston.

Whitey and Flemmi planned to squeeze every ounce of juice possible out of their plum position.

*****

With their F.B.I. boss, Larry Sarhatt, in their hip pocket, Connolly and Morris continued to file reports making Whitey and Flemmi look like the best informants since Judas Iscariot. Although Flemmi provided the bulk of information on the LCN, Connolly made it appear in his reports that Whitey was doing all the heavy lifting. Morris was obviously fine with this since he signed off on every report Connolly filed as if it were the gospel truth. In 1982, Sarhatt was replaced by James Greenleaf. But, by this time, the efforts of Whitey and Flemmi in fighting the LCN were legendary within the F.B.I.'s inner circle. So Greenleaf went along with the program without a peep.

In 1982, Connolly and Morris each had marital troubles. In January 1982, Connolly's wife filed for divorce. With the divorce decree finalized, the 41-year-old Connolly was officially a free man. Connolly had an eye for younger chicks, and soon was having an affair with buxom Elizabeth Moore, a stenographer in the F.B.I. office where Connolly worked.

While Connolly flaunted his affair with a younger woman, Morris was down in the dumps. Morris's marriage had been on its last legs for a while, partly because Morris's wife, Rebecca, hated the idea of Morris entertaining gangsters like Whitey and Flemmi in their home. Whenever Whitey and Flemmi were scheduled to appear, Rebecca Morris took a powder, leaving John Morris by himself to do the cooking and hosting.

Yet, man cannot exist on bread alone. It wasn't long before Morris was carrying on an affair in his F.B.I. office with his own secretary, Debbie Noseworthy. Since Morris was still married, he could not conduct an open romantic relationship in the office as the recently divorced Connolly did. So, whenever he felt the urge, Morris would hole up in a nearby hotel with Miss Noseworthy. Morris knew the rest of his staff was wise to his indiscretions, which made him mope around the office feeling ashamed and emasculated.

In June 1982, Morris was sent by his superiors to an F.B.I. training camp at the Federal Law Enforcement Training Center in Glynco, Georgia. The purpose of the camp was to get the F.B.I. up to snuff on illicit drug trafficking, which was supposedly under the jurisdiction of the Drug Enforcement Agency (D.E.A.). Because the F.B.I. loves to grab the glory in all high-profile cases, they didn't want their own agents under-trained in comparison to D.E.A. agents.

After a few days of boring classes and not being able to retreat to the hotel room at the end of the day to snuggle up with Miss Noseworthy, Morris decided to call in some chits from his top informants.

According to *Black Mass*, by Dick Lehr and Gerard O'Neil, "I called Connolly," Morris said. "And I reminded him of the offer Bulger and Flemmi had made: if I ever needed anything; just let them know. So I asked Connolly, 'Do you think they could arrange for an airline ticket for Debbie (Miss Noseworthy).'"

Connolly said no problem.

Connolly ran to Whitey with Morris's request, and Whitey said, "Sure, I'd like to help my old pal: Morris. He must be lonely down there in Georgia."

Whitey handed Connolly $1,000 in crisp new hundred-dollar bills, which Connolly stuffed into an envelope. Then Connolly rushed to Miss Noseworthy's desk and handed her the envelope. Miss Noseworthy opened the envelope and was startled to find a grand in cash.

"What's this for?" Miss Noseworthy asked.

"John wanted you to have this," Connolly said. "He's been saving it up for a situation just like this. He wants you to take the money and buy an airline ticket to Georgia to join him."

John Morris had just solicited cash from a gangster like Whitey so that he could cozy up with his girlfriend in Georgia. Whitey knew that was probably the best $1,000 he had ever invested.

Chalk up another black mark for the Boston branch of the F.B.I.

*****

The problem for Connolly and Morris was that Whitey and Flemmi were not the only F.B.I. informants in Boston. Other agents had cultivated different snitches. What those informants were saying did not make Whitey and Flemmi look too good. In 1981, an F.B.I. stoolie said Whitey was still involved in robbing banks and was using the spoils from the bank heists to fund his gambling and loansharking operations.

That was a mere distraction compared to the time a different informant told his F.B.I. handler that Whitey and Flemmi were up to their eyeballs dealing cocaine. Whitey's official stance on the streets was he hated drugs and would whack anyone bringing that filth into his Southie neighborhood. The truth of the matter was no cocaine dealer operated anywhere near Boston without paying tribute to Whitey. Although Whitey wasn't personally peddling the white powder, his pockets were bulging with cash contributed by Boston's drug dealers and there were plenty of them.

Other informant reports, saying Whitey was big into drugs, began flowing into the Boston F.B.I. office like a tidal wave. In February 1981, one F.B.I. mole said a thug named Brian Halloran was "dealing drugs" with Whitey and Flemmi. The feds knew Halloran had been a flunky for Whitey for years, but he was known mostly as a low-level hooligan, not a major drug dealer in cahoots with the biggest gangsters in Boston. Another informant independently confirmed the accusation that Halloran was working drug deals with Whitey and Flemmi. The biggest blow to Whitey and Flemmi's reputation was when yet another independent snitch said Halloran and his pal, Nick Femia, were shaking down as many as 30 Boston drugs dealers for a share of their profits, which they kicked upstairs to Whitey and Flemmi.

Amazingly, since John Morris was technically the superior of the F.B.I. agents who were turning Boston informants, and since these agents filed their reports directly with Morris, he was able to solve the problem by simply misfiling the incriminating reports, effectively making the reports disappear into thin air.

To make it appear Whitey was not profiting from the

sale of drugs, John Connolly concocted bogus reports indicating Whitey was appalled by the presence of drugs in Boston. Connolly filed reports saying Whitey was outraged, like Captain Renault in *Casablanca*, that someone was actually selling drugs in his town. And like Captain Renault, Whitey stuffed the illicit money into his pockets while uttering dubious denials.

In addition to making Whitey appear as the Robin Hood of Southie, Connolly went so far as to manufacture reports saying intelligence gathered from the great informant, Whitey Bulger, was responsible for the arrest and capture of several criminals, nationwide.

During the 1980 Memorial Day weekend, crooks broke into the Depositors Trust in Medford, Mass. Several days later, Connolly filed a phony report saying Whitey had called him and given him the names of the bank thieves. However, Jake Keating, the Chief of Police in Medford, said, on the day after the robbery, he had received several tips as to the bank robbers' identities, but none of the tips came from Whitey or John Connolly.

But then Connolly went one better.

In 1981, a mob killer named Joseph Barboza Baron was whacked in the distant city of San Francisco. This killing took place in front of the apartment of another West Coast wiseguy, Jimmy Chalmas. As far as the San Francisco police were concerned, Chalmas was their No. 1 suspect from the get-go, either as the actual shooter or the man who had set up Baron for the kill. In fact, Chalmas was interviewed by San Francisco homicide detectives the night after Baron's murder but they didn't have enough evidence to make an arrest.

A full three months later, after Chalmas had finally been taken into custody, Connolly had the nerve to file a report saying that Whitey had informed him that Chalmas was responsible for Baron's murder. In addition, Connolly said Whitey had provided concrete evidence to the San

Francisco police that led to Chalmas's arrest.

All of this was sheer bullshit, but no one in the F.B.I., including Larry Sarhatt, who was Connolly's boss at the time, questioned how a local mobster like Whitey, who had no power outside his fiefdom in Boston, could know so many intimate details about a murder committed 3,000 miles away.

Because of John Connolly's outright lies and the ignorance of his bosses, the legend of Whitey as a "top echelon F.B.I. informant" grew like Pinocchio's nose.

*****

In 1978, a new hooligan joined Whitey's crew. His name was Kevin Weeks.

Weeks, born on March 21, 1956, was a knockaround street guy who grew up in the Old Colony Housing Projects in Southie. Weeks was a good athlete, who took to the sport of boxing like a fish to water. He won several amateur boxing tournaments throughout New England.

In 1974, Weeks graduated without much distinction from South Boston High. Not exactly being college material, Weeks got a job as a security guard at the same South Boston high school. The school security job entailed Weeks breaking up fights between rowdy teenagers, or sometimes throwing a few punches himself. Since the pay sucked and his hands constantly hurt from all the slugging, Weeks figured he'd give higher education a shot. After a few months at the Commonwealth Prep School, Weeks decided he was not cut out for college, and soon he was back busting up fights at South Boston High.

In 1976, Weeks was fired from South Boston High for beating up a black student, a charge he categorically denied. While he was in court for a hearing on the assault and battery charge, Weeks ran into Billy O'Neil, who was there on an assault charge himself. O'Neil was part-owner, with his two brothers, of the Triple O Bar in Southie, one of

Whitey's favorite hangouts. O'Neil knew about Weeks's reputation as a brawler and he offered Weeks a job as a bouncer at the Triple O, where fights broke out almost every night. This is where Weeks hooked up with Whitey and, when he did, Weeks's life took a drastic turn deep into the underworld.

On Christmas Day 1978, Weeks, who was now working two jobs - at the Boston Transit System in the day and at the Triple O at night - got married to a wonderful girl named Pam. The invitee list for Weeks's wedding included friends and relatives. But it also included a Who's-Who of Triple O's elite customers, including Whitey and Flemmi.

On St. Patrick's Day 1979, Weeks broke up a particularly nasty fight at the Triple O among the usual St. Paddy Day drunks, busting a few heads in the process. His bosses rewarded Weeks's good work. Instead of bouncing inside the joint, the O'Neil's gave Weeks a less demanding job. He would now work the front door for 25 bucks a night and ten percent of the bartenders' and waitresses' tips.

Whitey, whom Weeks always called "Jimmy", was a regular customer a few nights a week at the Triple O, usually accompanied by Flemmi. Weeks said Whitey typically wore a western costume of sorts, unusual for a northern city like Boston: jeans, cowboy boots (Whitey also had the nickname "Boots"), and a tight leather jacket. Whitey, as is customary for the gangsters of his ilk, always sat at the end of the bar with his back against the wall so he could see if danger was coming through the front door.

Hearing Weeks was good with his fists and confirming it by observing Weeks in action a few times, Whitey began cultivating Weeks for an upwardly mobile move into a life of crime. Whitey preached to Weeks the absolute necessity of keeping away from drugs and booze. Whitey told Weeks both vices made people stupid. Whitey said if Weeks wanted to be a success in Whitey's world, being a boozer or a hopped-up cocaine head was a killer in more ways than one.

In Bed WithThe Feds

Whitey drilled into Weeks that people who drank to excess, or did drugs, were weak and untrustworthy. They might rat someday.

The turning point for Weeks was when Whitey told his underling, Nicky Femia, who was constantly strung out on booze and cocaine, to get lost permanently. That left a void in Whitey's crew, which Whitey filled with Kevin Weeks.

Soon, Weeks was a regular passenger in Whitey's cars, which were always fast and always equipped with police scanners so Whitey could listen to the inner workings of the Boston Police Department, the State Police, the D.E.A., and, of course, Whitey's pals in the F.B.I.

While he was working the door at the Triple O, Weeks got his first taste of action.

One night, Whitey told Weeks to take a ride with him. Weeks had busted a lot of heads at the Triple O, and Weeks thought one of Whitey pal's might have been one of the victims Maybe Whitey was using the ruse of taking a ride as a way to bust up Weeks. One thing Weeks knew for sure, no matter how much Whitey roughed him up, it was suicide to fight back. Weeks was resigned to take his beating like a man.

When Whitey pulled up to the curb by a bar on East Broadway, Weeks realized he was not in the car to catch a beating, but to administer one himself. A punk kid about 20-years-old was standing in front of the bar, and Whitey ordered him into the back seat of the car. After driving a few blocks, Whitey stopped and put the car into park.

Whitey turned around and read the kid the riot act, telling him never to touch Whitey's niece again. The kid had a knife in a sheath, but before the kid could do anything stupid, Whitey snatched the knife, and he slit it across the kid's throat. Lucky for the kid, Whitey had used the blunt end of the knife so the wound was not life threatening.

Then, like a maniac, Whitey began pummeling the kid's face. Weeks got into the act too, raining punches from all directions on the hapless victim. In seconds, the kid's nose and mouth were pouring blood all over the backseat upholstery, which enraged Whitey even more.

Whitey pulled out a leather sap, the kind Boston cops use to correct criminals, and administered a savage beating that left the kid unconscious on the floor of the car.

Mission accomplished, Whitey drove back to the East Broadway bar, where he and Weeks deposited the unconscious kid onto the sidewalk. From inside the bar, the kid's pals saw what was happening, and rushed outside. They were shocked and dismayed to come face-to-face with the most feared man in Boston, Whitey Bulger.

Whitey growled at them, "Anybody else want to bother with my niece?"

Without saying a word, the kid's pals picked up their friend and carried him inside the bar.

When Weeks and Whitey were back in Whitey's car, Weeks, still shaking from the incident, told Whitey, "I thought you cut his throat with that knife."

"The kid's lucky; I meant to," Whitey said. "I just held the knife the wrong way."

Weeks later discovered the girl was not Whitey's niece, but rather a daughter of a friend of Whitey's. To Weeks, it didn't make a difference who the girl was. Anyone who beats a girl deserves a beating himself.

A few days later, Whitey gave Weeks a thousand dollars for his role in the kid's whipping. Weeks was now firmly entrenched in Whitey's world, and he was getting paid pretty well for doing what he did best; beating the crap out of people.

One time, Whitey and Weeks were cruising the streets, when a double-parked car blocked them. The driver of the car was about 20-years-old and was engaged in a conversation with someone who was leaning into the driver's side window. Whitey beeped the horn and yelled for the driver to pull over so he could pass. The driver ignored Whitey. When Whitey beeped again, the driver shot Whitey the middle finger, which wasn't the brightest thing to do to a maniac like Whitey.

In a flash, Whitey and Weeks jumped out of their car and headed for the driver, whose finger was still erect in the air. Seeing Whitey and Weeks advance towards him, the driver jumped out of his car and made a beeline for Whitey, screaming and cursing.

Whitey smiled. Not wanting to get his hands dirty, he turned to Weeks and said, "Kevin, hit him."

And that's what Weeks did.

A single left jab put the driver on his back. Without a word, the driver's friends moved his car so Whitey and Weeks could continue their journey.

Almost on a daily basis, Kevin Weeks justified his existence in Whitey's world by using his fists. The pay was good and the adulation from the Boston crowd for being Whitey's right-hand man was intoxicating. At the time, Kevin Weeks was doing very well for himself.

But in Whitey's world, things change constantly, invariably in Whitey's favor.

Kevin Weeks bought into the "Whitey Bulger" legend. When the myth evaporated, Weeks would be the last to know.

Chapter Seven
The Trouble With Women

Even though Whitey was a full-time gangster, he always found time for the opposite sex, and he wasn't always nice about it. Besides banging the usual prostitute, or a girl Whitey had gotten drunk in a bar, Whitey had his first full-time post-jail fling with a pretty young thing named Lindsey Cir. Cir, like his former girlfriend Jacquie McAuliffe, was built like a brick shit house; the difference being Cir was a redhead while Jacquie was a blond.

It was 1965. Whitey had just been released from prison and had not yet made his bones in the Winter Hill Mob. Whitey first spotted Cir in a diner where she was waitressing. Whitey was in his mid-thirties at the time; Cir looked like she had just gotten out of high school (she was 21).

While Cir was serving Whitey breakfast, he made his pitch for a date. Cir turned him down, but she was nice about it. Cir told Whitey she was in the process of extracting herself from a relationship with a boyfriend who was causing her problems.

Almost every morning Whitey had breakfast at Cir's diner. Whitey admitted to Cir he had spent nine years in the can, but Cir did not seem turned off by Whitey's past.

One morning, Whitey finally got the break he was looking for.

Cir's boyfriend stormed into the diner. He grabbed her, shook her, and started screaming in her face. As startled customers looked on, Whitey calmly got out of his seat. He grabbed Cir's boyfriend by the collar and he flung him out the front door of the diner. Outside, Whitey went to work on him, until the man was reduced to a bloody mass of human flesh.

Whitey strolled back into the diner, and he finished his breakfast; but not until he assured Cir her boyfriend would not bother her again.

Soon, Cir became Whitey's steady squeeze. Cir discovered quickly that Whitey was a sex maniac who constantly wanted her to service him, even in the shadows of public places. Whitey often got the urge when he was driving Cir around town. When that happened, the nearest alley would do for a quickie, or maybe a public bathroom in a restaurant or an office building. Whitey abhorred using a rubber, and soon Cir was pregnant with Whitey's child.

This was not something Whitey wanted to hear.

Whitey insisted Cir have an abortion. But when it was clear Cir would do no such thing, Whitey, who was now rolling in dough working for the Killeens, agreed to support Cir and their child. Whitey had only one provision: his name could not be put on the birth certificate.

Whitey gave Cir the bullshit story that a man involved in the mob could not afford to have a child because his enemies might kidnap the kid for ransom. Cir agreed. When Whitey's blond and blue-eyed son Douglas was born (he looked just like Whitey), Cir put her ex-boyfriend – the man Whitey had wiped the sidewalk with – down as the boy's father on the birth certificate.

Although Whitey never married Cir, he treated her and their son like family, occasionally bringing them to his brother Billy's house for dinner.

In 1973, after Whitey had already been made the boss of the Winter's Hill Mob's Southie faction, Douglas, only six-years-old, died after a brief bout with Reye's Syndrome, a rare and fatal condition that's usually a reaction to aspirin. The disease causes swelling in the brain and in the liver.

Whitey paid for his son's funeral. Soon after, he gave Cir the gate.

By this time, Whitey had already hooked up with a blond named Teresa Stanley, who was built a lot like Jacquie McAuliffe.

Whitey was through with redheads.

*****

When she met Whitey Bulger, Teresa Stanley was a divorcee with four kids and living in the rundown Old Colony housing projects. Surprisingly, Whitey treated Stanley as if she was his wife, even sitting down for dinner every night with her brood as if he were their biological father. However, Whitey was a tyrant at the kitchen table, not allowing the kids to receive any phone calls during the dinner hour, or else.

Even though Whitey bought Stanley a nice house in a Boston suburb and took her on high-price vacations, Stanley was little more than Whitey's slave. Whitey ordered Stanley around with impunity, and yelled at her whenever she had more than one or two glasses of wine. They were together the better part of twenty years, and the only time Whitey ever laid his hands on Stanley was over her drinking.

One night, Stanley stayed out into the wee hours, decorating a house with her girlfriend Terry. The house was located right next to the home of Steve Flemmi's parents. About 3 a.m., Whitey stormed into the house looking for Stanley and was dismayed to find both women had been drinking. When Whitey noticed Stanley's slurred speech, he went berserk. He grabbed Stanley by the throat and started flinging her around the room like a rag doll. When Whitey was finished, Stanley had a black eye and bruises all over her body.

Stanley later told a friend, "I almost got killed for drinking a couple of glasses of wine."

The hypocrisy of Whitey's obsession with people

around him not drinking was obvious. In the mid-1980's, Whitey forced a married couple, Steven and Julie Rakes, to sell him their liquor store located near the Old Colony Housing projects. Whitey's used strong-arm tactics to acquire the liquor store because Whitey wanted to have a meeting place for his boys and make a few bucks in the bargain. Soon, the liquor store was raking in the cash. Whitey bragged to a pal he had the busiest liquor store in Southie. With all the boozers in the area, that's saying a lot.

Still, if anyone drank to excess around Whitey, he looked at them as if they were dogshit on the bottom of his shoe.

*****

Steve Flemmi was a lady-killer in many ways.

Beginning in the mid-1960's, Flemmi started playing house with Marion Hussy, who had a daughter, Debra, from a previous marriage, and two sons, Billy and Steven. After Flemmi returned from his stint on the lam, he bought Hussy and her kids a house in the town of Milton, just south of Boston. The house was a mini-mansion, complete with a swimming pool and tennis courts. Flemmi loved to invite his cronies, including Whitey and Teresa Stanley, for weekend dinners, which were usually prepared by Flemmi's mother, Mary, who had a reputation as a great Italian cook.

Flemmi, like Whitey, always kept a few babes on the side.

In 1972, Flemmi met 17-year-old Debra Davis, who was a clerk at the jewelry store where Flemmi occasionally visited to buy things for Hussy. Davis was thin, but curvy, with blond hair and blue eyes. When Flemmi, 38-years-old at the time, discovered the young lady was married and that her deadbeat husband was languishing in jail, he swooped in for the kill.

Soon, Flemmi set Debra up in a nice apartment in Brookline filled with the best furniture and electronics.

Flemmi showered Debra with clothes and bought her a swanky new car every year or two.

However, Flemmi had two problems he had to correct as far as Debra was concerned.

First, Debra was still married to the jerk in jail. She wanted a divorce, but her husband would not relent and sign the divorce papers. Fortunately, Flemmi had strong contacts in prison. One day, a crony of Flemmi confronted Debra's husband in the can and told him if he didn't agree to a divorce, Debra would soon be his not-so-grieving widow.

Scratch problem number one.

Second, there was the dilemma of Debra's pain-in-the-ass father, Ed Davis, who knew Flemmi for what he was: a married older creep who was using his daughter for sex. In 1975, Ed Davis got so incensed about his daughter's relationship with Flemmi, he took a hammer and destroyed the outside of a new car Flemmi had just bought Debra.

Unfortunately, Ed Davis never understood how dangerous Flemmi could be. One day in the summer of 1975, Ed Davis went boating with his pals in Boston Harbor and was never seen again. The story was Ed had somehow fallen overboard and drowned before anyone could save him. His body was never found. Readers can draw their own conclusions.

Scratch problem number two.

By 1980, after Debra hounded him for years, Flemmi finally divorced his first wife, left Marion Hussy, and moved in with Debra. A year later, when Debra reached 26 years of age, she began to tire of Flemmi and his unpredictable ways. She also knew Flemmi was seeing other women. Debra figured in a few years she'd suffer the same fate as Flemmi's first wife and Marion Hussy.

Debra decided to take a vacation with her mother, Olga, to Acapulco, where she met a Mexican millionaire named Gustav. Debra figured Gustav could give her everything Flemmi could without the baggage a man like Flemmi carried.

When Debra returned home, she told Flemmi she was leaving him for another man. This is where versions of Debra Davis's death diverge. One story is that Debra was killed because of Flemmi's jealousy. Another is that Whitey ordered her murder and actually killed her himself. The reason for the latter theory was that Flemmi had stupidly told Debra about his and Whitey's relationship with John Connolly. Whitey realized it was just a matter of time before Debra either ratted them out as informers or tried to blackmail them.

What is known is the following, which came from Flemmi's testimony at his 2003 trial.

According to Flemmi, at Whitey's urging, he lured Debra Davis to a house on 799 East Third Street, owned by Pat Nee's brother, under the ruse Flemmi had just bought the house for his parents. When Flemmi and Debra entered the house, Whitey was there waiting for them. Whitey sprung from the shadows, put his hands around Debra's neck, and kept squeezing until she was dead.

Then, with a pair of pliers, Flemmi pulled out Debra's teeth, one by one, so that her body could not be identified through dental records. Then, after wrapping her body in plastic, and with the help of Pat Nee, whom they had summoned to the house, they transported Debra's body in the trunk of a car to Quincy, where they buried her in marshland next to a bridge.

After several days, Debra's mother, Olga, began pestering Flemmi as to the whereabouts of her daughter. Flemmi visited Olga at her home and told her Debra had flown to Texas to be with her new boyfriend. Flemmi swore to Olga he'd keep looking for Debra until he found her.

In the meantime, Flemmi tried to cover all his bases. He had a pal visit Debra's dentist, who requested the dentist give him Debra's dental records. Of course, the dentist had little choice if he didn't want to wind up buried in the marshes himself. So he handed over Debra's dental records, which were promptly destroyed.

Olga Davis didn't believe a word Flemmi told her, so she filed a missing person's report. The F.B.I. came to her house and took Olga's statement. This is where Flemmi pulled the strings with his F.B.I. pals. The feds removed Debra's missing person's report from the F.B.I. database. In its place, they wrote a new report stating Debra had been spotted in Houston, Texas, having a fine old time in the company another man.

And then it became worse, much worse.

Flemmi lived in the same house with Debbie Hussy, the daughter of his common-law wife, Marion Hussy, since Debbie was three-years-old. It is not clear exactly when, but after Debbie became a teenager, Flemmi began having sex with his stepdaughter right under the nose of her mother.

Soon, Debbie began running with a wild crowd and started to use drugs on a daily basis. A hopeless junkie, Debbie was reduced to turning tricks on the streets to support her drug habit. There were rumors Debbie would pick up johns on the street, and take them to her mother's house if she knew nobody was home.

In his testimony in a later trial, Flemmi admitted his liaison with Debbie Hussy, but he claimed Marion Hussey knew what they were doing all along. According to Flemmi, Marion said nothing about the sexual relationship between him and her daughter.

However, Marion Hussy later testified in court she didn't know that her daughter and Flemmi were having sex until 1982. She found out when she returned home one day and saw Flemmi slapping Debbie around. Flemmi hold Marion he was hitting Debbie because of her drug use, but Debbie said that was a lie. Debbie blurted out that she had been having sex with Flemmi for years. Without hesitation, Marion Hussy threw Flemmi out of her house and out of her life.

For the next several years, Debbie continued in a downward spiral, stripping in raunchy sex clubs for a few bucks a night. Debbie would occasionally meet Flemmi for sex, after which he would give her money, which she immediately spent on drugs. Finally, Flemmi got Debbie an apartment, which she used to service her sex-for-sale customers, some of them African-Americans, which irritated the racist Flemmi even more.

Flemmi told the similarly bigoted Whitey, "She's bringing niggers into the house."

The reasons aren't exactly clear, but in January of 1985, Flemmi wanted Debbie Hussy dead. And like Debra Davis's murder several years earlier, Flemmi's partner, Whitey, would participate in the murder of a young woman.

Flemmi lured Debbie Hussy to a house he had just bought for his parents. It was right next door to the home of Billy Bulger. According to Kevin Weeks, when Debbie Hussey walked through the front door, Whitey was waiting downstairs and Weeks was in an upstairs bedroom. Weeks said he was heading down the stairs, when he heard a thud from the ground floor.

"When I walked into the parlor, Debbie, her brown hair falling against her shoulder, was lying on the floor," Weeks said. "I had never seen her before, and she certainly wasn't looking very good."

Weeks said Whitey then straddled Debbie and began strangling the life out of her. Debbie's eyes were bulging and her face and lips turned a dark blue. Weeks could see she was already dead. But Flemmi was not so sure.

"Stevie put his head on her chest, and said she was still alive," Weeks said. "To prove his point, he took a clothesline of rope, wrapped it around Debbie's neck, stuck a stick in it, and began twisting and twisting like it was a garrote."

When Flemmi was sure Debbie was dead, Weeks and Flemmi took Debbie downstairs to the cellar, while Whitey calmly climbed to an upstairs bedroom to take a nap. (Several of his confederates said Whitey was cold-blooded and emotionless, and would usually take a nap after he had participated in a murder.)

Down in the basement, Flemmi removed Debbie's clothes, and then he ripped out all of Debbie's teeth with pliers while Weeks dug a hole in the floor. Since the murder was a choking; there was no blood to clean up. Soon, two associates arrived at the house. They wrapped Debbie's body in a tarp and buried her in the marshes near the Neponset River.

Weeks was perplexed by the business-like way Flemmi had just participated in the killing of a woman he had known since she was three.

"Even though he had a long-term relationship with Debbie, this wasn't bothering him any more than it bothered Jimmy (Whitey)," Weeks said. "Stevie was actually enjoying it; the way he always enjoyed a good murder. Like a stockbroker going to work, he was just doing his job. He was cold and relaxed, with no emotion or change in his demeanor. He was just performing a night's work."

It's clear, both Whitey and Flemmi were stone cold murderers. It's also clear, Whitey treated his women much better than Flemmi treated his.

Chapter Eight
Whitey's Biggest Mistake

John Callahan was a successful businessman, who had more angles than a geometry teacher. Callahan was a regular at the exclusive wiseguy club, Chandler's, which by 1981 was controlled by the Winter Hill Mob, which meant Whitey Bulger.

Callahan was raised in Medford, Mass. After high school he joined the United States Air Force, not to protect his country, but as a way to wheedle a college education. After serving one tour in the air force, Callahan attended Yale and then Bentley College, where he earned his degree in accounting. After Bentley, Callahan took a job at the accounting firm, Ernst and Young. Making his bones at Ernst and Young, Callahan then landed a gig at a prestigious national firm, Arthur Anderson, which in 2002 was found guilty of cooking the books in the infamous Enron Scandal. But by then, Callahan was long gone in more ways than one.

After a few years at Arthur Anderson, Callahan was awarded a partnership in the firm. But Callahan's sights were set higher than being a partner in one of the country's biggest accounting firms. He wanted his own business, so he could afford to hang out with his buddies in Chandler's on an equal basis. In 1972, after already accumulating a huge clientele while working at Ernst and Young and then at Arthur Anderson, Callahan decided to strike out on his own, forming a consulting business.

In 1974, Callahan got his big break when he was hired by World Jai Alai, a company that ran the Basque sport of jail alai (zesta punta in Basque). Jai Alai is a sport of sorts, where men hurl goatskin-covered balls with a curved basket at speeds up to 188 mph. It's a game where huge bets are made. It's also a game that is known to be rigged at times. Callahan loved rigged games where he could rake in easy profits.

At the time Callahan was hired, Jai Alai was only legal in a few states like Rhode Island and Florida. Callahan's job was to expand the sport into other states, especially Nevada. Callahan started hiring people from his contacts in Chandler's, including infamous ex-F.B.I. agent Paul Rico, whom Callahan tapped as head of security, and Richard Donovan, who became Callahan's top assistant.

In 1976, after Callahan's underworld contacts were discovered by the lawyers at World Jai Alai, Callahan was asked to resign. Callahan agreed to step down without a court battle, but only if World Jai Alai hired his pal Richard Donovan as his successor and kept Rico on as the head of security. The reason for this was simple. He and Donovan with Rico's help had been skimming money off the top of the parking and concession stands to the tune of nearly a million dollars a year. They weren't about to give up that kind of dough without a fight.

A few months after Callahan stepped down, Callahan approached World Jai Alai with an offer to buy the company for thirty-five million dollars. Callahan was able to get so much cash was because he was in cahoots with several underworld figures, including Jack Cooper, who was a close pal of Jewish mobster Meyer Lansky. Twice, World Jai Alai turned down offers from Callahan to buy them out because they didn't trust Callahan or his associates.

This is where Roger Wheeler came into the act.

Roger Wheeler was an ambitious but honest businessman, who made huge amounts of money by taking the failing Telex Corporation in Tulsa, Oklahoma and turning it into a big moneymaker. Wheeler was aware of the tremendous profits in the racetrack business and in the casinos of Las Vegas. He wanted his own piece of the action. After several failed attempts at buying a racetrack or a casino, Wheeler discovered World Jai Alai was on the market for fifty million dollars. Wheeler did his due diligence (he and one of his sons were accountants) and determined that World Jai Alai was extremely profitable. He decided it would be a sound investment.

World Jai Alai, in turn, did its own due diligence on Wheeler. They discovered he was a legitimate businessman and agreed to sell him the corporation. To finance the deal, Wheeler put up seventeen million dollars of his own money and borrowed the balance from the National Bank of Boston.

This put John Callahan in a bind. Through Donovan and Rico, Callahan was robbing World Jai Alai blind. He knew it would not take Wheeler long to detect the thievery. Callahan approached Wheeler and offered to buy him out, but Wheeler turned him down.

Callahan figured, if Wheeler was out of the picture, Wheeler's wife and sons would have no choice but to sell World Jai Alai to him. To Callahan, the solution was obvious. Wheeler had to go, and Callahan knew exactly who to approach to thrust Wheeler out of the picture.

Back in Boston, Callahan set up a meeting with Whitey and Flemmi to talk about the Wheeler situation. Also at this meeting was Brian "Balloonhead" Halloran, who was pals with Callahan and itching to make a few bucks himself. Callahan explained to Whitey and Flemmi why it would be in their best interests if Wheeler were murdered. He threw in the fact that Paul Rico was onboard with the idea. Then, Callahan told Whitey and Flemmi he had the perfect man to do the job: Brian Halloran.

Whitey knew Halloran was a screw-up and a cokehead, who had never done a hit before. Quite frankly, Whitey hated Halloran's guts. Whitey made this clear to both

Halloran and Callahan by the way he contemptuously stared at Halloran throughout the meeting.

Whitey realized, however, that Callahan had a moneymaking machine at World Jai Alai. It would mean upwards of ten grand a week being funneled through Callahan to Whitey and Flemmi, if they agreed to the Wheeler hit.

Whitey wanted to talk over the situation with Flemmi, alone. So he abruptly ended the meeting, telling Callahan he'd think it over. After Whitey and Flemmi put their heads together, they agreed Callahan had a great idea, except for the part about Brian Halloran doing the hit. Because the money was too good to pass up, Whitey made the stupidest mistake of his criminal career in deciding to take out the upstanding businessman, Roger Wheeler.

A few days later, Whitey met with Callahan and told him the Winter Hill Mob would go for the deal, but only if their old crony John Martorano was Wheeler's assassin.

Callahan took a trip to Florida and approached his old drinking buddy from Chandler's, John Martorano, who was still on the lam for the horse race fixing indictments of 1979. During his exile, Martorano had depended on favors from Callahan to keep him one step ahead of the law. After hearing that Whitey and Flemmi had suggested him for the job and that ex-F.B.I. agent Paul Rico was also involved, Martorano listened to Callahan's pitch.

Later, after turning F.B.I. informant himself, Martorano testified in court at the 2008 murder trial of John Connolly.

Martorano told the court, "Callahan was trying to buy the business for a lot of money. He said if the deal went through, we'll give you $10,000 a week in cash, through the company, parking lot, vending, whatever."

Martorano agreed to do the hit. Martorano was to be paid $50,000 by Callahan (an unusually high amount for a hit), which he would split with Joe McDonald, a Winter Hill

Mob associate on the lam from the feds after being indicted for several crimes.

All Martorano needed were the details. That's where Paul Rico earned his keep.

Rico drove to Tulsa, where he tracked Wheeler's daily movements, trying to determine the best time and place to do the hit. Rico brought Joe McDonald along with him as a backup.

In the meantime, "Balloonhead" Halloran was still itching to make a buck. Halloran met with Callahan and asked Callahan if the Wheeler hit was still on. Callahan stalled Halloran, telling him there were still details to be ironed out before they could take out Wheeler.

Callahan ran to Whitey and he told him about the Halloran situation. Whitey was pissed at Callahan for involving a nobody like Halloran in the deal in the first place. Whitey didn't like any loose ends and Halloran was a loose end. Whitey figured $20,000 was enough dough to make Halloran happy and to shut him up. So, Whitey gave the cash to Callahan, who, in turn, gave it to Halloran.

Callahan invited Halloran to his apartment.

Callahan told Halloran, "Take the money. It's best you don't get involved in the Wheeler deal."

Then, echoing Whitey, Callahan added, "We should not have gotten you involved to begin with."

Halloran took the twenty grand, figuring he had made an easy score for doing absolutely nothing. For Halloran, it was always easy come-easy go. He blew the twenty grand in a few weeks on gambling, vacations, booze, and cocaine.

With Halloran out of the picture, Rico left Tulsa and met with Martorano in Florida. They decided Martorano and McDonald should fly to Oklahoma City, rent a car, and then drive to Tulsa. In Tulsa, they would get a hotel room and wait for Whitey to send the guns needed to do the job.

Rico had cased Wheeler's home and his place of

business in downtown Tulsa. Instead, he decided the safest place for the hit was the parking lot of the Southern Hills Country Club, where Wheeler had a regular tee time on early Saturday afternoons.

After arriving in Tulsa, the first order of business was for Martorano and McDonald to steal a car to use for the hit. They pinched a 1981 Pontiac for the intended purpose. To be safe, they stole the plates off another car and transferred them to the Pontiac. They took this precaution just in case an industrious cop spotted the Pontiac and tried to match the plates with the stolen car report. When the guns arrived from Boston, the table was set for Wheeler's demise.

On Saturday afternoon, May 27, 1981, Martorano and McDonald sat in the stolen Pontiac in the parking lot of the Southern Hills Country Club. As a disguise, Martorano wore a false mustache, beard, horned-rimmed glasses, and a baseball cap.

At approximately 4 p.m., Wheeler exited the clubhouse of the country club and headed to his black Cadillac in the parking lot.

Martorano spotted his mark. He casually got out of the Pontiac, and he paced, not too fast and not too slowly, towards Wheeler's car. After Wheeler got behind the wheel, but before he was able to shut the driver's side door, Martorano shot Wheeler once right between the eyes.

After Wheeler keeled over dead, Martorano casually walked back to the Pontiac. McDonald put the car into gear, and they exited the parking lot at a leisurely pace.

Two little girls, who had been playing at the country club's pool right next to the parking lot heard the fatal shot. They saw Martorano get into the Pontiac, but they didn't get the license plate number (not that it would have made a difference since the plates didn't belong to the Pontiac).

The Tulsa detective assigned to Wheeler's murder was Mike Huff. It didn't take Huff long to discover Wheeler had been involved in a business dispute with Callahan, and that Callahan had a close association with Winter Hill Mob members, including Whitey.

Pursuant to protocol, the Tulsa F.B.I. contacted the Boston F.B.I. for guidance in the Wheeler murder investigation. This inquiry fell into John Morris's lap, which meant there was no real inquiry at all.

Morris asked John Connolly to go through the motions. Connolly duly "interviewed" Callahan, who told him, on his scout's honor, that he had nothing to do with Wheeler's death. This effectively absolved the Winter Hill Mob and Whitey of the crime. As payment for Morris's "trouble," Whitey sent him the usual case of wine.

Callahan, however, had misjudged Wheeler's wife and two sons. Not only did they refuse to sell World Jai Alai to Callahan; they used their considerable fortune to investigate Wheeler's murder themselves. This supplemented the official investigation being done by Detective Huff. Both investigations came to the same conclusion; i.e.. John Callahan was somehow involved in Wheeler's murder, despite what John Connolly and the Boston F.B.I. said.

When news got back to Whitey that Callahan was still the prime suspect in Wheeler's killing, Whitey knew one thing for sure: the only people who could link the Winter Hill Mob to Wheeler were "Balloonhead" Halloran and John Callahan, which immediately made them two dead men walking.

Halloran was already under the surveillance by the Federal Bureau of Alcohol, Tobacco, and Firearms for his involvement in several drug deals, when he got involved in the murder of George Pappas, another cocaine dealer. It seemed that Pappas owed big money to Jerry Angiulo, the head of the Boston La Cosa Nostra. Pappas had refused to pay Angiulo the money back. Pappas said he was going to jail for a five-year bit and that it meant he didn't have to pay Angiulo until he got out of the can.

Angiulo saw it differently.

Angiulo ordered one of his made hitmen, Jackie Salemme (brother of Frank Salemme), to get in touch with Pappas and handle the situation. In October 1981, Salemme ordered Pappas to meet him at 4 a.m. in the Four Seas Restaurant in Boston's Chinatown. Salemme brought Halloran along in case he needed him, which turned out not to be the case and a big mistake.

There was no one in the dining room at the time of the shooting (the Chinese waiter was in the kitchen). When the waiter returned to their table, Pappas was dead, and Salemme and Halloran were gone.

However, someone had accidently dropped a set of keys under the table. That someone was Brian Halloran, who proved again he was not the type of person who should ever be involved in something as serious as a hit.

Since Salemme was a made man in the LCN, Angiulo arranged for Salemme to take it on the lam until the heat died down. On the other hand, since Halloran was a cocaine-addicted bully, whom no one liked, Angiulo did not offer him the same protection.

Federal Bureau of Alcohol, Tobacco, and Firearms agent Bill Murphy had been tailing Halloran for days, but had lost him earlier on the night of the Pappas hit. When Murphy went to the office the next day, he heard about the Pappas murder. Murphy also learned that detectives had matched up a car key on the set of keys left under Pappas's death table to a white Buick Regal, which was left in the Four Seas Restaurant's parking lot. This was the same car, driven by Halloran, that Murphy had been following for days.

Murphy obtained a conditional warrant to search Halloran's Quincy apartment. The warrant was only in effect if one of the keys on the key chain found at the Four Seas Restaurant allowed entrance into Halloran's apartment. Sure enough, Murphy turned the key in the lock and it

Whitey's Biggest Mistake

opened the door to Halloran's apartment.

Halloran was smart enough to hide out after the Pappas hit, especially after he reached into his pocket and found out his keys were missing. Knowing he was a dead man if the Italian mob caught up with him before the cops did, Halloran gave himself up to F.B.I. agent, Leo Brunnick, whom Halloran had dealings with in the past.

Halloran sat down with Brunnick and his partner, Gerry Montanari. The first words out of Halloran's mouth after "hello" were "I know who killed Roger Wheeler."

Halloran then got total diarrhea of the mouth, telling the agents everything he knew about the Wheeler hit. Halloran said he attended a meeting with John Callahan, who had wanted Wheeler out of the way, so Callahan could take over World Jai Alai. Halloran said Whitey and Flemmi were also at this meeting. Halloran said he left the meeting believing he was the man assigned to do the hit, but a few weeks later Callahan gave him $20,000 *not* to do the hit.

Halloran also told the feds, after the news about Wheeler's death hit the newspapers, that Callahan invited him for a few drinks at the Pier Restaurant in Southie. After both men had belted down a few, Callahan told Halloran that John Martorano, under orders from Whitey, had been the shooter in Wheeler's death.

Not totally buying Halloran's tale, Brunnick and Montanari wired Halloran for sound. They then sent him back on the streets to get corroboration of his story, in addition to any other information Halloran could garner that could put Winter Hill Mob members in the can for a very long time.

The fact that Halloran was wired spread throughout the Boston F.B.I. office like wildfire.

John Morris found out about Halloran's confession and his subsequent wiring. He relayed the information to John Connolly, who called Whitey with the bad news.

Unfortunately for Halloran, when the word hit the streets he was wired, nobody would say an incriminating word to him. This led to the feds to place Halloran, his wife, and their two sons, in a safe house in Cape Cod until they could figure out what to do with him.

In a few days, Halloran began having uneasy feelings about the F.B.I. Since only the feds knew he was wired, why did every mobster he met while he was wearing the wire clam up? Halloran began getting the feeling the feds were not working in his best interests.

On May 11, 1982, after he told his wife he thought he was being set up by the F.B.I., Halloran left Cape Cod without notifying his F.B.I. handlers. He took a bus to Boston where he planned to rent a car, and use it to go on the lam with his wife and kids.

Screw the F.B.I.

When he reached Boston, Halloran inexplicably went straight to the Topside Lounge in Southie to have a few belts. It was a fatal mistake.

F.B.I. agents Leon Brunnick and Gerry Montanari wrote in a special report after Halloran was killed that Montanari had received a phone call from Halloran at 4:40 p.m. He was trying to reach Brunnick. After identifying himself, Halloran left Montanari a phone number where Brunnick could reach him. It was the phone number of the pay phone inside the Topside Lounge.

A few minutes later, Brunnick called the phone number. Halloran answered immediately as if he had been sitting on the phone.

"What's up? I hear you've been looking for me," Halloran said.

Brunnick told Halloran he was a moron for leaving the safe house in Cape Cod.

"Go back to your family," Brunnick told Halloran. "Stop bouncing around."

Whitey's Biggest Mistake

Without committing one way or another, Halloran hung up the phone and went back to bending his elbow at the bar.

Halloran sat next to an acquaintance named Michael Donahue, who was just passing time before he went home for dinner. While they were downing their drinks, Halloran asked Donahue if he could drop him off at Halloran's apartment when they left the bar. Donahue said sure. Why not?

Halloran was taking his time, while Donahue's wife, Pat, was getting impatient waiting for her husband to come home to enjoy her special pork chop dinner with their three boys, ages 8, 11, and 13.

While Halloran and Donahue sat at the Topside Lounge bar, Halloran was spotted by a local thug named John Hurley. Hurley had his ear to Southie's sidewalks and knew Halloran was a rat. He also knew Whitey wanted Halloran dead.

Hurley hurried to a furniture store in Southie, where Whitey sometimes held court. Sure enough, Whitey was there with his right-hand-man, Kevin Weeks. After Hurley told Whitey the good news about Halloran, Whitey was as happy as a camel on Hump Day. He thanked Hurley, and then told Weeks to take Whitey's Olds Delta 88, equipped with a police scanner, and meet him at Jimmy's Harborside Restaurant, just down the block from the Topside Lounge.

Weeks did exactly as he was told. A few minutes after Weeks arrived at Jimmy's Harborside Restaurant, Whitey pulled up next to him with the "Tow Truck", a souped-up blue Chevy Malibu, which, if pushed, could go upwards of 200 miles-an-hour. The Tow Truck was also equipped with devices that shot oil onto the ground and dispersed smoke into the air, making a quick getaway more easy to accomplish (Whitey was a big fan of James Bond movies).

As a disguise, Whitey wore a long, blond wig and a bushy-blond mustache. Weeks spotted another man in the back seat of the Tow Truck. He wore a mask, so Weeks couldn't determine his identity (people have said this man was Pat Nee, but that was never verified).

Whitey told Weeks that Halloran was in the Topside Lounge. He asked Weeks to get closer so he could determine exactly when Halloran emerged from the bar. Weeks found a good spot in the parking lot of Anthony's Restaurant directly across the street from the Topside Lounge. From that vantage point, Weeks got a clear view of the front door of the Topside Lounge. Weeks and Whitey were communicating to each other on walkie-talkies. Weeks's job was to alert Whitey when Halloran exited the bar.

Weeks described Halloran's murder in his book *Brutal*.

"I wasn't there ten minutes when Halloran got up," Weeks said. "I got on the walkie-talkie and told Whitey, 'The Balloon is rising.' A minute later, I saw Halloran come outside with another man and they got into a blue Datsun. I thought Jimmy might call off the hit because of the other man being in the way."

Weeks thought wrong.

Donahue was driving the Datsun. As soon as Halloran sat down in the front passenger seat, the Tow Truck sped up alongside the Datsun, facing in the opposite direction. Whitey pulled out a .30 caliber carbine with thirty rounds in the magazine and commenced firing into the Datsun. The masked man in the back seat started firing at the Datsun too.

The Datsun began to roll away into traffic (by this time Donahue was probably dead), and it stopped about twenty yards from where the shooting had begun.

"It was a beautiful Tuesday night in May and people were still walking along the waterfront, dressed in business suits and casual wear, looking to enjoy the night," Weeks said. "Most of them started to panic and were screaming. Others seemed paralyzed by the shooting and just stood there, transfixed by the scene around them, staring and not moving, maybe not even realizing bullets were flying around their heads."

Whitey made a U-turn and he pulled up next to the Datsun.

Amazingly, Halloran was still alive.

Halloran had spilled out of the Datsun and was trying to stagger away. Whitey aimed out the window of the Tow Truck and fired a barrage of bullets into Halloran. Even after Halloran fell to the ground, Whitey kept firing until his gun was out of bullets. Witnesses saw Halloran's body jerking one way and then another from the force of the bullets.

Satisfied Halloran was toast, Whitey sped away. One of the Tow Truck's hubcaps hit the curb of the sidewalk and fell into the street about fifty yards from where Halloran lay still alive, but barely. Whitey later sent an underling to retrieve the hubcap so there would be no evidence linking the Tow Truck to the murder scene.

When the police arrived, Michael Donahue, an innocent man who was just giving a ride to an acquaintance, was found dead. And Brian Halloran, bleeding like a sieve from numerous bullet wounds, was babbling like an idiot. Halloran had been shot 22 times, but only one time in his "Balloonhead," and that was just a flesh wound.

Halloran screamed at the cops, "I don't want to die. Get me to a fucking hospital!"

When a cop asked Halloran who had shot him, he accused Jimmy Flynn, a thug who was searching the streets to kill him on a different matter. There is no proof Whitey wore a blond wig and blond mustache to impersonate Flynn, but it is certainly possible since throwing the ball and hiding the hand was ingrained in Whitey's M.O.

An ambulance came and Halloran was loaded inside. But he didn't make it. Brian Halloran died before he reached the hospital.

Twenty-two bullets tend to do that to a man.

The Halloran hit sent shockwaves throughout the Boston F.B.I. office, which spread to the fed's main headquarters in Washington D.C. There was no question two F.B.I. informants, Whitey Bulger and Steve Flemmi, were somehow involved in the Wheeler murder and the Halloran hit. Yet, there was internal dissent as to how the F.B.I. should proceed with the investigation of the two rats.

Bob Fitzpatrick was the fed in charge of the Boston office. He said Whitey and Flemmi had to be cut loose before they did any more damage to the fed's reputation. Conversely, Sean McWeeney, the Washington D.C. fed boss, saw things differently. McWeeney wanted the Mafia badly, and if it meant shielding two mobsters from Boston, then that's the price the feds would have to pay to crush the hated LCN.

For decades, under J. Edgar Hoover, the F.B.I. adamantly refused to acknowledge the existence of the Mafia or La Cosa Nostra. There were rumors Hoover was especially close to Italian mobster Frank Costello, and that Costello off tipped Hoover whenever there was a fixed horse race. Hoover, a degenerate horseplayer, would have one of his aids bet a fixed horse race for him. Later, he would gleefully count his winnings when Costello's "prediction" hit pay dirt. The notion that the top law enforcement officer in the country would profit from an illegally fixed horse race is almost beyond belief - almost.

There were also rumors, which persist to this day, that Hoover, who had the face of a constipated bulldog, was a closet homosexual. It was said that he carried on a decades-long love affair with his top aide, Assistant F.B.I. Director, Clyde Tolson. Whenever dinner invitations were sent to Hoover, he always brought along Tolson as his date for the night. Tolson was five years Hoover's junior, and light-years better looking. The happy couple ate two meals a day together for decades. After they died, they were buried just yards away from each other. They could almost hold hands.

This burial arrangement was hinted at when Hoover wrote to Tolson in 1943, "Words are mere man-given symbols for thoughts and feelings, and they are grossly insufficient to express the thoughts in my mind and the feelings in my heart that I have for you. I hope I will always have you beside me."

President Richard Nixon once referred to Hoover as, "That cocksucker."

Nixon never confirmed whether he was referring to Hoover's nasty demeanor, or Hoover's sexual orientation.

Then, there were other rumors, supposedly backed up with glossy photographs, where Hoover was exposed as a cross-dresser, with an affinity for flowery red dresses. Supposedly, the Italian mob had set up Hoover in a hotel suite with several other men who had the same sexual proclivities. Gossip has it that booze flowed as the glossy photographs were taken. Depending on one's point of view, the photos could have been taken at an innocent costume ball, or taken as proof that Hoover hit from both sides of the plate.

One Italian mobster reportedly once told his pals, "Hoover will never bother us. He saw the pictures, and his career would be over if we ever released these pictures to the public."

In 1972, when Hoover died, the F.B.I.'s attitude towards organized crime, especially the Mafia (LCN), made a 180-degree turn. When Washington fed chief, Sean McWeeney, made the call that burying the Mafia was their primary concern; Whitey and Flemmi were deemed indispensable. His decision trumped any notion about closing the files on Whitey and Flemmi, even if the dynamic duo might have been involved in a tiny killing, or two.

After Whitey and Flemmi got the all clear from John Connolly, there remained the little problem of what to do about John Callahan. Through Connolly, Whitey learned that the F.B.I. in Tulsa and in Boston were asking embarrassing questions about Callahan's involvement in the murder of Roger Wheeler. Connolly, Whitey, and Flemmi all agreed John Callahan was not a tough guy. If law enforcement applied the screws, Callahan would fold like a five-dollar suitcase.

In the 2008 murder trial of John Connolly, where he was convicted of the second-degree murder of John Callahan (Judge Sanford Blake gave Connolly 40 years as if it were a weekend in Acapulco), prosecution witness John Martorano described what happened to Callahan and why.

Martorano testified that the original notion of killing Callahan came from Connolly. In late July of 1982, Martorano was summoned by Whitey from Florida to Boston. Instead of driving, which would have been safer for a man on the run, Martorano flew commercially under the name Richard Aucion. At his Southie meeting with Whitey, Martorano was immediately inundated with statements made by Connolly to Whitey concerning Callahan's durability.

"We are all going to go to jail if Callahan doesn't hold up," Whitey told Martorano.

Whitey then hit Martorano with a sharp body blow, which caused Martorano to lose his breath. Whitey told Martorano, before Brian Halloran went down in a hail of bullets, Halloran told his F.B.I. handlers that John Callahan said it was Martorano who had whacked Wheeler. To make Martorano feel even worse, Whitey insisted he killed Halloran solely to protect Martorano. Of course, Whitey failed to mention the fact that Halloran told the feds he personally met with Callahan, Whitey, and Flemmi to discuss putting the kibosh on Wheeler.

Despite all the evidence that Callahan was potentially a loose cannon, Martorano was still against hitting his best bud. Callahan and Matorano had been pals for years, and despite what Connolly said about Callahan, Martorano insisted that Callahan was a stand-up guy.

"What do you mean Callahan is a stand-up guy?" Whitey said. "He already gave you up to Halloran!"

Although he was a remorseless and brutal killer, Martorano had never killed a friend before. To tilt the scales in favor of whacking Callahan, Whitey laid down a deadly trump card.

"Can Callahan do twenty years in prison?" Whitey asked Martorano. "Because that's what he's facing."

Martorano mulled that question a bit; then he honestly told Whitey that Callahan liked the good life too much to spend two decades in the can, even for his close chums in the Winter Hill Mob.

Finally, Whitey and John Martorano both agreed, in the interest of the Winter Hill Mob, that John Callahan would have to become a casualty of war.

In order to distance themselves from any possible spillover, Whitey insisted that Callahan had to be whacked, not in Boston, but in the sunny state of Florida. To grease the skids for Callahan's demise, John Connolly wrote up a phony F.B.I. report implicating Callahan in numerous drug deals with a homicidal crew of Cubans in Miami. Connolly and Whitey reasoned, when Callahan turned up dead, the spotlight would shine south, away from Boston.

Martorano flew back to Florida to set up Callahan's murder, but Callahan had disappeared into thin air. Unbeknownst to Martorano, Callahan had left the country to visit his ancestor's motherland in Ireland. Martorano left message after message for Callahan, but he got nothing back as a response. On the verge of thinking maybe someone else had already taken out Callahan, Martorano finally got a phone call from his old buddy explaining his absence. But Callahan was in Boston, and Martorano, as per instructions from Whitey, needed Callahan in Florida to do the dirty deed.

Whenever Martorano traveled to Plantation, Florida, he stayed at Callahan's condo, and even drove Callahan's Cadillac, instead of his own staid Dodge Van.

"Come down to Plantation," Martorano told Callahan. "We'll do some bouncing around the bars. I'll pick you up at the Fort Lauderdale airport."

Callahan liked Martorano's idea and agreed to go.

On August 2, 1982, Callahan jumped on a jet and flew to Florida, happier than a witch in a broom factory. When Callahan arrived at the airport, Martorano met him at the gate, smiling and backslapping. Martorano was so happy to see his old pal, he even carried Callahan's luggage to the airport parking lot.

Inside the lot, as Martorano slid open the Dodge van's back door and flung in Callahan's suitcase, Callahan jumped into the front passenger seat. Martorano scanned the parking lot looking for stragglers, but he saw none. Just before Callahan could inquire as to their drinking destination for the day, Martorano pulled out a .22 caliber pistol he had hidden in the back of the van and shot Callahan once in the back of the head.

"I didn't want to kill Callahan," Martorano testified in court. "He was my pal and we hung out together. But Whitey Bulger and Steve Flemmi out-voted me two to one, so Callahan had to go."

After he shot Callahan, Martorano hid Callahan's body on the floor of the van. Then Martorano got behind the wheel and exited the airport's parking lot.

Joe McDonald, who had been operating as a lookout, followed Martorano. They drove to a garage where Martorano had stashed Callahan's Caddy. When Martorano and McDonald moved Callahan's body to the trunk of the Caddy, Callahan let out a dreadful moan. McDonald then fired several shots into Callahan's head and the moaning stopped.

Whitey's Biggest Mistake

Martorano and McDonald emptied Callahan's pockets. They snatched Callahan's keys, his cash, and his watch. They left these items in the bathroom of a Cuban bar in Little Havana. Then they drove to the Miami airport and ditched the Caddy with Callahan's body inside the trunk. A few days later, someone smelled a stench emanating from the trunk of the Caddy and called the Miami police.

Just to be safe, after Callahan's body was discovered, John Connolly closed out Flemmi as an F.B.I. informer, but he kept Whitey on the F.B.I.'s rat-pad. Everything else remained the same. Whitey and Flemmi still reported to Connolly any ongoing developments concerning the Italian mob. Just to keep John Morris quiet, Whitey, through John Connolly, gave Morris another case of wine and an envelope containing one thousand dollars.

From this point on, even though Flemmi gave the F.B.I. the bulk of the information concerning the New England LCN, John Connolly made sure Whitey got all the credit. This made Whitey, but not necessarily Flemmi, untouchable to law enforcement in the city of Boston.

This was just another case of an Old Harbor Village projects denizen doing favors for his former neighbor.

Chapter Nine
"Bucky Barrett – Freeze!"

The murders of Brian Halloran and John Callahan were just the start of a 1980's murder spree orchestrated by Whitey and Flemmi. They spree including the slaying of bank robber Arthur "Bucky" Barrett, who became a victim of his own success.

Barrett was known in the Boston underworld as a drug dealer in partnership with Joe Murray. He was also an expert safecracker, bank robber, and dealer in stolen diamonds. In 1980, Barrett participated in the infamous $1.5 million bank robbery of the Depositors Trust Bank in Medford, Mass.

Barrett's niece, Sandra Patient, told the *New Hampshire Junior Leader*, "My uncle had a skill, and was one of the best at what he did. He was probably one of the 10 best in the world then, but it just happened to be taking jewels and cracking safes."

On Memorial Day weekend, Barrett, along with three police officers and two other confederates, broke into the Depositors Trust Bank. They spent the entire three-day weekend looting safe deposit boxes that contained cash, jewelry, and other valuables. (This bank heist was the subject of a book entitled *The Cops Are Robbers: A Convicted Cop's True Story of Police Corruption* by Gerald W. Clement and Kevin Stevens. It was later turned into a made-for-TV movie called *The Cops are Robbers*, staring Edward Asner and James Keach.)

There is no valid estimate of how much money and valuables were stolen (people who stash cash in safe deposit

"Bucky Barrett – Freeze!"

boxes are not likely to have reported that money as income to the IRS), but $1.5 million seems like an extremely low figure.

As is the custom in this sort of thing, when a thief robs a bank, he must kick up a nice percentage of the loot to the bosses of that area's predominant organized crime family. In the case of Barrett, he considered his boss to be Frank Salemme, a made LCN member and Flemmi's old partner in crime. Barrett gave Salemme a $100,000 cut. As his part of the deal, Salemme was supposed to protect Barrett from shakedowns from men like Flemmi and Whitey.

"He got in with a tough crowd," Patient said of her uncle Barrett. "He made some tough decisions, made his choices in life, but he never murdered anyone. He never hurt anyone like that. He didn't deserve what happened. He just decided he wasn't giving Whitey all the money Whitey wanted."

In 1983, three years after the bank robbery, Whitey and Flemmi figured it was time Barrett ponied up a big chunk of change from the bank heist. They also figured, if they operated in a secretive manner, Frank Salemme, who had his own problems with the law, would be none the wiser.

Flemmi and Whitey came up with a plan to shake down Barrett, and they took Kevin Weeks along for the ride. They lured Barrett to the infamous house on 779 East Third Street, with the ruse they had hot diamonds they wanted Barrett to move for them.

When Barrett entered the house he was greeted by Kevin Weeks, who shook Barrett's hand and said, "How you doing? Nice to meet you."

Before Barrett could respond, Whitey burst from the shadows holding a Mac-11 nine millimeter machine gun.

Whitey barked, "Bucky Barrett, freeze!"

Flemmi joined Whitey and Weeks, and they tied Barrett to a kitchen chair with chains and handcuffs. At this point, Weeks thought it was a simple shakedown and not an execution.

While Weeks sat in another room, Whitey and Flemmi peppered Barrett with questions; mingled with a few slaps, punches, and kicks for emphasis. The main purpose of the interrogation was to learn how much money Barrett had earned from the bank heist, and how much money Barrett was presently making in drug deals with Joe Murray. Weeks figured Whitey needed this information for the future shakedown of Joe Murray, which, for some reason, never occurred.

Finally, Barrett offered Whitey a deal. Barrett said he would pay Whitey $40,000 a month from that point on. But Whitey figured a bird in the hand was worth more than forty grand a month in the bush. And he wanted his money – now.

Whitey forced Barrett to phone his wife and tell her he was bringing some pals over to do business, and for her to leave the house immediately with the kids and stay away for a few hours. After Barrett told Whitey where he had money hidden in his house, Whitey, accompanied by Flemmi, left 779 East Third Street and drove to Barrett's house in Squantum, a neighborhood in Quincy. They left Weeks in the kitchen with Whitey's machine gun pointed at Barrett's chest.

A few hours later, Whitey and Flemmi returned to 779 East Third Street about 47 grand richer. They then dispatched Weeks to a Chinese restaurant in downtown Boston to retrieve another ten grand owed to Barrett.

When Weeks returned, Whitey told Weeks, "Bucky's going to go downstairs and lay down."

At this point, Weeks knew Barrett was a goner, but there was nothing he could do about it.

While Barrett was plodding down the steps, Whitey put a handgun to the back of Barrett's head and fired.

"Bucky Barrett – Freeze!"

Nothing happened.

Whitey adjusted his gun and fired again. The second time was a charm. Bucky Barrett's blood and brain matter splashed against the basement floor and walls.

His part of the job completed, Whitey went upstairs to take his customary nap.

Weeks said, "I noticed that Jimmy seem to calm down after the murder, almost as if he had taken a Valium."

But for Flemmi and Weeks the work was just starting. While Weeks dug a hole in the basement floor, Flemmi took off all Barrett's clothes and he stuffed them in a large black garbage bag. Then Flemmi tugged out Barrett's teeth, one-by-one, with a pair of pliers. He put the teeth in the same bag with Barrett's clothes for later disposal far away from 779 East Third Street.

When the hole was deep enough, they stuffed Barrett's body down into his grave and covered it with two bags of lime to hasten the body's decomposition.

After Whitey had finished his nap, Weeks drove Barrett's car to Savin Hill, while Whitey and Flemmi followed in Whitey's car. Weeks parked Barrett's car on top of the hill, and then he jumped in Whitey's car for a trip to Castle Island.

Whitey parked in Castle Island's parking lot. While Weeks and Flemmi watched out for nosy passers-by, Whitey paced the length of the pier and flung the black garbage bag containing Barrett's clothes and teeth into the water.

That was the end of Arthur "Bucky" Barrett, at least for the time being.

Chapter 10
The Valhalla

Despite being a stone cold killer, Whitey was a true patriot: not of the United States of America, but of his ancestral homeland in Ireland. Whitey contributed regularly to the Irish Republican Army (IRA). His hero, if Whitey had any, was Joe Cahill, the titular head of the IRA. John Hurley, the Irish-born bloke who had tipped off Whitey to the whereabouts of Brian Halloran, arranged a meeting between Whitey and Cahill. The purpose of the conference was to coordinate the sending of a shipment of guns from America to the freedom fighters in Ireland.

Cahill was a convicted gunrunner, so he could not gain admittance into the United States. But our neighbors to the north in Canada have no such restrictions. It was a piece of cake for Cahill to fly into Montreal, and then sneak into the United States on a bus transporting Boston Bruin fans from a hockey game between the Bruins and the Montreal Canadians back to Boston. Cahill took advantage of this service even though he wouldn't know a hockey puck if it hit him between his eyeballs.

When Cahill arrived in Southie, his first stop was the second floor meeting room of the Triple O Bar. There Cahill met with Whitey and his crew. Cahill impressed upon them that the boys across the Pond badly needed their help in their fight against the British oppressors in Northern Ireland. Also, at this meeting were Irishman Pat Nee, a big IRA supporter, and the drug-dealing Joe Murray, who just happened to have an armada of trawlers, which he used to ship drugs in and out of the country.

The Valhalla

Only this time Murray's boats would be used, not for drugs, but to ship guns to Ireland. Whitey and his boys, including Steve Flemmi, acquired the illicit guns. Flemmi was so tight with the Irish in the Winter Hill Mob that Whitey fancied him a bollixed Italian and an Irishman by association. Flemmi even convinced his brother, Mike, a decorated Boston police officer, to contribute his bulletproof vest, which Mike reported stolen from his car.

This was the plan:

Whitey and his men would load one of Murray's boats, the *Valhalla*, with enough guns and ammunition to stock a small army. Then the *Valhalla* would steam off from Boston and travel into international waters, where it would meet an IRA ship named the *Marita Ann*. The crew then would transfer the guns from the *Valhalla* to the *Marita Ann*, and the *Marita Ann* would return to Ireland with its booty.

Cahill figured the cost would be about one million dollars for the amount of guns and ammunition needed. Whitey showed no concern about his ability to raise that amount of cash. All Whitey had to do was send his men around to every drug dealer in the Boston area and demand the money, or else.

As expected, the drug dealers coughed up the cash. No problem. Some dealers even offered their own guns for the cause, as did various Irish gangsters throughout the region.

To convert the million or so dollars into guns and bullets, Pat Nee had an unorthodox idea. Instead of buying stolen guns, Nee flipped through the pages of a magazine called *Shotgun News*. Amazingly, Nee discovered anything they could get on the streets, they could also obtain legally through mail order magazines. For the next five months, Nee did the ordering, using a fictitious name. He had the guns delivered to the Columbia Yacht Club in South Boston. When the money ran out, Nee determined it was time to put the gunrunning operation into motion.

Volunteers were needed to man the *Valhalla*. By

definition, volunteers do not get paid for their services. This quickly narrowed down the number of potential shipmates, but Whitey can be very persuasive when necessary.

Whitey, with the help of Joe Murray, cajoled veteran drug smuggler and trained seaman, Bob Anderson, into being the Captain of the *Valhalla*. Anderson needed a first mate and an engineer, and he settled on John McIntyre for the dual role. McIntyre was basically a skilled fisherman, but he was even more skilled at working on ship engines, like the one on the Valhalla.

Both Anderson and McIntyre were loyal to the IRA cause, and as payment of sorts, Murray and Whitey told them they could keep the profits from any fish they caught during their gunrunning expedition. The IRA's Joe Crawley was also drafted into service; i.e., to monitor the cruise and make sure none of the guns disappeared into the hands of Winter Hill Mob associates who were pressed into ship duty by their boss.

Whereas Whitey was brilliant in making money; he was not so sharp when it came to other things, like the weather for example. For some inexplicable reason, Whitey, along with Joe Murray and Patrick Nee, insisted the *Valhalla* make its run in mid-September when hurricane season is at its peak. Anderson knew this was pure folly, but he also knew his only other choice was to jump into the sea wearing cement shoes.

As the sun set on September 13, 1984, five vans formed a procession which advanced approximately 31 miles from downtown Boston north to Gloucester Harbor, located on the eastern end of Cape Ann directly between Ipswich Bay and Massachusetts Bay. Whitey followed the convoy at a distance. He pulled over and parked his Chevy Malibu on a high hill that offered a clear view of the harbor. His driving companion was Kevin Weeks.

Weeks said, "That night Jimmy and I found a spot with a view of the dock, as well as the road from opposite

The Valhalla

directions. Things were quiet, until about an hour after we had gotten there, we got the call on our walkie-talkies from one of the drivers of the vans. He said 'We're on our way,' meaning 'Go, the coast is clear.' Since our job was to provide security. Jimmy and I sat in the Malibu, and we watched as five vans pulled up to the dock."

Whitey and Weeks observed from a distance as the ordnance, boxed in crates or packed in duffle bags, was loaded onto the *Valhalla*. An hour later, the vans were empty. Weeks received another call on his walkie-talkie, which informed him the mission was complete from that end. Satisfied they had done all they could for the cause, Whitey and Weeks departed from the hill in the Malibu and headed back to Boston.

Right off the dock, the *Valhalla* ran into a shitload of trouble. When the Valhalla arrived just south of Nova Scotia, it ran into the back end of a hurricane that was headed out into the Atlantic. Fifteen-foot waves pounded the vessel, causing the amateur sailors to lose their lunches all over the deck and off the sides of the boat.

On the *Valhalla's* third night at sea, Anderson saw a blip on his radar screen, and he yelled to Crawley that they were being followed.

The question was: "By whom?"

Anderson feared their pursuers might be the Canadian Navy, whose job was to patrol the waters looking for dope smugglers. Anderson told Crawley to have the crew put all the guns and ammunition above deck and cover them with tarpaulins. Anderson figured, since he wasn't getting paid, he wasn't about to take a pinch for gunrunning. So, if the Canadian Navy closed in on them, the guns were going overboard; the IRA be dammed. This was something Crawley did not want to hear, since his boys back in the old country badly needed those arms.

As a last desperate tactic to avoid detection, Anderson stopped the ship and dropped his fishing nets to give the appearance the *Valhalla* was simply on a trawling trip. The *Valhalla* floated in one place for several hours, and whatever fish the men did catch, Anderson wrapped up and put on ice as his payday.

As night turned into day, Anderson realized his radar screen no longer displayed a blip. He ordered the crew to raise the fishing nets and put the guns and ammunition back below deck. Because all of this maneuvering took precious hours, the *Valhalla's* rendezvous with the *Marita Ann* was delayed. Crawley sensed this development was not a good thing for his boys back home.

After the *Valhalla* was at sea for about a week, they ran into another hurricane, this one much more severe than the first one they had encountered. The waves reached fifty feet, blowing out the glass windows surrounding the wheelhouse, where Anderson was desperately trying to keep the *Valhalla* afloat. The flying glass slashed Anderson's hands. McIntyre was now doing double-duty as an engineer and medic. He stopped the bleeding by wrapping Anderson's hands with electrical tape; i.e., the same tape he was using to repair the engine, which, by this time, was flooded and shaking as if it had Parkinson's. Soon, the electricity also went out.

If Anderson and McIntyre thought they would get help from the Keystone Cops-crew that had been assembled for the mission, they were miserably mistaken. The thugs, bank robbers, and drug dealers, who comprised the rest of the *Valhalla's* crew, did what they did best at sea. They barfed all over the ship and all over themselves. There was more order in an insane asylum than there was on the *Valhalla*, which once again proved the old adage, "You get what you pay for."

Finally, after 14 days at sea, the *Valhalla* limped along, about 200 miles off the coast of Ireland. This was when Anderson got a very crude welcome from a representative of the IRA, who was nearby on the *Marita Ann*.

Instead of, "We're glad to see you," the voice that

The Valhalla

crackled through the Valhalla's radio (which was still operative thanks to McIntyre) said, "You're two fuckin' days late!"

Pissed at the way he was being treated by non-seafaring simpletons, Anderson figured, "Let's transfer the guns and ammunitions to them, and get the fuck back to Boston."

Anderson pulled the *Valhalla* alongside the *Marita Ann*. But the seas were so rocky it caused the *Valhalla* to repeatedly crash into the *Marita Ann*, damaging the *Marita Ann's* hull. This made the IRA crew onboard the *Marita Ann* angrier than Alec Baldwin having his picture taken by the paparazzi.

Seeing it was impossible to move the guns and ammunitions directly from ship to ship, Anderson suggested they use a small dinghy to do the dirty work. Anderson looked around at his motley crew and quickly realized only John McIntyre was capable of ferrying the small boat between the two bigger ships. It took McIntyre 14 trips between the vessels to transfer all the weaponry from the *Valhalla* to the *Marita Ann*.

That done, Anderson pointed the *Valhalla* toward Boston and prayed no more hurricanes were on the menu.

Unfortunately, the *Marita Ann* never made it safely back to Ireland.

Before it could dock, the British Royal Navy and the British Royal Air Force surrounded the *Marita Ann*. It was obvious to the IRA and to Whitey's boys back in Boston, someone had exposed the trip for what it was, even before the Valhalla had set sail from Boston. But they were wrong about who the rat was, not that it made a difference.

Sean O'Callaghan was a former IRA hitman, who had decided to jump ship and side with the law. O'Callaghan followed the IRA's activities closely. The inside information he gathered went straight to the Irish Garda, who then tipped off British authorities.

O'Callaghan knew the *Marita Ann* had been dry-docked for many years. When he noticed the *Marita Ann* was getting ready for another sea venture, he knew something was up. O'Callaghan poked around the IRA a bit and discovered that a shipment of guns was on its way on a trawler from Boston, and that it would arrive in Irish waters to meet up with the *Marita Ann*. O'Callaghan informed the law, and the *Marita Ann* was a sitting duck when it tried to dock in Ireland.

Back in Boston, Whitey was not very happy. He didn't know Sean O'Callaghan from a hole in the wall. He assumed the informant was someone inside his own crew.

When the *Valhalla* docked, it did so in South Boston, not in Gloucester Harbor from where it had shoved off. Anderson dismissed his ragtag crew, except for John McIntyre, who was the only maritime expert onboard other than himself. Anderson figured he and McIntyre could make the needed repairs themselves, but not until they had a good night's sleep.

Anderson went straight home, but McIntyre went to the home of his estranged wife in Quincy. Since she had a restraining order prohibiting McIntyre from visiting her, McIntyre's wife refused to answer the front door. Undeterred, McIntyre, who had stopped at a few pubs on the way, climbed onto the second-floor balcony, where he threw himself on the floor and fell into a drunken stupor. A neighbor across the street, believing he was witnessing a burglary, called the cops.

The Quincy police arrived and found McIntyre in a heap on the balcony. They roused McIntyre, and when they checked McIntyre's ID, they found an outstanding drunk-driving warrant, which McIntyre had failed to answer in court. The police then arrested McIntyre on two charges: the outstanding warrant and for violating his wife's restraining order.

McIntyre was arrested late on Friday night and knew

The Valhalla

he would not appear before a judge until Monday morning. Stewing in the can, McIntyre got to thinking. He had just spent two of the worst weeks of his life on a tin can mingling with the worst characters known to man. McIntyre had worked his butt off, but he hadn't made a dime.

Then McIntyre made a fatal mistake. He began blabbering to the local police about Whitey Bulger, drugs, gunrunning, and the Irish Republican Army. The local police thought McIntyre was a drunken lunatic. However, since Whitey's name was mentioned, they were compelled to investigate McIntyre's allegations.

The Quincy police called D.E.A. agent Steve Boeri, who heard Whitey was getting paid by drug dealers, but he did not have an ounce of evidence to prove the allegations. Boeri grilled McIntyre, and McIntyre spilled his guts. He not only admitted to the IRA gunrunning operation, but he also copped to transporting drugs into Boston on Joe Murray's ships.

Boeri unsuccessfully tried to convince McIntyre to go into the Witness Protection Program immediately, so that he would be alive to testify in court against Whitey, Murray, and the others in the illicit drug operation. But McIntyre was adamant. He was staying in Boston, and if the law wanted him to gather further drug information, he was up to the task.

Boeri decided to enlist the help of the feds in this matter. Boeri contacted F.B.I. agent Roderick Kennedy, and both men debriefed McIntyre at F.B.I. headquarters in Boston.

Guess who overheard this meeting?

That's right. It was Whitey's old pal, John Connolly, who immediately contacted Whitey and told him about McIntyre's government cooperation.

Whitey knew what he had to do. He decided to contact Joe Murray, since McIntyre worked for Murray and was ratting on Murray too. At first, Murray suggested they send

McIntyre on one of Murray's ships to South America, where Murray had drug connections who could make McIntyre disappear.

But Whitey wanted the pleasure of eliminating the informer himself.

Whitey told Murray the plan was to contact McIntyre with the ruse of bringing him into a big drug deal. But McIntyre would have to invest $20,000 of his own money. Both Whitey and Murray knew McIntyre didn't have two nickels to rub together. If McIntyre agreed to the deal, the only way McIntyre could get the money was from McIntyre's handlers in the F.B.I. or in the D.E.A. If McIntyre said he had the dough, Whitey planned to whack McIntyre and keep the government's twenty grand to boot. The thought of such a Daily Double made Whitey's Irish eyes twinkle.

On November 30, 1984, Joe Murray met McIntyre on the South Boston waterfront. Pat Nee was driving, and Murray sat in the front passenger seat.

Murray asked McIntyre, "You got the twenty grand?"

McIntyre assured Murray he had the cash.

"Then get in the back seat," Murray said.

McIntyre did as he was told. He sat next to two cases of Miller Light beer, which were stacked up on the back seat alongside him.

After McIntyre gave Murray the twenty grand, Nee dropped off Murray in front of a Boston bar. Then Nee told McIntyre he had to deliver the two cases of beer to a party. McIntyre was not smart enough to realize he would be the guest of honor.

After Nee parked in front of 779 East Third Street, he opened the back door, took out a case of beer, and told McIntyre, "Pick up the other case and follow me. We'll stop for a few drinks, then I'll drive you home."

As soon as McIntyre entered the kitchen, he knew he

The Valhalla

was a dead man. Standing there were Kevin Weeks and Steve Flemmi, and they were not smiling. McIntyre tried to make a break for the front door, but Weeks tackled and subdued him. After McIntyre was under Weeks's control, Whitey emerged from behind the refrigerator, brandishing a Mac-10 pistol equipped with a silencer.

"Pick him up and put him on a chair," Whitey said.

Weeks and Flemmi grabbed McIntyre by his shoulders, dragged him to a kitchen chair, and forced him into the chair. In seconds, McIntyre was bound to the chair with chains and handcuffs.

Whitey put his face close to McIntyre's.

"We know you're a snitch, you piece of shit!" Whitey said.

McIntyre started whimpering.

"I know. I was weak," he said.

"Relax, you're going to be okay," Whitey told McIntyre. "I just want some information. When we're through here, we're sending you to South America. And you're never coming back."

Whether McIntyre believed Whitey or not, he began blabbing about everything he had ever done wrong in his entire life, including telling Whitey he had tipped the D.E.A. about a large shipment of marijuana Joe Murray was presently transporting on one of his boats. This pissed off Whitey to no end, since his part of this deal was supposed to have netted Whitey around $3 million.

After a few more smacks and Whitey poking him with the point of the gun, McIntyre told Whitey the complete details of what caused him to join Team America, including the names of the agents he was working with. McIntyre also admitted the D.E.A. had come up with the twenty grand for the proposed drug deal, which was now in Joe Murray's possession.

McIntyre insisted to Pat Nee, the IRA fanatic of the

Winter Hill Mob, he had not been the rat on the Valhalla deal. Nee believed him, but Whitey was not finished with his grilling.

With the Mac-10 pistol pointed in McIntyre's face, Whitey demanded to know every intimate detail, including the dollar amounts of drugs Joe Murray was dealing, in addition to how and when the transactions were made. Whitey, who wouldn't trust the Pope, figured Murray was shorting him on his cut, and if anyone could provide proof it was McIntyre.

After six hours of intense questioning, Whitey figured he knew everything McIntyre knew about Joe Murray's drug operation. They undid McIntyre's shackles and pushed him down the steps to the basement.

Below deck, after they shoved McIntyre into a chair, Whitey began strangling McIntyre with a length of thick rope. But Whitey was not an expert in strangling like he was in shooting. Besides, McIntyre, at six-feet-two-inches and 225 pounds, was not a fragile girl like Debbie Hussey and Debra Davis had been.

After about a minute of struggling with the rope around his neck, McIntyre puked all over Whitey's brand-new cowboy boots. This did not please Whitey at all. So, he pulled out a .22 pistol with a silencer.

"Would you like one in the head?" he asked McIntyre

"Yes sir," McIntyre said. "Please."

Whitey walked around McIntyre, and he fired one into the back of McIntyre's noggin. McIntyre fell to the basement floor.

Steve Flemmi bent down and listened to McIntyre's chest, searching for a heartbeat.

"He's still alive," Flemmi said.

Whitey gritted his teeth and fired several more shots into McIntyre's head and face.

Whitey smiled. "He's dead now."

The Valhalla

Chalk that up as another Whitey-orchestrated murder initiated by F.B.I. agent John Connolly.

Whitey climbed upstairs for his customary after-murder nap, and Weeks and Flemmi began their usual cleanup routine: Weeks dug the hole in the ground, and Flemmi pulled out McIntyre's teeth with a pair of pliers.

As an added touch, Flemmi also tugged out McIntyre's tongue. He waved McIntyre's bloody tongue in Weeks's face and said, "He won't be needing this anymore."

Weeks just shook his head and continued digging.

The twenty grand of the government's money was divided four ways: Whitey, Flemmi, Murray, and Weeks each got five grand apiece. For some reason, Pat Nee, whose brother's house was used for the murder, and who drove John McIntyre to the murder scene, got nothing.

Whitey never did like Pat Nee.

Chapter 11
Down With La Cosa Nostra

While Whitey and Flemmi were raking in cash from their illegal activities, the F.B.I., intentionally blind to what Whitey and Flemmi were doing, was elated with the information they were garnering from the bug in Jerry Angiulo's social club at 98 Prince Street. Oblivious to the fact that the feds, with Whitey and Flemmi's assistance, had his club wired, Angiulo said things on tape that were criminal in nature. Among other things, Angiulo showed how much he hated the Irish, especially Irish cops, whom Angiulo had been paying off for decades.

On one tape Angiulo was heard saying, "It takes a special guy to be a cop to begin with. Disturbed upstairs. That's why all the Irishmen are cops. They love it. Alone they are a piece of shit. When they put on the uniform and get a little power, they start destroying everything."

Angiulo had been extremely successful in beating the feds in court all throughout the 1960's and 1970's. In 1972, Angiulo was accused of hiding money and secretly owning the Berkshire Downs Racetrack in Springfield, Mass. When Angiulo appeared before the House Select Committee on Crime, famed Italian-American singer and actor, Frank Sinatra, testified on Angiulo's behalf. There were rumors Sinatra and Angiulo were in cahoots with Sinatra being the front man on the record, as the vice president of the racetrack. But nothing came of the Committee's investigation, Angiulo walked away whistling like a bird and thumbing his nose at law enforcement, especially the F.B.I.

This made Angiulo, in his own mind, an expert on the law. Angiulo rightfully conceded, however, that the Racketeer Influence and Corrupt Organizations (RICO) Act was a deadly law, which could be used by the government to take him down.

On tape, Angiulo was heard explaining to his underlings how RICO worked.

"They only have to prove we committed two out of thirty-two fuckin' federal and state crimes over a ten-year period to put us in the fuckin' can," Angiulo said. "If you break one of those crimes this year, and within ten years you break another one, they will take your fuckin' head off."

Then Angiulo went on to explain how he would beat RICO at its own game. Angiulo reasoned incorrectly that one of the thirty-two crimes; i.e - infiltrating a business, applied only to legitimate businesses, not illegitimate businesses. (I'm not making this up.)

"They can stick RICO!" Angiulo told his consigliere, Larry Zannino. "Our argument is that we are an *illegitimate* business."

"We're shylocks!" Zannino said.

"Yeah, we're shylocks," Angiulo said. "We're fuckin' bookmakers too. We're selling marijuana."

"We're not infiltrating," Zannino declared.

"We're illegal here," Angiulo said. "Arsonists. We're every fuckin' thing."

"Pimps. Prostitutes!" Zannino said.

"The law does not cover us, "Angiulo proclaimed. "Isn't that right?"

Zannino said, "That's the argument."

But then Angiulo contradicted his own reasoning when he said, dejectedly, "This law was made for people like us."

Angiulo was also caught on tape discussing Whitey and

Flemmi, which made John Morris and John Connolly turn blue.

"Whitey has all of Boston and Stevie has all of the South End," Angiulo told Zannino. "We're all partners in their operation. We could use them too. If I called these guys right now, they'd kill any fuckin' body we tell them too."

Zannino was also caught on tape discussing an incident which had happened years back concerning Jerry Matricia, one of Angiulo's underlings. While in Las Vegas, Matricia was supposed to bet $51,000 for Whitey and Flemmi on a fixed horse race. But before he got to the race track, Matricia stopped at the craps tables and blew the whole wad.

"If you fuck someone close to us, I'm going to give you a shake right now," Zannino said on tape he told Matricia. "Do you know the Winter Hill Gang is us? These are nice people. These are the kind of people that straighten things out. Anything I ever asked them. They're with us. We're together. And we cannot tolerate them getting fucked. Okay?"

Then there was the little problem of a debt owed Angiulo by the Winter Hill Mob. Angiulo claimed, when he made the agreement to share the loansharking and gambling operations in South Boston, the Winter Hill Mob was supposed to pay Angiulo 5% of their take, which, by 1982, amounted to $245,000. Whitey, who had not paid one cent to Angiulo in four years, agreed money was owed, but he said it was only $195,000.

After Howie Winter went to jail, according to the Angiulo tapes, Whitey began getting greedy.

Richie Brown was a bookie who paid the Angiulos to stay in operation. To the Winter Hill Mob, Brown paid nothing. Howie Winter never complained about Brown, but with Winter in jail, Whitey felt differently. Whitey approached Brown, and he said if Brown wanted to stay healthy, he had to pay Whitey $1,000 a week. Brown told

Whitey he belonged to the Angiulos, and if Whitey had a problem to go see Danny Angiulo, Jerry's younger brother and the muscle in the family.

And that's exactly what Whitey did, accompanied by Flemmi.

At a meeting in Danny Angiulo's office, Whitey told him the Winter Hill Mob was short of funds and they needed Richie Brown's cash to stay competitive in the streets.

After his meeting with Whitey and Flemmi, Danny Angiulo was heard on tape telling his brother Jerry, "I told Whitey 'Don't say you're broke. I know of fifty guys who pay you one thousand a month. That's fifty thousand a month!'"

In the end, Whitey backed off and Brown stayed with the Angiulos.

The problem for John Connolly and his boss, John Morris, was explaining the taped conversations to their superiors at the F.B.I. After all, Angiulo said the Winter Hill Mob had committed murders for him. Angiulo also said on tape that the Winter Hill Mob was raking in tons of cash from numerous illegal activities.

Connolly wrote in a report to his superiors, contrary to what Angiulo said on tape, "Our source (Whitey Bulger) is not a hit man for Jerry Angiulo as has been contended."

John Morris followed Connolly's lead when he wrote in a report that it was curtains for the Winter Hill Mob after Howie Winter went to jail.

Morris wrote, "The Winter Hill Mob does not merit further targeting at this time or anytime in the foreseeable future."

Cha-ching. Ring-up another case of wine for John "Vino" Morris.

On September 19, 1983, the feds decided they had enough evidence on the Angiulo crime crew to start making arrests. In raids at several locations, including the social club at 98 Prince Street, the feds nailed a dozen Italian mobsters connected to Angiulo, including Larry Zannino. They also arrested three other Angiulo brothers: Danny, Frankie, and Jimmy. Along with the Italian mobsters, the feds confiscated $700,000 in cash and negotiable securities.

F.B.I. agent Ed Quinn arrested Jerry Angiulo while Angiulo was sitting at a table (with his back against the wall, of course) at Francesco's Restaurant in Boston's North End.

As Quinn was cuffing Angiulo, the waiter arrived at Angiulo's table with his order of Pork Chops Italiano. Angiulo sneered at Quinn. Then he turned to the waiter and said, "Don't worry. I'll be back before my pork chops get cold."

On September 20th, based on 850 hours of taped conversations recorded by the feds over a three-year period, a Boston Grand jury issued indictments against six members of the Angiulo clan including the four Angiulo brothers, Larry Zannino, and Sammy Granito. The six men were charged under the RICO Act, with murder, loan sharking, obstruction of justice, obstruction of law enforcement, interstate travel involving racketeering, and the operation of illegal gambling enterprises.

The 58-page indictment read, "The purpose of the 'criminal enterprise' the defendants belonged to included 'to control, supervise, finance, participate in, and set policy concerning the making of money by illegal means' and 'to commit crimes, including murder, as a matter of duty.'"

Jerry Angiulo and Larry Zannino were held without bail. Bail was set at $1 million for Danny, Jimmy, and Frankie Angiulo and $750,000 for Sammy Granito.

Since he had the good sense to suffer a heart attack while he was being arrested, Larry Zannino was not present in the courtroom when the indictments were read.

In the indictments, Jerry Angiulo was described as "underboss" to Raymond Patriarca, whose base of operation was in Providence, R. I. In the indictment, Patriarca was said to be the "boss" of the crime organization La Cosa Nostra in "Massachusetts, Rhode Island, and elsewhere."

Patriarca was also named as a co-conspirator in the indictment, but he was not indicted. It wouldn't have made a difference. Patriarca died a year later at the age of 76, and the Angiulo mob trial, after numerous delays, didn't start until June of 1985.

Jeremiah T. O'Sullivan, chief attorney in the Justice Department's New England Organized Crime Strike Force, said the indictment was "only the first stage." O'Sullivan said the objective of the Justice Department was to destroy "La Cosa Nostra as a functioning conspiracy in the United States."

This was the same Jeremiah T. O'Sullivan who four years earlier had kept Whitey and Flemmi from being indicted in the horse race-fixing scandal, because he wanted to keep them actively ratting out the Angiulos and the Italian LCN.

After the indictments were handed down, the defendants' attorneys claimed that the wiretaps, which were the entire case against the Angiulo clan, were illegally obtained. Federal Magistrate Lawrence Cohen said he would rule on that matter at a later date.

Judge Cohen did admit, "If the Government loses on its wiretap, it's going to lose its entire case."

However, O'Sullivan knew the fix was in. He also knew he had a better chance of being honored by the Sons of Italy than he had of losing his treasured wiretaps.

*****

Despite the fact Whitey and Flemmi were invisible as far as the F.B.I. was concerned, the local Quincy police force held a different view of the twin devils of deceit.

Detective Dick Bergeron had worked with D.E.A. agent Steve Boeri to flip John McIntyre. When McIntyre went missing, Bergeron knew the Winter Hill Mob was responsible. Through his informants in Quincy, Bergeron discovered, not only did the Winter Hill Mob control the illegal activities in South Boston, but also in Quincy and other areas around South Boston. To add insult to injury, Whitey was now living within Quincy's boundaries.

Bergeron wrote in an internal Quincy police document, "Subject Bulger is residing in a condominium at 160 Quincy Shore Drive, Quincy, which is located in a luxury apartment complex called Louisburg Square. The apartment unit is 101."

Going through court records, Bergeron discovered the condo was purchased in 1982 for $96,000 – all cash.

Bergeron also wrote, "The shades in said unit are usually pulled down, and cardboard is taped to the small windows on the outside entry door."

And here's the kicker. The condo was not in Whitey's name, nor in the name of his longtime girlfriend, Teresa Stanley. The condo was recorded as being owned by an attractive blond named Catherine Greig.

Catherine Grieg graduated Southie High in 1969 and was voted "best looking girl" in her class. Greig wrote in her senior yearbook that she "wanted to have a medical career." However, Greig didn't have the time nor the ambition to be a doctor or a dentist or even a veterinarian for that matter. Instead, she enrolled in a two-year program at the Forsythe School for Dental Hygienists. Greig did so well, upon graduation she landed a job working in the lab of a well-known local periodontist.

Even though Greig exuded class and beauty, her choice of men was decidedly crass. When she was only 20-years-old, Greig married Bobby McGonagle of the infamous McGonagle brothers. Bobby's siblings, Paulie and

Down With La Cosa Nostra

Donny, were later murdered by Whitey: one by accident (Donny) and one on purpose (Paulie).

The problem with Bobby McGonagle was he couldn't tell one Greig sister from the other. In 1973, Catherine discovered Bobby was fooling around with her twin sister, Margaret. Catherine gave Bobby the boot, which, considering her later actions, was probably the smartest thing Catherine Greig ever did in her life.

Months later, Greig began dating Whitey, who by this time had already whacked her two brothers-in-law. When Greig and Whitey became an item, she was 24 and Whitey was 46, and still ostensibly living with Teresa Stanley.

As was reported in *Whitey Bulger*, by Cullen and Murphy, Whitey immediately began showering Greig with sparkling jewelry and a fur coat, which sure comes in handy during winters in frigid Boston.

One of Greig's co-workers said about the May-December relationship between Greig and Whitey, "After all she had been through with her ex-husband, I think she just wanted to be loved. And Jimmy (Whitey) was very good to her. Certainly in a material way he was."

Whitey, a real woman-killer (remember Hussy and Davis), handled his female relationships like a cockeyed juggler at Barnum and Bailey's. Whitey's usual nightly schedule was to have dinner with Teresa Stanley and her brood and then jump into bed with the much younger Grieg later on.

But not always.

Whitey had a few chickadees on the side, and all too many nights Catherine Greig slept alone. This compelled her, even before the age of 30, to undergo breast implants and a facelift that included eyelid surgery. The good news for Greig was Whitey liked his women to look fantastic, so he footed the bill for all of Greig's physical enhancements.

Whitey continued his dual life with Stanley and Greig

for almost 20 years, and it ended with a switcheroo in midstream.

But we'll get to that later.

*****

Police Detective Dick Bergeron became angered and obsessed with Whitey invading Bergeron's Quincy territory. Through his usual criminal informants, Bergeron discovered Whitey not only was spending loads of time in Quincy, but was, in fact, involved in the selling of huge amounts of drugs, most notably cocaine. Of course, Whitey didn't get his own hands dirty dealing the drugs. But Whitey did get a cut out of every gram of coke sold in Quincy by shaking down the dealers who were doing the actual street sales.

Bergeron wrote in a confidential police report, "Whitey Bulger and Steve Flemmi now appear to have broadened their horizons into drug trafficking. With their expansion on the drug market, they will be helping people destroy their lives."

Bergeron consulted his contacts in the D.E.A. He found out the D.E.A. had reports identical to what he had on Whitey and Flemmi. A confidential D.E.A. memo said, both in South Boston and in Quincy, Whitey and Flemmi were, "Attempting to control drug trafficking in the region by demanding cash payments and/or a percentage of profits for allowing dealers to cooperate."

As a result, the Quincy police and the D.E.A. began a joint operation called "Operation Beans," in which Bergeron worked closely with D.E.A. agents Al Reilly and Steve Boeri. All throughout 1983 and 1984, Operation Beans kept close tabs on Whitey and Flemmi. Although the F.B.I. was not a part of the surveillance, as a courtesy, the D.E.A. told the Boston F.B.I. Whitey and Flemmi were knee-deep in drugs So far, the D.E.A. did not have enough evidence for an arrest and an indictment. This information did not sit too well with Boston's top Organized Crime

Down With La Cosa Nostra

F.B.I. agent, John Connolly.

In early 1985, Connolly's supervisor and partner-in-crime, John Morris, had gotten a promotion, and was transferred to the Miami F.B.I. office to work on organized crime problems in South Florida. Morris was replaced by John Ring, who did not like the fact Connolly was so close to Whitey and Flemmi. Nor did Ring appreciate it that Connolly spent a lot of time with the two gangsters in social settings. Though Ring dressed down Connolly for his close association with the mobsters, he did nothing to prevent Connolly from doing so.

Ring knew Connolly was the Boston F.B.I.'s fair-haired boy as far as F.B.I. headquarters in Washington was concerned. If push came to shove, Ring figured, despite being Connolly's boss, the big shots in Washington, D.C. would most likely accept whatever Connolly said as the gospel truth. So, to keep the peace, Ring bit his tongue concerning Connolly and his mobster associates. He basically sat back and tried to protect his own turf.

Now that they were cognizant of the D.E.A.'s damning surveillance on Whitey and Flemmi, the Washington F.B.I. office began seriously contemplating dropping both as government informants.

When Connolly heard the scuttlebutt about Whitey and Flemmi's removal, he fired off a memo to his superiors saying, "James Bulger and Steve Flemmi are not involved in drugs. They don't do drugs and they hate drug dealers. They would never allow drugs in South Boston."

Connolly also said "The D.E.A.'s allegations concerning James Bulger and Steve Flemmi are unsubstantiated and the D.E.A. has provided absolutely no evidence to back up their speculation."

Connolly urged the Washington F.B.I. office not to close Whitey and Flemmi as informants because of their "past, present, and future valuable assistance."

What possible future "valuable assistance" Whitey and

Flemmi could provide for the F.B.I. concerning the taking down of La Cosa Nostra was problematic for Connolly to explain. Both Whitey and Flemmi were not expected to testify at the trial of Jerry Angiulo and his pals. In the Boston F.B.I.'s own words, "The arrest of the Angiulo brothers and their associates decimated the LCN in Boston."

Despite all of the evidence that warranted Whitey and Flemmi's dismissal as F.B.I. informants, they remained safe under the F.B.I.'s umbrella due to Connolly's influence.

Due to the lack of cooperation and clear obstruction by the F.B.I., Operation Beans sputtered out like a flame against the wind. The efforts of Quincy Police Detective Dick Bergeron along with D.E.A. agents Al Reilly and Steve Boeri, came to naught.

Chalk up another triumph for Connolly, Whitey, and Flemmi.

But their winning streak would not last forever.

Chapter 12
Stacking it Away

Like all astute businessmen, Whitey planned for the future.

It is not known exactly when it started, but Whitey traveled frequently all around the United States, Canada, and even Europe (especially Ireland), with the purpose of stashing money in numerous safe deposit boxes around the world. Whitey knew it was just a matter of time before his F.B.I. charade was exposed. When the split finally came splattering down, Whitey would be prepared. John Connolly would tip him off in advance of any imminent bust, and Whitey would just disappear to any of more than a dozen places where his cash would be waiting for him. This was before the airlines frisked passengers looking for bomb material so Whitey was able to travel just about anywhere in the world carrying copious amounts of cash, which he usually kept in a money belt strapped around his waist.

In September 1987, Whitey decided to take a jaunt to Montreal, Canada. Teresa Stanley accompanied Whitey on this trip, which was ostensibly being made for Teresa to visit her daughter, Karen, who was married to the Montreal Canadian NHL hockey star, Chris Nilan.

Nilan, who came from Roxbury, Mass. and went to Northeastern University in the heart of Boston, was a perfect match for Whitey. Whitey was a legitimate tough guy, and Nilan was known not so much for his ice skating and puck handling skills, but exclusively for his willingness and ability to fight on the ice. To this day, Nilan is one of only nine players in NHL history to record more than 3,000 career penalty minutes, and he has the highest penalty minute per-game average ever at 4.42 minutes per game. Nilan also recorded the most penalties in one game: 10 penalties for a total of 42 minutes. The latter record means Nilan sat in the penalty box for 70% of the game.

Obviously, Chris Nilan loved to fight, and Whitey loved guys who loved to fight.

Whitey is notorious for avoiding the camera. Yet in 1986, after the Montreal Canadians won the coveted Stanley Cup, Whitey graciously posed for a picture with Nilan. This photo displayed a beaming Nilan with his arm wrapped around the Stanley Cup, and a benignly smiling Whitey, dressed in a dark-blue, double-breasted sports jacket, gray trousers and solid blue tie, with his arm wrapped around Nilan's shoulder.

Sure, Whitey loved homeboy Nilan and Nilan's spirited hockey style. But the main reason for Whitey's trip to Montreal was to shuttle nearly one hundred grand in cash into a Montreal safe deposit box. Whitey was no slouch when it came to accumulating bogus driver licenses and other pieces of false identification. These precautions came in handy when Whitey finally went on the lam. He had the cash and brand new identities to go with him.

Whitey called his right-hand man, Kevin Weeks, to drive Whitey and Stanley to Logan airport.

Weeks said, "It was about five in the afternoon, but by the time we got to the airport, Jimmy (Whitey) was already in a bad mood. We'd been halfway there when Teresa forgot her license and her birth certificate, so we had to go back for them. He (Whitey) started screaming and yelling, and he was plenty aggravated when we finally arrived at Logan."

As part of his luggage, Whitey carried an overnight bag containing $80,000. This was in addition to another ten grand Whitey had crammed into his money belt and close to ten grand in Stanley's possession. Weeks walked Whitey

Stacking it Away

and Stanley to the check-in counter, where Whitey placed his bag on the conveyer belt to be X-rayed.

A female airport security guard saw the X-rayed contents of Whitey's bag, and she nearly had a heart attack.

She stammered, "I'm sorry, sir, but you have a large amount of money in this bag. And I have to take a look at it."

Then Whitey almost had a heart attack.

Whitey tugged the bag out of the woman's hand, telling her, "Fuck this shit! I ain't going nowhere!"

She immediately called for assistance.

At this point, Whitey didn't know whether to shit or go blind.

Weeks spotted a male security guard coming to her aid. So Kevin Weeks did what he was paid to do. He threw a shoulder into the male security guard, knocking him over a counter and out of play.

"At that moment, Jimmy was trying to take off his money belt," Weeks said. "But the belt had a knot in it As he struggled to pull off the belt, the knot kept getting tighter around his waist."

Finally, before the floored male security guard got back into action, Whitey extricated the belt from his waist and flipped it to Weeks.

Weeks immediately made a beeline for the airport exit.

Whitey saw that Weeks was being pursued by another male security guard. Whitey quickly followed Weeks, while Stanley guarded the bag containing the eighty grand.

Weeks fled through the revolving door. Just as his pursuer entered the revolving door, Whitey stuck his foot in the door, trapping the security guard inside.

Safely out of the terminal, Weeks sprinted to his car and exited the airport.

Whitey returned to the terminal and started giving hell

to every security guard in sight.

He told whoever was in charge, "Is this how you treat citizens? You can't hold me! You got nothing on me! I ain't traveling nowhere!"

State trooper William Johnson tried to detain Whitey. Johnson demanded identification from Whitey, which Whitey testily provided.

When one of the security guards tried to interview him, Whitey told him, "Shut the fuck up!"

This is when Johnson put his hands on Whitey and pushed him up against the wall.

"One more word out of you and I'm going to lock you up," Johnson said.

Whitey just smirked.

Johnson soon realized he had no legal cause to detain Whitey and Stanley any longer. He seized the cash on Stanley, and it turned out to be $9,993, seven dollars under the maximum amount allowed for airline passengers to carry on board a plane. Besides, Johnson knew who Whitey was and what he was capable of doing, so he allowed Whitey and Stanley to exit the terminal.

Free to go, Whitey grabbed Stanley by the hand and dragged her out of the terminal. Stanley carried the $9,993 in her purse, and Whitey held the bag containing the $80,000.

However, if you believe the Boston newspapers, there was a woeful ending to this drama.

In 1998, after Whitey was already in the wind, William Johnson, then 50-years-old, killed himself with a self-inflicted gunshot wound to the head. The *Sun Journal* ran a story saying Johnson had committed suicide because of his downward career spiral after the Logan Airport incident with Whitey.

According to the *Sun Journal*, Jane Johnson, William Johnson's sister, said Johnson's troubles began the week after the incident with Whitey at Logan Airport.

The *Sun Journal* wrote, "That was when Johnson heard that David Davis, then-head of the Massachusetts Transit Authority which runs Logan Airport, was seeking a report on the Whitey Bulger incident. Johnson said Davis had come to him for the report on the insistence of Bulger's brother, then State Senate President William Bulger, now president of the House Committee on Government Reform. Johnson said he refused to hand over the report because Davis would not give him a receipt."

"In the end Johnson wound up patrolling the airport's parking lot. He told the *Boston Herald* earlier this year, 'I was ordered back in the cruiser and told to watch for people ripping off car radios.'"

"Jane Johnson said her brother, who was a decorated 22-year state police veteran and former Green Beret, never recovered from the direction his career took after a chance encounter with one of Boston's infamous mobsters."

However, Weeks said the explanation for Johnson's suicide didn't ring true to him.

"Other state troopers told me Johnson had mental health issues," Weeks said. "Even though the trooper had plenty of problems before he met Jimmy (Whitey), it made a much better story to link his suicide to the scene at Logan eleven years earlier."

Chapter 13
The State Versus the Feds

Thomas J. Foley was a Massachusetts state detective who had his eyes on Whitey and his crew. In 1984, Foley was appointed to the State Intelligence Unit on Organized Crime. The unit was headed by Dave Mattioli, under the supervision of Lieutenant Charlie Henderson. The State Intelligence Unit on Organized Crime worked with the F.B.I., which meant John Connolly would be privy to any actions the unit took concerning Whitey and Flemmi.

On the F.B.I. side, Foley worked with Nick Gianturco, who was close pals with John Connolly and Whitey. Gianturco was so close with Whitey they exchanged presents at Christmas. Whitey was also clever enough to give Christmas gifts to Gianturco's boss, Jim Ring, whom Whitey called "The Pipe," because he always had a pipe stuck between his teeth.

When he first began working with the F.B.I. on organized crime, Foley didn't know the relationship between Whitey's crew and the F.B.I.

But soon, Foley became suspicious.

Foley first became aware of Whitey's control of the Boston underworld when he read a report by *President Reagan's Commission on Organized Crime*. In this report, Whitey's last name was misspelled as "Bolger," but the facts were clear, precise, and to the point. Whitey was identified as a "bank robber, murderer, and drug trafficker."

Before the issuance of the presidential report, Whitey was virtually unknown outside of Boston. Now, Whitey was

The State Versus the Feds

identified as a crime lord to law enforcement throughout America. Because of his newfound notoriety and the arrests and convictions of the LCN hierarchy in Boston, Whitey knew he would become target No. 1 for law enforcement in the state of Massachusetts, except for his pals in the local F.B.I.

Yet, when Foley and the F.B.I. started working together on organized crime, their target was not Whitey, Flemmi, or any members of the Winter Hill Mob. Instead, they concentrated on an obscure alleged LCN member named Frank Oreto Jr.

According to Foley's book *Most Wanted: Pursuing Whitey Bulger*, the state police did most of the outside dirty work out, while the F.B.I. stood cozily inside, listening to wiretaps between sips of coffee and bites of stuffed jelly donuts.

"Clearly there were two different work ethics in play when it came down to the State Police and the F.B.I.," Foley said. "We did most of the street work; they manned the interior jobs, monitoring the recorders. We worked late hours; them not so much."

While the Otero investigation was underway, and the unit was busily transcribing the wiretaps to present to a judge for an indictment, Foley saw John Connolly snooping around.

Foley said, "Seeing Connolly, you'd almost think he was Mafia, not fed. He had the chunky ring, the slicked-back hair, the jet-black Italian suit, the glad-to-see-ya smile. He could have been John Gotti's younger brother. But I give him this: The guy exuded likability."

Connolly cozied up to Foley. Connolly told him how close he was to Billy Bulger, but Connolly never mentioned his relationship with Whitey, who was still on record as an F.B.I. informant with Connolly as his handler.

After the joint state and F.B.I. operation took Frank Otero off the streets, Foley spoke with his immediate supervisor, Dave Mattioli.

He said, "I want to work on Whitey Bulger; both him and Flemmi."

Mattioli told Foley neither Whitey nor Flemmi had been arrested since the mid-1960's.

Foley shot back, "Come on! Does anybody think he's gone straight?"

Mattioli admitted Foley had a point. But before he could authorize a Winter Hill Mob investigation, Mattioli said he'd had to check with Boston F.B.I. boss, Jim Ring, who was still getting his Christmas pipes and tobacco from Whitey.

Foley talked over his idea of going after the Winter Hill Mob with another state cop named Jimmy White, who loved the idea.

A few days after Foley's request, Foley and White were called into Mattioli's office.

Mattioli told Foley and White, "I've run it by Ring, and he says no. We can't do Bulger and we can't do Flemmi."

Foley and White were flabbergasted. It was White who spoke first.

"Why the hell not?" he asked Mattioli.

Mattioli snapped back, "Because they're not LCN, and the F.B.I. is only doing LCN."

It was Foley turn to mouth off to his boss.

"Come on Dave, the LCN is way down," Foley said. "He's (Whitey) the biggest thing in Boston now, maybe ever. You know that. Everybody knows that. Just by himself, he's bigger than the whole LCN right now."

But Mattioli's hands were tied by the F.B.I. bureaucrats.

"Guys, I know," Mattioli said. "But the F.B.I. wants to go after LCN. Okay? So that's it. LCN."

Foley's next joint state police and F.B.I. taskforce assignment was dubbed "Operation Mist," and their main target was another low-level Italian gangster named Angelo "Sonny" Mercurio. Mercurio operated out of a Boston restaurant named Vanessa's. When the Boston F.B.I. wrote an affidavit to the court for permission to wiretap Vanessa's, Foley noticed that Whitey's name was mentioned in the affidavit as an informant against the LCN.

Whitey was supposedly seen going in and out of Vanessa's to meet with various Italian mobsters, including Mercurio, to get information for the feds. And Whitey, as a result, was considered by the F.B.I. to be an integral part of the F.B.I.'s effort to bring down the LCN. But neither Foley nor his partner Jimmy White, who were doing intense surveillance on Vanessa's, had ever seen Whitey anywhere near Vanessa's.

Foley said, "We checked with a couple of other troopers working the case. Nobody had ever seen Whitey, or heard him, or heard anything about him on all the hours of talk we had listened in on. And yet the F.B.I. claimed he was so important. I didn't get it. Whitey was cited by the F.B.I. as someone on the inside, and yet there was no indication that he'd ever been one."

Foley asked around the F.B.I. about this strange situation, but all he got from F.B.I. agents was a shrug of the shoulders and a look that said, "Mind your own business."

It's obvious John Connolly, with the help of Jim Ring, had cemented the idea into the minds of the F.B.I. big shots in Washington that Whitey was a key informant in the F.B.I.'s quest to decimate the LCN. In truth, the Italian wiseguys the F.B.I. were after wouldn't give Whitey the time of day; let alone make him privy to important LCN information.

Whitey's world continued to spin in his favor.

Chapter 14
Globed

In 1986 and 1987, everything went hunky-dory for Whitey. He was raking in the cash, he had two beautiful girlfriends, and he was under the protective umbrella of John Connolly and the F.B.I.

Then came rocky 1988 and the *Boston Globe*.

Four *Boston Globe* reporters; i.e., Dick Lehr, Kevin Cullen, Gerard O'Neil, and Christine Chinlund, were all working on articles that concerned the Bulger brothers, Billy and Whitey. Both brothers were ostensibly on opposite sides of the law. Cullen came up with an intriguing hypothetical. Since Whitey, known throughout Boston as the "King of Crime," had never been arrested for years, maybe he was an F.B.I. informant.

As the reporters snooped around for information, they made calls to high ranking members of the F.B.I., including John Morris and the chief of the Federal Organized Crime Force, the aforementioned Jeremiah T. O'Sullivan. The reporters asked O'Sullivan, point blank, if Whitey was an F.B.I. informant.

O'Sullivan, his nose twitching, blurted out, "I don't buy it!"

That statement, of course, was a bold-faced lie, since O'Sullivan knew back in 1979, during the horse race-fixing case, that Whitey and Flemmi were singing like canaries to the feds.

In 1989, the same Jeremiah T. O'Sullivan was the lead prosecutor in a federal investigation into improprieties concerning properties bought with tainted money at 75 State Street. One of the people purportedly involved in the scandal was Billy Bulger, who was still the boss of the Massachusetts State Senate. However, there was absolutely no evidence Billy had done anything wrong concerning the development of property at 75 State Street. In fact, it seemed political opponents were simply maliciously impugning Billy.

After a thorough investigation, O' Sullivan issued a statement, "No witness has ever alleged Senator Bulger was criminally involved in this matter. And any inferences that he was so involved are not supported by the weight of the evidence."

All this was well and good and the right thing for O'Sullivan to say. Yet, it was a statement made by Billy in his self-serving autobiography - *While the Music Lasts* - that was better left unsaid.

Billy wrote, "The media was correct in depicting O'Sullivan, the federal attorney, as a dedicated and efficient dragon slayer. What they did not take into account was that he was so honest."

Jeremiah T. O'Sullivan was a lot of things. But, in view of O'Sullivan's outright lies about Whitey and Flemmi not being F.B.I. informants, "honest" was not one of them.

Did Billy know his brother Whitey and Flemmi were F.B.I. informants, and that O'Sullivan was not telling the truth when he denied the fact?

There is no direct evidence Billy ever knew a damn thing about Whitey and Flemmi singing to the Feds. In fact, one of the stipulations Whitey supposedly demanded from Connolly, when he first decided to become a rat, was that Billy be kept in the dark.

Supposedly.

However, although this author was born in the day, it wasn't yesterday. The readers can draw their own conclusions.

Let's get back to the *Boston Globe's* probe into the Bulger Brothers. John Morris, a weak and treacherous man, was starting to crack. Whether it was through guilt or fear, Morris agreed to meet with *Boston Globe* reporter Gerard O'Neil. According to *Black Mass*, this meeting took place at Venezia's Restaurant, a stylish eatery on the waterfront overlooking Dorchester Bay.

As they sipped espresso and munched Italian desserts, O'Neil posed the question about the possibility of Whitey having lived such a charmed life because he was secretly an F.B.I. informant.

Morris almost choked on his cannoli.

He told O'Neil, "You have no idea how dangerous he (Whitey) can be."

Then Morris began talking fast, in bursts, as if his life depended upon it. Morris told O'Neil all about the cozy relationship between the F.B.I., and Whitey and Flemmi. Morris also told O'Neil how Connolly and Whitey were almost joined at the hip. If you smacked Whitey, a red mark would appear on Connolly's face.

Morris started blabbing about the nice little dinners the F.B.I. agents, including himself and Connolly, had with the heads of the Winter Hill Mob. In particular, Morris mentioned a feast at the home of Flemmi's mother, which Billy Bulger had unexpectedly walked in on.

"There we were," Morris told O'Neil. "The two (Bulger) brothers were sitting on one side of the table and the two F.B.I. agents on the other side of the table."

Morris later admitted the reason he had agreed to meet with O'Neil was because Connolly informed him that Billy Bulger had already agreed to be interviewed for a future article in the *Globe*. In actuality, Connelly claimed the *Globe* was setting up Billy in order to go after Whitey and Whitey's connection to the F.B.I. Connolly told Morris to play down

Whitey's F.B.I. involvement. Instead, Morris, most likely exhausted from all the stress, aggravation, and all the lies, did exactly the opposite.

There was speculation Morris's motivation for speaking with O'Neil was that he figured, if Whitey and Flemmi were outed as rats for the F.B.I., the local LCN would kill both of them; thereby relieving Morris of the anxiety of possibly being whacked by the two notorious killers.

Morris said to the *Globe*, "My principal concern was my own skin. I was trying to minimize the damage in my own career."

However, Morris denied he was trying to induce the Boston LCN to handle the Whitey/Flemmi situation.

"No, absolutely not," Morris said. "What I was trying to do was get them closed as F.B.I. informants. My line of thinking there wasn't very clear. I think that part of it, if Connolly surfaced, that would mean that I would be surfaced. And I think at that point in time I wanted my own involvement surfaced."

Morris's line of reasoning makes no sense. It only shows what a mutt John Morris really is and always has been. All Morris had to do to rectify the situation was to tell his F.B.I. bosses in Washington D.C. the truth about its favorite informants, and throw himself at the mercy of the feds. If Morris had come clean sooner, there would have been a good chance Whitey would have been arrested long before he went on the lam, and some of Whitey's victims would still be alive.

Next, there was the curious phone call made by F.B.I. agent Tom Daly to the *Boston Globe*. Kevin Cullen was sitting at the newspaper's city desk when he took Daly's call. Suddenly, Daly started blasting Cullen, the *Boston Globe*, and everyone connected with the *Boston Globe*. Daly was irate that snoopy *Globe* reporters had somehow contacted, by mail, Tony Ciulla, the rat from the 1979 horse race-fixing deal.

Ciulla had refused to go into the Witness Protection Program because he knew the Boston F.B.I. was just as corrupt as most Boston crooks. So, the *Globe*, being one of the best publications on investigative journalism on the planet, had little difficulty locating Ciulla. Consequently, Ciulla figured Whitey would have no difficulty in locating Ciulla either. The fact Whitey and Flemmi had never been indicted in the horse race-fixing case hardly mattered, since Ciulla had fingered them anyway. It was only through the efforts of the Boston F.B.I. and prosecutor Jeremiah T. O'Sullivan that the Winter Hill Mob bosses emerged from the horse nonsense unscathed.

F.B.I. Agent Daly told Cullen on the phone, "I'm annoyed you didn't call me first. First off, Ciulla will not talk to you. I also know the *Globe* has interviewed Billy Bulger. Ciulla told me to give you a message. 'Be very careful about what you say about Whitey. Whitey is a dangerous guy and you don't want to piss him off.'"

F.B.I. agent Daly then hit Cullen with an uppercut below the belt.

Daly said, "Whitey Bulger is the type of guy, if you write the truth he has no problem with you. But if you embarrass him or his family, or write something untrue, then this is what Ciulla said, 'The guy would never live with that. He would think nothing of clipping you.' Especially you, Kevin. I mean in all sincerity I'm not trying to be dramatic. He's extremely dangerous. I know you live over there in South Boston."

After the telephone conversation with F.B.I. Agent Daly, you couldn't blame Cullen for being scared, pissed, or both. Cullen rightfully assumed the little extra oomph at the end of Daly's phone conversation was either from the F.B.I. or from the great Whitey Bulger himself.

In September 1988, the *Globe's* series on the Bulger brothers finally saw the light of day. They say sunlight is the best disinfectant, but sunlight also makes the roaches scatter and scatter they did. When F.B.I. supervisor Jim Ahern took the podium at a hastily-arranged press conference, the F.B.I. was in full damage control. When the press asked Ahern about Whitey's F.B.I. informant status, Ahern was apoplectic.

Ahern bellowed, "That is absolutely untrue! We specifically deny that there has been special treatment of this individual (Whitey Bulger)!"

Soon after the *Globe* article surfaced, Whitey called for a summit meeting between him and Flemmi, and Morris and Connolly. Flemmi suggested that he and Whitey should drop out of the F.B.I. informant program to ease the pressure from the press.

John Connolly was adamantly against releasing Whitey and Flemmi as F.B.I. informants. Connolly's reasoning was that Whitey was such a respected and revered figure in the Boston crime world –to both Irish and Italian gangsters - no one would ever believe Whitey was eating cheese. Connolly turned out to be right since it was later discovered that both Whitey's Irish pals and members of the Boston LCN dismissed the allegations as unfounded. Instead, they believed the story was either planted by the press or based on comments from disgruntled gangsters who were looking to make a deal for themselves.

Connolly and Whitey had an ace in the hole inside the Boston press crew that they would utilize quite often, especially when the heat became stifling. His name was *Boston Globe* Pulitzer Prize-winning columnist Mike Barnicle, who was fired in 1998 for fabrication and plagiarism. Whenever Connolly, the F.B.I., Billy Bulger, or Whitey needed good press, Barnicle was their go-to guy. In fact, a competing newspaper once called Barnicle "Billy Bulger's water carrier."

A good example of Barnicle's "Bulger Protection Program" surfaced in 1991, when Whitey ostensibly won

$1.4 million in the state lottery. The winning ticket had been bought in Whitey's own liquor store - the South Boston Liquor Mart - a business Whitey had "purchased" after allegedly threatening the former owner, Steven "Stippo" Rakes.

During the Christmas Holidays of 1983, Rakes, who had bought the store in mid-1983 with his wife, Julie, had three unexpected visitors to his home. It seems Whitey wanted a new base of operations for his illegal businesses, and Stippo's liquor store was the perfect location for it. When the visitors arrived at the Rakes's home, Julie was minding the store, and Steven was home watching their two young daughters.

The men who stalked into Rakes's kitchen were Whitey, Flemmi, and Kevin Weeks.

According to Rakes, Whitey spoke first.

"There are other liquor store owners who want you killed," Whitey said. "We'll do you a favor. We'll buy the store from you."

Rakes told Whitey, "The store is not for sale."

Suddenly, one of Rakes's little girls wandered into the kitchen. Flemmi pulled out a handgun and innocently placed it on the table. With Flemmi's encouragement, Rakes's little girl began fingering the gun.

Then Flemmi said, "Isn't she cute?" Flemmi paused for effect. "It would be a sin for her not to see you."

By this time Rakes was shaking like Barney Fife holding a gun.

Whitey took out a paper bag, and he threw it on the table. It contained $67,000 in cash.

Whitey smiled. "We either buy the store, or we kill you. The choice is yours."

Figuring he had no choice, Steven Rakes sold Whitey his liquor store. Whitey changed the name from "Stippo's" to the "South Boston Liquor Mart."

Globed

Kevin Weeks disputed Rakes's reason for selling his liquor store. According to Weeks, it was Rakes's sister, Mary, who had approached Whitey and told him Rakes wanted to sell his liquor store. She wanted to know if the Winter Hill Mob might be interested.

Whitey told Weeks, "Stippo wants to sell the liquor store. A legitimate business wouldn't be a bad idea. What do you think?"

Weeks told Whitey, "It doesn't hurt to listen."

After having a friend go over Rakes's books to determine a fair selling price, Whitey put $100,000 (not $67,000) in a paper bag. Another 25 grand, but only on paper, was added onto the bill of sale to make it look like Whitey had not underpaid Rakes. Then Whitey, Flemmi, and Weeks went over to Rakes's home to complete the transaction.

According to Weeks, when they got to Rakes's home, Whitey told Rakes to count the money. In the middle of counting the money at his kitchen table, Rakes looked up and said, "I don't know about this. My wife doesn't really want to sell."

Immediately, Whitey, Weeks, and Flemmi got the same idea. Rakes, a shrewd businessman, was trying to shake down Whitey for more cash.

Whitey just shook his head at Rakes's remark.

"We agreed on this price," Whitey said. "The money is here, and you're not getting any more money out of us."

As if on cue, Weeks (not Flemmi as Rakes claimed) pulled out a gun, and he put it on the kitchen table. Rakes's daughter was already in the room sitting on Whitey's lap, and she innocently touched the handle of the gun.

According to Weeks, "Whitey pushed the gun back to me and told me to put it away. Then Whitey took the little girl off his knee, and he placed her standing on the floor."

After the girl had been removed from the kitchen by

an aunt, Whitey told Rakes, "Listen, we had a deal. We agreed upon a price, and now you are trying to get more money out of us. You were the one who came to us to buy the store. We didn't come to you."

Rakes took the hundred grand and the deal was done.

In July of 2013, Weeks told this same story on the stand at Whitey's trial. Rakes was scheduled to testify to present his side of the story. But two days before Rakes was to take the stand, the government decided not to use Rakes as a prosecution witness.

John "Red" Shea, who once worked for Whitey selling drugs and did hard time in prison without becoming a rat, told *Fox News*, "I guess the government didn't want Rakes to contradict its star witness (Kevin Weeks) on the witness stand."

One day after Rakes discovered he was not being called to testify in Whitey's case, Rakes was found dead in Lincoln, Mass, 15 miles from his home in Boston. Rakes did not have any signs of obvious trauma. Nonetheless, the death was suspicious because Rakes did not have any identification on him, and there was no visible means of him getting to the spot where his body was found.

The day after Rakes was found dead, his ex-wife, Julie Dammers, said, "I can assure you my ex-husband did not commit suicide."

That turned out to be the truth because on August 1, 2013, Middlesex police arrested William Camuti for the murder of Steven Rakes. It seems Camuti owed big money to Rakes. He invited Rakes to a McDonald's in Waltham, where the two men were supposed to discuss how they could make money working together so Camuti could pay off his debt. While Rakes was not looking, Camuti slipped cyanide into Rakes's ice coffee.

Rakes drank the laced coffee, and a few minutes later, Rakes keeled over dead in Camuti's car. Camuti drove around for a while before depositing Rakes's body in a wooded area in Lincoln. Camuti was charged with murder, misleading the police, and unlawful disposition of human remains.

Now let's get back to Mike Barnicle and his kid glove treatment of Whitey and Billy Bulger.

In late July 1991, a man named Michael Linskey bought a lottery ticket at Whitey's South Boston Liquor Mart. The ticket turned out to be a winner to the tune of $14.3 million. However, when Linskey presented the ticket to state authorities, he claimed he was actually partners in the ticket with Linskey's brother Patrick, Kevin Weeks, and the infamous Whitey Bulger. Why Weeks was brought into the picture is anyone's guess.

Every crook in Boston knew if you made illegal money, you had to kick up a piece to Whitey or your health would not stay good for very long. Apparently, Whitey used this same logic when it came to someone buying lottery tickets in his liquor store. Only a fool would believe the Linskeys, who had no apparent connection with Whitey except to buy liquor and lottery tickets at his store, would go partners with Whitey in anything, unless they were forced to. But Linskey, probably feeling an invisible gun in his back, kept to his story, and Whitey was awarded a stash of lottery cash.

According to the July 30, 1992 issue of *The Telegraph*, Linskey was to be paid $537,336 a year for 20 years. It was later discovered that Whitey took the same deal to save on the taxes.

When *The Telegraph* phoned the South Boston Liquor Mart to find out if Whitey had made the same arrangement with the state that Linskey had, whoever answered the phone declined to comment, except to say, "We have no comment. We wish you would stop calling. He (Whitey) is entitled to buy a lottery ticket like anyone else in the state of Massachusetts."

Barnicle, as he had many times before, came to a Whitey's rescue. This happened after Whitey and Flemmi were dropped from the F.B.I. as informants, but not from being pals with John Connolly, who, even after his 1990 retirement from the F.B.I., had his tentacles deep into the Boston F.B.I.'s secret operations.

Barnicle wrote this in his *Boston Globe* column entitled "Give Whitey a Break":

"In a blatant display of prejudice against local Irish gangsters, some narrow-minded bigots are hinting that the lottery was rigged just because a friend of Whitey Bulger won $14 million and split the ticket four ways. Hey, good things happen to good people, right? Of course there is an army of malcontents who refuse to believe that the result of a mere game of chance is on the level when the cash cow moos at the doorstep of a man – Bulger – who, according to illegal eavesdropping by F.B.I. agents and their cheap equipment (And I will show you how lousy their stuff was), runs a vastly overrated criminal enterprise in the area.

"So lay off Whitey Bulger. For the first time in his life, he got lucky, legitimately, and won the lottery. Knowing him, he probably already has handed money out to St. Augustine's, figuring that when he goes – and the odds on that are better than winning Mass Millions – there will be some people left behind who will say, 'Not a bad guy.'"

Later on, Barnicle and some of his pals said this column was a tongue-in-cheek satire piece. But others say Barnicle was just doing what he always had done: speak nicely of Bulger family members.

After all, as Dionne Warwick once said, "That's what friends are for."

Chapter 15
Three Doesn't Go into Two

Whitey spent the early 1990's still in bed with two women - Teresa Stanley and Catherine Greig - but with only one at a time. Grieg knew all about Stanley, but Stanley, although she must have known Whitey was as faithful as a fifty-dollar hooker, didn't even know Catherine Greig existed.

In 1994, Catherine Greig was tired of being the second woman. After all, she had been Whitey's girl for almost two decades, and the pretty young thing she had been when she first met Whitey had turned into a middle-aged woman with no marriage prospects in sight.

To bring the situation to a head, Catherine Greig picked up the phone and called Teresa Stanley.

"We have to talk about Whitey," Greig told Stanley.

Stanley felt a thick lump in her throat.

After Stanley confirmed Whitey had left her domicile for the night, Greig told Stanley she be right over. When Greig arrived at Stanley's house, she asked Stanley to get into Greig's car. Grieg was intent on showing Stanley something Stanley didn't want to see: the love nest Whitey had shared with Greig for many years in Quincy.

Stanley was suffocated by the silence in the car. She knew this was not going to be pleasant, and she was right.

When they arrived at Greig's residence, the tension evaporated like smoke from a cigarette. As the two ladies sat comfortably in Greig's living room, Grieg told Stanley all about her two-decade love affair with Whitey. Grieg also told Stanley she was tired of Whitey's double life, and the two women should get together to force Whitey to choose one woman and forget the other.

As part of Whitey's normal routine, Whitey showed up at Grieg's apartment, this time with Kevin Weeks in tow. When he strutted through the front door, Whitey was confronted with both women in his life. Stanley and Grieg sat in the living room together looking like the Nuremburg jury.

Whitey knew what was up. As usual, he took control of the situation.

He grabbed Stanley's hand and barked, "Let's go!"

But Stanley would have none of that.

Stanley not so politely informed Whitey that Grieg had spilled her guts about everything, and that Whitey would have to pick one woman and discard the other. She also called Whitey several unflattering names, including two-timing bastard, lowlife, and cheating son-of-a-bitch.

Whitey's answer was to turn to Grieg and to proceed to strangle her, just as he had strangled Debbie Davis and Debra Hussy many years before. Luckily, Kevin Weeks was younger and stronger than Whitey. He extricated Whitey's hands from around Grieg's neck. Then, with Whitey fermenting in rage, Weeks grabbed Stanley and pushed her out the front door. While Grieg sat on the floor gasping for breath, Whitey stormed out of the house too.

After Whitey calmed down a bit, he had a heart-to-heart with Stanley about the situation. Because of Grieg's jealous actions, Whitey promised he would never see her again. Stanley bought Whitey's explanation for the time being, and Whitey kept his word for maybe a week. Soon, Whitey was back to his two-woman daily routine. And neither Stanley nor Grieg was brave enough, or had enough integrity, to tell Whitey to take a flying leap.

Three Doesn't Go Into Two

As Mel Brooks said in *History of the World - Part I*, "It's good to be king."

Whitey, probably feeling a little guilty about his treatment of Stanley, took her on an expensive tour of Europe with stops in London, Venice, and Dublin. But Whitey being Whitey, he always mixed a little business with pleasure.

On each of his stops, Whitey visited his safe deposit boxes and infused them with additional cash. Whitey heard whispers from his old pal John Connolly that indictments were coming down soon. And with Whitey in possession of several passports with different aliases, Whitey knew he would have no trouble blending in with the European crowds, who didn't know Whitey Bulger from Whitey Ford.

Chapter 16
On the Run

John Connolly had lived a charmed life as an F.B.I. agent, and he planned to live a similar life after his retirement from the feds in 1990.

After Connolly put in his papers and was given a grand old retirement party by his F.B.I. chums, the first chit Connolly called in was one he figured was owed him by Billy Bulger, who was still the President of the Massachusetts State Senate. Billy contacted Boston Mayor Ray Flynn, and made a pitch for Connolly to be the new Boston Police Commissioner. Instead, Flynn decided to promote from within the Boston Police Department, and he gave the post to his buddy, Lieutenant Francis Roache, who had been the acting Police Commissioner since 1989.

Deprived of a high-profile gig, Connolly took a better-paying job as Director of Security/Public affairs for Boston Edison, which was established back in 1886. His old pal, retired F.B.I. agent John Kehoe, recommended Connolly for this prestigious position. At this point, Whitey and Flemmi were no longer F.B.I. informants. But Connolly, even though he was retired from the feds, still knew when a pin dropped in the F.B.I.'s Boston Office.

In 1994, a few days before Christmas, Connolly heard from his F.B.I. moles that trouble was brewing for the bosses of the Winter Hill Mob. It seems that an ambitious United States Attorney from Massachusetts named Donald Stern had set his sights on Whitey and Flemmi. But Stern's first order of business had been to contact the Boston F.B.I.

On the Run

to confirm the two gangsters had been past F.B.I. informants. Unfortunately, Stern didn't know telling the Boston F.B.I. anything about Whitey was like telling John Connolly, which, in turn, was like telling Whitey himself. The leaker inside the F.B.I. was an old Connolly chum, Dennis O'Callahan, who had risen to the No. 2 spot in Boston's F.B.I. office.

Connolly knew it was just a matter of days before the indictments came down, so he ran to Whitey's headquarters at the South Boston Liquor Mart. When he got to Whitey's joint, Kevin Weeks was standing next to the counter, but Whitey and Flemmi were nowhere in sight. Consequently, Connolly relayed the message through Weeks. The pending indictments concerned the extortion of two local Jewish bookies, Chico Krantz and Jimmy Katz, who had been contributing to the Whitey and Flemmi Retirement Fund for many years.

"The indictments are imminent," Connolly told Weeks. "They are trying to put them together over the holidays. That way they can pinch them all at once."

To make sure Weeks understood the severity of the matter, Connolly made Weeks repeat, word-for-word, everything Connolly had just told him.

Satisfied Weeks had gotten all the information correctly, Connolly told Weeks, "Only four people in the F.B.I. office know about this. So get this word to Jimmy (Whitey) and Stevie right away."

As soon as Connolly left, Weeks dialed Whitey's beeper number. Whitey called back and told Weeks he was busy Christmas shopping with Teresa Stanley. Weeks told Whitey it was urgent for Whitey to pick him up in front of the liquor store, pronto. Then Weeks dialed Flemmi's number, but he got no answer.

When Whitey arrived at the South Boston Liquor Mart, he picked up Weeks, and then he drove Weeks and Stanley to Neiman Marcus in Copley Plaza. After double-parking his car, Whitey told Stanley to get lost for a while, while he and Weeks did a little walk-talk, in case Whitey's car was bugged.

When Weeks told Whitey the bad news, Whitey barely blinked. He had been prepared for this moment for many years. In fact, he had been looking forward to the time when he could enjoy life and not worry about who owed him money or whom he must kill to stay on top of the Boston underworld. Whitey told Weeks to make sure he contacted Flemmi. When Teresa Stanley returned to the car, Whitey informed her their Christmas shopping was over. The good news, he told her, was that they were going on a little road trip to locations, which were not yet determined by Whitey.

Whitey told Stanley, "We're going on the road. You know, 'On the Road,' like in that book by that Greenwich Village hippie writer, Jack Kill-the-Quack, or something like that."

Stanley, ever the good soldier, smiled and said, "Sure. What the heck? I like books."

This turn of events meant Teresa Stanley was in and Catherine Greig was out. That's all that mattered to Stanley in the whacky world of Whitey Bulger.

Whitey didn't know if the feds, at that very moment, were staking out Stanley's home, so he told Stanley, "We'll buy what we need on the way to wherever we are going."

Whitey always had large amounts of cash on him, and millions more stashed in safe deposit boxes throughout the world. So, before Flemmi even knew what was happening, Whitey, with Stanley playing Tonto to Whitey's Long Ranger, was officially on the lam.

In the meantime, Weeks went back to the South Boston Liquor Mart, where he put in another call to Flemmi. Unlike Whitey, who knew for months things were looking bleak, Flemmi had prepared very little for a life on the run. In fact, Flemmi had another Boston F.B.I. agent in his hip pocket. He figured his guy would let him know if the roof was about to fall on his head.

In other words, Flemmi, because he had been in cahoots with the feds for almost 30 years, thought he was bulletproof to being arrested.

He thought wrong.

In the late afternoon, Flemmi made his appearance at the South Boston Liquor Mart. Weeks told Flemmi, just as Weeks had told Whitey, that indictments were coming, possibly at any moment. Weeks also told Flemmi that Whitey was already in the wind and suggested it would be wise if Flemmi got lost too.

Flemmi yawned. Then he told Weeks, "My guy is right on top of it. I'll be hearing from him."

Weeks spoke again, this time more slowly and more distinctly.

"I'm telling you only four guys in the Boston F.B.I. office know about this," Weeks said. "They're being very careful about the whole situation. Maybe your guy ain't one of the four guys in the know."

Flemmi said he'd think about it and then left the South Boston Liquor Mart whistling "Jingle Bells."

In order to enjoy Christmas with his family, Weeks put Flemmi and Whitey's situation on his pay-no-mind-list for a few days. Weeks figured Whitey was gone, and Flemmi was smart enough to disappear too. So why not enjoy his kids enjoying Santa?

A few days after Christmas, Weeks was shocked when Flemmi strolled into the South Boston Liquor Mart like he didn't have a care in the world.

"What are you nuts?" Weeks told Flemmi. "You should be long gone by now, like Jimmy (Whitey)."

Flemmi shook his head at Weeks like Weeks was a wayward child.

"I told you my guy's on top of things," Flemmi said.

"Now stop breaking my balls."

Weeks couldn't believe what he was hearing.

"I hate to repeat myself, but I told you a few days ago only four people in the Boston F.B.I. office know what's about to come down," Weeks said. "Listen to me; take a few weeks off. It's cold as a witch's tit here in Boston. Go someplace where it's warm. Get a nice suntan. Drink a few pina coladas. If what Connolly says is true, you have a head start. If not, come back in a few weeks and freeze. But get out of Boston now."

Flemmi told Weeks to perform an anatomical impossibility on himself, then he stormed out of the South Boston Liquor Mart.

On the evening of January 5, 1995, Flemmi, who had just spent his final New Year's Eve celebration as a free man, decided to take his 25-year-old Chinese girlfriend on a grand tour of Schooner's Restaurant - a High Street bistro that was closed for renovations. The joint was owned by Steven Hussey - the brother of Debbie Hussy - whom Flemmi had watched Whitey choke to death. Unfortunately, D.E.A. agents and Massachusetts state troopers spotted Flemmi entering the restaurant.

When Flemmi and his girl emerged from Schooner's, they slid into her white Honda with Flemmi behind the wheel. Before Flemmi could crank the engine, he realized he was boxed in by what he hoped was the law. If it wasn't the law, then Flemmi was being set up to be whacked.

A D.E.A. agent pointed his gun at the Honda and screamed at the frightened couple inside, "This is the D.E.A., Steve Flemmi! Stay right where you are!"

Flemmi still wasn't sure who these armed people were. Many times a ruse like this is used by gangsters to whack somebody. So Flemmi did what bad guys do when they think they are about to be riddled with bullets. He dove under the dashboard. The young Chinese girl didn't move a muscle. Her petrified face looked like an advertisement for

On the Run

"Scream 10."

According to *Most Wanted*, a D.E.A. agent named Doherty ripped open the driver's door with his gun pointed at the cowering Flemmi.

"Steve Flemmi, you are under arrest!" Doherty said. "Put your hands up on the dashboard where I can see them."

By this time Flemmi must have realized if this was a hit, he'd be dead already. Still, Flemmi didn't like to cooperate with the law too much. Few gangsters do. So, Flemmi smirked, and ignored Doherty's commands.

Doherty was no jerk and didn't like being treated like one. He pressed his gun up against the side of Flemmi's head and increased his finger's pressure on the trigger.

"Hands on the dashboard!" Doherty barked. "Or I'll blow your fucking head off. Now!"

Flemmi sat up straight, and he slowly put his hands on the dashboard.

Doherty, the cold metal of his gun still making contact with Flemmi's head, said, "Okay, out of the car! Slow and easy! Any quick movement and you're dead!"

Flemmi obeyed, and the next thing he knew he was spread-eagled facedown on the pavement. As Doherty attempted to cuff Flemmi, Flemmi cried, "Come on now. What's going on here? Come on!"

Doherty snapped the cuffs shut, and then he frisked Flemmi. Doherty found a large hunting knife on Flemmi and a can of mace. But no gun. Doherty dragged Flemmi to his feet. Flemmi was now a captive of the State of Massachusetts.

Flemmi's girlfriend, who was a Chinese nationalist and somewhat of an activist herself, was patted down too. When no weapons were found on her, she was released and told to find herself another boyfriend, preferably one not featured on "America's Most Wanted."

It's a simple fact; if Flemmi had listened to Weeks, he would have been enjoying a nice vacation, most likely in a warm climate. Instead, Flemmi was going on another sort of "vacation," which would consume the rest of his natural life.

Like actor Robert Mitchum said at the end of the flick, *The Friends of Eddie Coyle*, "Life is tough, but it's tougher when you're stupid."

Also arrested in the same roundup was Flemmi's old partner in crime, Frank Salemme, who was not an F.B.I. informant and, therefore, not tipped off to the imminent pinch. John Martorano was soon arrested in Florida.

Right about the time the feds pinched Flemmi, the state police surrounded Teresa Stanley's house in South Boston. They circled around the back, and they smashed in the back door with a battering ram. As several agents searched the house – even looking in the closets and under the bed – it was obvious no one was home and no one had been home for quite some time.

Undaunted, the state police sped to Catherine Greig's home in Quincy. Greig saw them coming, and she rushed outside to meet them face-to-face. The cops said they were looking for Whitey, and if they could please search her home to make sure Whitey was not hiding in her closets or under her bed.

Grieg asked the police to produce a search warrant, and when they couldn't, she told them to perform an anatomical impossibility on themselves, one at a time, or all at once. It didn't make a difference. This shocked the cops because those words came out of the mouth of a very attractive and outwardly respectable lady, who obviously didn't like police officers too much.

While all the commotion was going on in and around Boston, Whitey was in his car somewhere in Connecticut driving Stanley back home. It seems Stanley missed her children, and was quite pissed at not celebrating Christmas

On the Run

with her family.

Suddenly, a report came over the car radio saying Flemmi had been arrested. Whitey did a screeching U-turn, and he told Stanley her family reunion would have to wait until he could sort things out.

Whitey had phony identification on him that said he was Thomas Baxter, from Selden, Long Island. He was also within a few hours driving distance of several safe deposit boxes rented out to the same Thomas Baxter. So money was not a problem. Whitey knew Weeks had not been arrested. He also knew there wasn't any F.B.I. evidence that would make Weeks's arrest imminent.

So from this point on, Kevin Weeks became a faithful Kato to Whitey's Green Hornet. Weeks turned into Whitey's go-to guy for anything Whitey needed to avoid being infected with the same disease presently contaminating Flemmi: incarceration.

Whitey knew his beeper was now useless, so he bought telephone calling cards or he used pay phones to contact Weeks to keep tabs on the situation in Boston. Whitey and Weeks had previously networked through a series of pay phones in the Boston area. They had also communicated on several home phones listed to Weeks's relatives. So, it was relatively easy for the two men to stay in touch.

For the next six weeks, Whitey and Stanley did numerous one-and-two-night stands in several hotels and motels all along the East Coast. While Whitey was on the run, the F.B.I. made a little visit to the office of State Senator Billy Bulger. Billy's secretary told the feds Senator Bulger was indisposed at the moment, and could they please leave their card so he could contact the feds when he got un-indisposed, which meant when he was good and ready.

Eventually, Billy relented and phoned the feds. Although Billy's language was not as salty as Catherine Greig's, his helpfulness to the feds was the same. Billy claimed he hadn't heard from his brother, didn't know where his brother could be located, and didn't expect to hear from his brother in the near future, or in the far future, for that matter.

This turned out not to be the truth.

On December 6, 2002, Billy Bulger, retired from the Senate, and now President of Massachusetts University, was called to testify before the House Committee on Government Reform. The chairman, Representative Dan Burton, a Republican from Indiana, asked Billy if he had had any contact with his brother Whitey, now 73-years-old, who had been indicted in 1995 and was still missing.

The 68-year-old Billy Bulger immediately took the Fifth, saying, "The Constitution provides this right to 'protect innocent men who might be ensnared by ambiguous circumstances.' I find myself in such circumstances."

Earlier that week, the *Boston Globe* had printed an article saying that in private grand jury testimony the previous year, Billy admitted he had talked by phone with Whitey in January 1995, just a couple of weeks after Whitey went into the wind. Billy said the phone conversation was set up by Kevin Weeks, and took place at the home of Billy's former driver "to avoid detection."

The conversation between the two brothers was, according to Billy, a simple case of, "How are you doing? Fine. And you?"

Billy did admit in his private grand jury testimony that he gave Whitey legal advice. After all Billy was still a lawyer. But that was all the milk Billy was going to spill about Whitey.

"I do have an honest loyalty to my brother and I care about him," Billy told the secret grand jury. "I don't feel an obligation to help everyone to catch him."

There was a split verdict as to Billy's performance before the House Committee on Government Reform.

On the Run

Massachusetts Governor-Elect Mitt Romney expressed concern, but hardly any anger. All Romney said was, "I was disappointed that University of Massachusetts President Bulger could not find a way to answer the questions."

However, the trustees of Massachusetts University did all but kiss Billy's butt.

Grace Fey, the chairman of the Massachusetts University trustees, issued a statement, saying, "President Bulger invoked constitutional rights available to every citizen. That is a reasonable and prudent decision in light of the circumstances. My respect and admiration for President Bulger are stronger than ever."

However, soon after Billy's testimony, Governor Romney had a change of heart, and he forced Billy to resign his prestigious and well-paying post as President of Massachusetts University. From that point on, Billy has lived his life in relative obscurity.

Years before his testimony in front of the House Committee on Government Reform, Billy wrote in his 1996 bio *While the Music Lasts: My Life in Politics*, "There has been much speculation in the press; many lurid allegations about my brother. From everything I could see, he appeared to have taken every step to separate himself from the environment that led to his early behavior. It's left to me, as it has been to others, to speculate what, if anything is valid in the dark rumors published about him.

"I am confident much of it has been circulated as an oblique political attack on me. I know some of the allegations and much of the innuendo to be absolutely false. Other matters I cannot be sure about; one way or another. I have no way of knowing and can only hope. But he is my brother and I love him, and pray he will not damage himself again."

However, after Whitey was captured and charged with numerous crimes, Billy said he still felt his brother was innocent of all charges.

After Whitey disappeared from Boston and was sought by every law enforcement officer in America and beyond, Billy said in his bio, "It's been known for many years that a 'get out of jail' card has been available to anyone who would give testimony against my brother. As long as this behavior is countenanced, prosecutors may and do buy testimony, with all the dangers attended to such purchases.

"In the well-publicized case against my brother, *all* the evidence has been purchased. Inducements more precious than money - release from prison, the waiver of criminal charges - have been offered time and time again. Some who have insisted they had nothing to offer at the beginning of their incarceration have had second thoughts and suddenly 'remembered' things they could barter for advantages. Without such testimony, there would be no accusations."

So, according to Billy, not one shred of evidence of his brother's three decades of crime can be accepted as gospel truth. Without lying rats seeking to better their own lot, Whitey should be considered as clean as a newborn baby.

"*All* of the evidence has been purchased," Billy wrote.

ALL OF THE EVIDENCE.

Billy Bulger is either the most naïve man in the word, delusional, or as big a liar as his brother Whitey is a rat.

*****

Next it was John Connolly who was forced to do a little tap-dance for Whitey. Because of present circumstances, Connolly was beginning to fear Whitey like bad seafood.

While still with Stanley and moving from one nightly rental to another, Whitey ordered Kevin Weeks to tell Connolly he wanted to talk to him about what could be done to alleviate the pressure from the feds. Whitey felt the indictments against him and Flemmi were a bad rap. The charges all concentrated on illegal gambling, which the feds had told Whitey he was free to engage in as long as he and

On the Run

Flemmi kept dishing the dirt on the Italian mob. Of course, by 1995 the Italian mob was moribund in Boston, and the dirty F.B.I. agents, including Connolly, whom Whitey and Flemmi had conned for years, were now either retired or stationed somewhere far from Boston.

Weeks arranged for Whitey to phone Francis X. Joyce, who was awarded a prestigious state job by the patronage of Billy Bulger. In other words, Joyce owed the Bulgers a favor. When Joyce's phone rang at a prearranged time, it was John Connolly who answered the phone, not Joyce. Whitey was on the other end and he was red-hot, which made Connolly sweat like he was in a sauna.

Forgetting Connolly had been retired from the feds for almost five years, and also forgetting Whitey had been off the F.B.I.'s rat rolls for the same amount of time, Whitey tore into Connolly about Whitey's supposed "immunity" to run a gambling empire with impunity.

Connolly hemmed and hawed, but mostly he sweat.

Whitey wanted a deal. He told Connolly, if he surrendered to the feds, both Whitey and Flemmi would have to be guaranteed bail, giving them a chance to better arrange a lifetime getaway to parts unknown.

But Connolly, who no longer had any clout in F.B.I. matters, told Whitey bail for him and Flemmi was probably not in the cards.

Connolly's comment got Whitey to thinking. Whitey was safe now, so why should he put himself on the line to get bail for Flemmi, who was quickly becoming a bad memory?

It was at this moment that Whitey decided he would never again return to Boston. What happened to Flemmi was Flemmi's problem. After all, if Flemmi had listened to Whitey's advice, relayed to Flemmi through Kevin Weeks, Flemmi would not presently be behind bars. As for John Connolly, he was, obviously, no longer of any use to Whitey. In fact, he could be a liability down the road.

His mind made up, Whitey bid Connolly good-bye.

They never spoke again.

Now, Whitey's biggest problem was what to do with Teresa Stanley, who was starting to annoy Whitey's with childish cries of, "I wanna go home." Whitey had enough problems of his own without Stanley constantly whining, so he contacted Kevin Weeks and told Weeks he was ready to trade in the old-model girlfriend for the newer-model girlfriend. Weeks contacted Catherine Grieg, and she was happier than a vampire working at a blood bank.

Whitey had chosen her after all.

Whitey drove back to Boston, where he ditched Stanley in the parking lot of Chili's Restaurant. After spending the last 33 years with Stanley, there is no record of Whitey kissing her good-bye. However, Whitey might have said something like, "Goodbye and good luck," before kicking Stanley to the curb.

With the Stanley load off his mind and off his back, Whitey hustled to Malibu Beach in Dorchester, where the radiant Catherine Grieg was waiting with him in Weeks's car, parked in a secluded spot in the parking lot. Sitting in the back seat of Weeks's car were Greig's two constant companions - Nicki and Gigi - two black toy poodles, whom, thanks to Whitey, she would never see again.

According to Weeks, "Jimmy (Whitey) strode calmly out of the darkness. He was wearing a Stetson hat, a black leather jacket and black jeans. At first, Jimmy didn't show any emotion. Then he smiled and said to us, 'How you doing?' Cathy ran out to him and gave him a big hug. The two of them embraced for a long minute, making a dramatic scene right out of *Casablanca*."

The last sounds you heard were Humphrey Bogart and Ingrid Bergman rolling in their graves.

Whitey and Greig then disappeared into the sunset (that's more like a John Wayne movie), minus Greig's two

On the Run

toy poodles, which Weeks brought to Greig's twin sister Margaret. If you recall, Margaret was the sister who Cathy Greig's ex-husband, Bobby McGonagle, had constantly mistaken for Cathy.

It's hard to determine which pair of siblings had the more tortured existence together - the male Bulgers or the female Greigs.

*****

As soon as Whitey and Greig hit the road as Thomas and Helen Baxter, Whitey got to thinking. Where could they go where nobody ever heard of Whitey Bulger, and more important, could care less?

The northeastern United States was definitely out, and Florida was dangerous territory since it was a known hideout for men of Bulger's ilk. The West Coast was a possibility - Whitey liked to be near the waters of the Pacific Ocean – but, at the moment, Whitey was tired of driving and running. He wanted to put down some roots somewhere until he could get his mind around the fact he would never see the Boston Bruins play a home game again, ditto the Red Sox.

Maybe Whitey read a travel brochure, or possibly a travel magazine. But Whitey came to the conclusion Grand Isle in Louisiana, 50 miles south of New Orleans, would be a grand place to settle, at least for a while.

The Chamber of Commerce of Grand Isle advertises Grand Isle's allure as follows:

GRAND ISLE – UNIQUELY LOUISIANA SINCE 1781. Grand Isle is a remote oasis nearly hidden within Louisiana's expansive shoreline, Grand Isle is your passport to adventure in a state known for being a "Sportsman's Paradise." Renowned for its world-class fishing and birding habitat, Louisiana's only inhabited barrier island offers unblemished views of the Gulf of Mexico, miles of beaches, and boundless wildlife. Couple this with southern hospitality and mouthwatering seafood, and you'll discover why visitors have fallen in love with Grand Isle for two and a half centuries.

Whitey wasn't exactly enamored with fishing. Most fish Whitey became acquainted with had been dead, cooked, and on his plate. But after he saw a Grand Isle rental cottage on stilts overlooking the Gulf of Mexico, Whitey became quite interested and he rented the place. The price was only 400 bucks a month, which, because of Whitey's bulging safe deposit boxes, was basically tipping money.

Whitey, being Whitey, he and Grieg kept mostly to themselves. But they did become friendly with a dense local young couple, who thought Tom and Helen Baxter were the cat's meow. Their names were Penny and Glenn Gautreaux. Tom Baxter's expansive demeanor enthralled them, along with the fact Tom spread his money around as thick as the meat on a Subway sandwich.

Although they had four children, Penny and Glenn weren't exactly world-beaters. They were basically living hand-to-mouth and day-by-day. Penny worked as a meter reader for the town, and Glenn took on work whenever it suited him. This backward couple was the perfect foil for a man of Whitey's wiles, and especially his cash.

During his time at Grand Isle, besides lavishing the Gautreaux's with food and drink almost every night, Whitey bought the family a stove, a refrigerator, and a freezer.

In 1998, after the F.B.I. had traced Bulger to the Grand Isles (Whitey and Grieg had already flown the coop), Penny Gautreaux told the *Boston Globe*, "He was a very nice man. He treated us like family. He was kind. He really had a nice personality. How could you not love him?"

When Penny Gautreaux was brought before a grand jury in Boston in November of 1998 to discuss Whitey's fling in Grand Isle, she told the grand jury the gifts from "Uncle Tom and Aunt Helen" were given out of the goodness of their hearts.

"He wanted to give them to us as a gift for cooking for

him," Gautreaux said.

Lanny Schexnailere, owner of Island Appliance Sales, waited on Whitey when he bought the appliances for Penny Gautreaux. The total bill was $1,900, which Whitey paid for with crisp new hundred dollar bills.

Schexnailere had previously met Whitey at a barbecue in the Gautreaux's backyard.

"I was introduced to him as Uncle Tom," Schexnailere said. "Someone told me that Tom was a long-lost uncle, who had left the family when he was a baby and was raised by other people. I figured maybe he made it big and came back to help the family."

Penny Gautreaux told the Boston grand jury that Tom Baxter had called her twice since he skipped Grand Isle in July of 1996. But she swore she hadn't talked to "Uncle Tom" since the F.B.I. tracked him to Louisiana in early 1997. Penny also said she hadn't the slightest idea where Uncle Tom and Aunt Helen could possibly be hiding, now could she?

Penny told the *Boston Globe* Uncle Tom truly loved her, her husband, and her four children, and even the Gautreaux's black Labrador retriever.

"He gave us inspiration and courage," Penny said. "He'd say to my husband Glenn, 'Get off your lazy butt; you've got beautiful kids. You need to make something out of your life.' If my husband was sitting down drinking coffee, he'd say, 'Go to work.' Stuff I couldn't make him do, Tom could."

Despite tremendous evidence to the contrary, Penny refused to believe what the F.B.I. said about the man she now knew was Whitey Bulger, not Tom Baxter.

"I figured they (the F.B.I.) made it bigger than what it is," Penny said. "Really, I hate them more than him."

Penny and Glenn Gautreaux were not the only Grand Isle residents fooled by Whitey.

Grand Isle Police Chief Roscoe Besson Jr. wanted to kick himself in the pants when the F.B.I. visited Grand Isle in January 1997 with a picture of a man Besson knew as Tom Baxter. Besides the picture, the feds showed Besson a wanted poster, which said there was a bounty of $250,000 on Whitey's head.

Besson ruefully remembered the morning when he had stopped cars on Louisiana Highway 1 to allow Whitey unimpeded walking access.

"I stopped the traffic and let $250,000 get across the street," Besson told the *Globe*. "If he had taken off running, I'd have been on him like gravy on rice."

However, Whitey didn't run; he just smiled and waved at Besson in a "thank you" gesture.

"If I see a guy with long stringy hair, nasty looking, I stop them," Besson said. "I want to know who they are. Tom (Whitey) was clean-cut. I'd see him walking. This is a tourist community. He and Helen were just traveling around."

Chief Besson's daughter, Chrisel Page, owned a beauty salon in town frequented by Helen Baxter (Greig). Helen had her hair trimmed every week. She also had her hair colored L'Oreal light ash blond or extra light platinum blond.

"I really enjoyed Helen's company," Page said. "She was a real nice lady and a generous tipper."

Page's husband was a sheriff in the Jefferson Parish sheriff's department. After Greig's first visit to Page's salon, instead of driving Grieg to the salon in the 1995 black Mercury Marquis he had purchased in Selden Long Island under the name Tom Baxter, Whitey let Greig walk to the salon alone.

"Tom spotted my husband's police car out front the first time Helen visited my salon," Page said. "I guess Tom just stayed away after that."

On the Run

Whitey and Greig left Grand Isle in February of 1996, but returned in May. When they visited the Gautreauxs, the Gautreauxs had unexpected (to Whitey) houseguests. They were Thomas "Blackie" Rudolph and his wife, Mary, who were Glen Gautreaux's former in-laws; i.e., the parents of Glenn's ex-wife. Right off the bat, Blackie didn't cotton to Whitey.

"He had this attitude like he was the boss," the 64-year-old Blackie told the *Boston Globe*. "He was rude in front of my wife, and he insulted Mary by saying her cooking wasn't as good as Penny's."

Mary Randolph thought Whitey was a male chauvinist pig.

"He thought women should be seen and not heard," Mary said. "And he bragged that all he had to do was clap his hands and his wife would jump. He told me and my husband, 'I have control of my woman.' But I think he was joking. He was trying to be a macho man."

Blackie was also insulted by Whitey's attitude about hard work.

"I told him I worked every day of my life since I was 15-years-old," Blackie said. "But he said he never had to work because he always had people working for him."

Then there was the issue of who was the tougher man: Blackie or Whitey. Whitey bragged to Blackie that he was in better shape than Blackie; intimating Blackie wasn't in the same class with Whitey when it came to brute strength.

So Blackie made Whitey an offer Whitey could refuse. Blackie challenged Whitey to a pushup contest.

Blackie sprung to the floor and immediately did several one-handed pushups.

"Then I told him I would do more one-handed pushups than he could do with two hands," Blackie said. "But he said he was much older than me and it wasn't a fair test. I slapped my driver's license on the table to show him my age, but he refused to do the same."

The pushup contest never happened.

As much as Blackie and Mary Randolph disliked Whitey, they felt different about Greig (Helen).

"I really enjoyed Helen because she was very quiet," Mary said. "She was always a loner. We walked the beach one time, and she talked about missing New York. Helen was nice."

On Whitey and Greig's second trip to Grand Isle (May 19, 1996 to July 7, 1996), instead of renting the small $400-a month waterfront cottage on stilts, they rented a two-bedroom house on Cott Lane, a dead-end street around the corner from Penny and Glenn Gautreaux. The owners of the house were Henry and Barbara Wellman, who were retired and lived next door. Henry Wellman said Tom Baxter paid the $1,700 rent up front with $100 bills.

Barbara Wellman said Tom and Helen Baxter were "quiet, polite, articulate, and clean as a whistle." Barbara also said she had the impression Tom Baxter was retired, because he told her he "never could travel all his life, and finally he can. And he never wants to go home."

Considering the law was waiting for Whitey in Boston with a set of handcuffs, that remark may have been Whitey's lifetime understatement.

Henry Wellman thought Tom Baxter was a man's man. Tom (Whitey) gave Henry his copies of *Soldier of Fortune Magazine* when he had finished reading them.

"To be quite honest," Henry said. "I wish we had more tenants like them. They didn't bother anyone. If they were criminals, I don't know which side I'm going on."

Henry was delighted one day when Tom blasted a group of drunks who had gathered across the street from their houses; looking for trouble and mostly finding it.

The shapely Helen Baxter had paraded past the men, and they ogled Helen as if she was Marilyn Monroe standing on a sidewalk steam grate with her dress up in the air, like in "The Seven Year Itch."

Tom Baxter didn't like that one bit.

"Hey, what are you looking at?" Tom bellowed from across the street. "Haven't you seen a real woman before?"

"I was proud of him," Henry Wellman said. "To tell the truth, I liked him. He didn't give me no reason not to."

When the Baxters departed Grand Isle on July 7, 1996, they told the Wellmans they were going to San Diego, which is approximately 134 miles and a two-hour car ride from Santa Monica, where Charlie and Carol Gasko were finally arrested on June 22, 2011.

*****

While cruising the country in his car with Catherine Grieg, Whitey began thinking about John Morris's betrayal, which was evident in the 1988 *Boston Globe* articles concerning the Bulger brothers. Whitey knew it was Morris who had leaked to the *Globe* that Whitey and Flemmi were engaged in a "you wash my back and I'll wash yours" routine with the feds. This meant Whitey was a rat, and the Boston underworld exterminates rats. So, in Whitey's mind, Morris was trying to get Whitey whacked. Morris's betrayal stuck in Whitey craw for many years, and while he was in the wind, Whitey decided to do something about it.

Whitey let his fingers do the walking in the *Yellow Pages*, and then he used several pay phones to find the exact location where Morris was presently serving the feds. It took a while, but Whitey discovered Morris was stationed at the F.B.I. Academy in Quantico, Virginia. Whitey dropped a few dimes, and he got the main switchboard at Quantico. The operator told Whitey Morris was a very busy man, and for Whitey to state his business.

"Tell Morris Mr. White called, and I'll call him back," Whitey told the operator.

Whitey figured, after Morris heard the name "Mr.

White," Morris would automatically assume Whitey himself was the caller. And Whitey was right.

A few days later, "Mr. White" phoned the main switchboard at Quantico, and he was immediately put through to John Morris.

After assuring Morris that Whitey was indeed Mr. White, Whitey got down to business.

"You miserable fuck, you tried to get me killed!" Whitey said. "You started this fucking thing, and you better use your brains to figure a way to straighten this out for me. Because if I go down, you're going down with me."

It's not certain if Morris was more afraid of going to jail, or of Whitey whacking him. But Morris knew one thing for sure. If Whitey could find Morris at Quantico, he could find Morris anywhere and then put two bullets in Morris's head, assuming Whitey didn't torture him first.

A few minutes after he hung up the phone, Morris clutched his chest. He had been stricken with a massive heart attack. After he was rushed to the hospital, Morris flat lined twice on the operating table.

When Morris was well enough to walk and chew bubble gum at the same time, he did a two-step to the feds. He offered to spill all he knew about Whitey and Flemmi, as long as he received complete immunity from prosecution.

And so it was done. John Morris retired and became a rat like Whitey and Flemmi, causing Whitey to become America's most famous fugitive since Dr. Richard Kimble.

*****

While Whitey slithered from place to place with Catherine Greig, he became unhinged about his former paramour Teresa Stanley's new boyfriend: a known piece-of-crap-junkie and F.B.I. informant named Alan Thistle.

This was right after Whitey discovered the feds had confiscated the $1.9 million in lottery money Whitey "won" in 1991, as well as $199,000 Whitey had hidden in a Boston bank's safe deposit box. To make his aggravation a trifecta, the feds also discovered a safe deposit box Whitey owned in Clearwater, Florida and had that money impounded too.

What Whitey really couldn't stand was Stanley living with a rat. To matter worse, Thistle was ensconced in the house Whitey had bought for Stanley on Silver Street in South Boston. Thistle even had the audacity to work out in Whitey's private home gym.

Whitey sent Kevin Weeks to pay Stanley a little visit.

Weeks banged on Stanley's front door and found her home alone.

"Right off the bat I told her 'What are you going out with Alan Thistle?'" Weeks asked.

Stanley would not be cowered by the hulking Weeks.

"He's (Whitey's) with Cathy," she said. "I have my life to live."

"He's (Thistle's) an informant for law enforcement," Weeks said. "He's just pumping you for information. Everything you tell this guy, he's going back and tell the government."

"Well, it's too late," Stanley said.

"What do you mean it's too late?" Weeks said.

Stanley then handed Weeks the business card of F.B.I. agent John Gamel.

"I already spoke to him," Stanley said. "He came by the house, and I told him everything. I told him that when Jimmy and I were in New York, we used the name Mr. and Mrs. Thomas Baxter. I even told him about the Grand Marquis he bought in Selden, Long Island."

His head spinning, Weeks exited Stanley's house.

It was the last time he ever saw her. Teresa Stanley died of lung cancer in August of 2012. She was 71-years-old.

Weeks could do nothing but wait for Whitey to contact him, and on the Fourth of July weekend Whitey did just that. Weeks told Whitey the bad news about Teresa Stanley talking to the feds.

"Thank God you told me," Whitey told Weeks.

Whitey also told Weeks he needed new phony identities for himself and Greig. Weeks, using Whitey's brother Jackie's photo, had a document counterfeiter create Whitey a bogus driver's license, social security card, and birth certificate.

Weeks met with Whitey and Greig at the Water Tower in Chicago. And in the blink of an eye, Tom and Helen Baxter became Mark and Carol Stapleton. Weeks then went back to Boston. But in July of 1996, Whitey and Greig, flaunting their new identities, took the train to Penn Station in New York City.

Whitey knew, as most gangsters do, New York City is a great place to go on the lam. First, there are over eight million people milling about, and the vast majority knows how to mind their own business. Second, in New York City, Whitey was virtually unknown to the average person on the street. Whitey may have been a big shot in Boston, but in the Big Apple, he was nothing more than a nondescript tourist taking in the sights.

Mark and Carol Stapleton spent several months in New York City, staying in numerous hotels and feasting in all the fancy restaurants. (It's likely Whitey had a safe deposit box in New York City too.) They may have seen the Statue of Liberty and taken a trip around Manhattan on the Circle Line. They could have gotten lost in the crowds in Yankee Stadium, especially when the Red Sox came to town.

But they mainly stayed in New York City because Whitey needed Weeks to get him additional phony identifications; the more the better. Then, as soon as he felt the heat, Whitey could then transform himself and Greig into a different married couple. Since Boston was out as a potential meeting place for Whitey and Weeks, New York City, a short train ride from Boston, was the next best choice.

In November 1996, when the cold weather in New York City was almost as bad as in Boston, Weeks met Whitey and Greig at the New York Public Library at 42nd Street and 5th Avenue. They went to a ritzy hotel restaurant where Weeks gave Whitey enough phony identification to last Whitey a lifetime.

After dinner, the three tourists walked over to Penn Station, where they waited for Week's train to depart for Boston.

As Weeks boarded the train, Whitey told him, "I'll be in touch."

But Weeks never heard from Whitey again.

Before Weeks knew Whitey was a rat, he said in his book *Brutal*, "I think about him a lot. I figure he's out of the country now. I hope they never catch him."

That's a long way from calling Whitey "The Biggest Rat," as Weeks did in court at Whitey's 2013 trial.

Five years in prison, which is what Weeks served after becoming an informant, tends to change your perspective about someone, especially someone as despicable as Whitey Bulger.

Chapter 17
The First Rat Makes a Deal

In March of 1997, while Whitey was still on the run, Steve Flemmi and Frank Salemme were set to go to trial along with mob associate Bobby DeLuca and hitman John Martorano. Whitey was to be tried in absentia. The charges were racketeering, which fell under the umbrella of the much-feared RICO act.

Frank Salemme hired attorney Anthony Cardinale to represent him and DeLuca, (Cardinale, who was born in New York City's Hell's Kitchen, had previously been John Gotti's attorney.) As part of the discovery process, Cardinale had Salemme and DeLuca listen to the secretly recorded F.B.I. tapes, which were being presented as evidence against both men.

Suddenly, Salemme and DeLuca heard F.B.I. voices on the recording referring to informants, including a man called "The Saint," Anthony St. Laurent. Salemme and DeLuca told Cardinale of their discovery and it got Cardinale to thinking.

Cardinale had heard the rumors throughout the years that both Whitey and Flemmi were F.B.I. rats. If that were true, it might be the key to getting his clients acquitted. Figuring "what the heck," Cardinale made a bold move that sent electroshocks throughout the courtroom.

On March 27, 1997, Cardinale prepared a motion, which he handed Judge Mark Wolf. The motion read, "Defense counsel seeks the disclosure of the identity of various individuals who may have served as government

The First Rat Makes a Deal

informants/operatives in conjunction with the investigation and/or the prosecution of this case."

In this motion, Cardinale named Whitey as a possible F.B.I. informant, but he didn't mention Flemmi, who was also a defendant in this trial and ostensibly still a fine buddy of Frank Salemme.

As was reported in *Black Mass*, Cardinale explained why he did not name Flemmi as a suspected F.B.I. Informant.

"I was just a little uncomfortable," Cardinale said. "Keep in mind, one of the last things you want to do in a situation like this - I mean this guy (Flemmi) is a defendant in this case – and if you believe he was a rat essentially his whole life, one of the last things you want to do is pull the trigger on the guy when you're not ready, and the guy rolls, and he hurts your client. I thought if the finger was pointed at Flemmi too early and he rolled, he could not only try to hurt Salemme, but a number of many other people. It could be a disaster.

"Besides, the word on the streets was about Bulger. Nobody had said anything about Flemmi. Even among the Italians. They always said 'Bulger is capable of anything.' But Flemmi, they considered like almost one of them."

Judge Wolf ordered the F.B.I. to come clean as to Whitey having been an F.B.I. informant. The F.B.I. hemmed and hawed, and they tried to do everything possible not to admit Whitey was a cheese-eating jumbo rat.

Finally, the Justice Department's Paul Coffey said to Judge Wolf, "I hereby confirm that James J. Bulger was an informant for the Boston Division of the Federal Bureau of Investigation. Because Bulger, as a fugitive, was now trying to escape responsibility for his many alleged crimes, Bulger had forfeited any reasonable expectation that his previous informant status will remain confidential."

Coffey did not name Flemmi as an F.B.I. informant, and was, in fact, trying to convince Flemmi, as well as

Flemmi's lawyer, Kenneth Fishman, that it was in Flemmi's best interest to turn state's evidence against Salemme, DeLuca, and Martorano. Since Flemmi had already been a rat for more than 30 years, Coffey tried to persuade Flemmi and Fishman that a little more singing would do Flemmi more good than harm.

On January 6, 1998, it was a blustery day outside the Boston Federal courtroom, and it was about to get more chilly inside the courtroom, especially for the defendants. For the past few months, unbeknownst to the other defendants, Flemmi had been singing like Sinatra to the government about all the crimes he had committed with Whitey. Flemmi claimed he was allowed to act in such a manner because the F.B.I. had promised Flemmi and Whitey immunity for all crimes, except murder.

In court before Judge Wolf, as the other defendants' fumed, Flemmi's attorney, Kenneth Fishman, claimed Flemmi's relationship with the government as an informant should be enough to have the charges dropped against him.

Fishman told Judge Wolf, "The focus here is on the promises made to my client, Steven Flemmi, by the F.B.I. In exchange for his very unique and special cooperation, he would be protected, he would not be prosecuted."

Prosecutor Fred Wyshak was so incensed at this that he almost swallowed his tongue.

Wyshak cleared his throat, and then he told the judge, "This is preposterous! Bulger and Flemmi never had any official deal saying they would not be prosecuted for their crimes! What were Flemmi and Bulger – Junior G-Men with a license to kill?"

For the next year, witness after witness paraded into court, including numerous F.B.I. agents who were in on the deal Whitey and Flemmi had with the Boston F.B.I. When it became clear Flemmi was an informer, Frank Salemme had to be physically separated from Flemmi in the courtroom, otherwise Salemme might have had a murder

The First Rat Makes a Deal

charge on his docket.

One of the key witnesses, former prosecutor Jeremiah T. O'Sullivan, used an old Mafia trick to avoid testifying. When it was his turn to speak in court about the unholy alliance between Whitey, Flemmi, and the law, O'Sullivan, then 54-years-old, had the good sense to have a heart attack. And then he had a relapse. Consequently, O'Sullivan never did take the stand to testify.

However, Teresa Stanley, under the promise of immunity, did testify. It was obvious Stanley, then 57-years-old with hair as white as Santa's beard, still held a grudge against Whitey for two-timing her with Catherine Greig.

Stanley related the facts concerning her two decades with Whitey; emphasizing the way Whitey shoved Stanley out of the way to romance Greig.

Stanley fumed in court, "He (Whitey) was leading a double life with me and a double life with the F.B.I."

The chief witness for the prosecution was none other than John Morris, who was now a broken-down-valise of a man. Like Stanley, in exchange for his testimony, Morris was given full immunity from prosecution.

Morris told the court he and John Connolly had been working closely with Whitey and Flemmi for many years. Morris mentioned the bribes he took from Whitey, including $7,000 in cash and several cases of wine. Morris dropped a bombshell when he said he was afraid of Whitey, not only because of Whitey's reputation for violence, but also because Whitey's brother Billy was a political hotshot and could cause Morris much harm. (There is no evidence, however, that Billy Bulger ever did anything untoward concerning Morris.)

When Flemmi's attorney tried to get Morris to concede he had given Flemmi and Whitey immunity from prosecution, the weary Morris said, "Immunity is a very formal process, and there's actual documentation. There was none for Flemmi and Bulger."

Near the end of his eight days of testimony, the prosecution asked Morris if John Connolly was in on the deal to allow Whitey and Flemmi to commit crimes as long as they sang the right Mafia tune to the government.

Morris said, "I felt he (Connolly) participated in it. But I'm responsible for my own actions."

While John Morris was spilling his guts in court, John Connolly was launching a campaign to discredit Morris and his testimony.

Every day after Morris had spilled his guts in court, Connolly, still working for Boston Edison, held an impromptu press conference on the courthouse steps.

After calling Morris's testimony "utter nonsense," Connolly told the assembled media Morris, "was the most corrupt F.B.I. agent in history."

Connolly admitted Whitey and Flemmi were F.B.I. informants, whom he worked closely with for many years. But Connolly said he had always done things by the book concerning Whitey and Flemmi. If any rules had been broken, it was Morris who had broken them for his own personal gain.

Connolly told the press he likened the way he handled informants to a circus, where he was the ringmaster taming the animals, Whitey and Flemmi.

Connolly said, "I was no John Morris in the office with a No. 2 lead pencil. My job was to get in there with the lions and tigers."

Then Connolly added, "And I am no liar like Morris."

Connolly repeated his rants on local television, talk-radio programs, and in several local magazine articles.

To cover all bases, Connolly not only pleaded his case to the press, but he got his mates still working in the Boston F.B.I. office to give him secret documents which would discredit the testimony of several F.B.I. agents who had testified for the prosecution. Connolly handed these

The First Rat Makes a Deal

documents to Flemmi's lawyer, Kenneth Fishman.

As if that wasn't enough, Connolly started writing anonymous letters to the court, claiming Frank Dewan, an intrepid Boston police sergeant, who had stalked Whitey and Flemmi for decades, had, in fact, planted evidence to implicate the dirty duo in crimes they had not committed.

All of Connolly's bluster evaporated after he conducted a particular interview with the Boston press. Finally putting his foot in his mouth, Connolly said, "I do not need immunity from corrupt acts. I did not commit corrupt acts. I would refuse immunity for those reasons. I don't need it."

As soon as Connolly misspoke, the prosecutors ran to Judge Wolf and asked him to get Connolly on the stand to testify without immunity.

On October 13, 1998, Connolly appeared in court with his lawyer, Robert Popeo, in the wings for backup. Connolly outwardly exuded confidence and disdain for the court proceedings. But to seasoned court observers, Connolly looked like he had just swallowed a dozen bad oysters.

First up to bat was Anthony Cardinale, the lawyer for Salemme and DeLuca.

Cardinale said, "Mr. Connolly, in 1982, did you give any cash to an F.B.I. secretary Debbie Noseworthy, now Debbie Morris."

Cardinale's tactic was to get Connolly to lie in court, thereby exposing Connolly to a charge of perjury. But Connolly wouldn't bite.

As the entire courtroom bent forward anticipating the answer, Connolly calmly reached into the breast pocket of his suit jacket, and he extracted an index card, from which he read: "Upon the advice of my counsel, I respectfully decline to answer at this time and rely upon my rights under the United States Constitution not to give testimony against myself."

The former F.B.I. poster boy, with a head of hair like Elvis, had taken the Fifth Amendment not to incriminate himself. How amusing.

Cardinale kept peppering Connolly with questions; which included delivering bribes of wine and cash to John Morris, and whether, throughout the years, Connolly had informed Whitey and Flemmi when trouble was brewing for them with the law.

Each and every time Cardinale queried; Connolly eyed the index card, and he spoke the words transcribed on it like he was browsing the *Boston Globe*.

In twenty minutes, Connolly took the Fifth 46 times.

Finally, Judge Wolf had heard enough. He summoned Connolly's mouthpiece, Popeo, to the bench, and he asked him if Connolly was prepared to answer every question with the same tedious recital.

Popeo told the judge, "To each and every question put to the witness, he had been advised to invoke his privilege under the Fifth Amendment."

Judge Wolf shook his head, and then he told Connolly, "Mr. Connolly, you may go."

Connolly slunk out of the witness chair.

As John Connolly slithered out of the courtroom, his fine pompadour, now filled with torrents of sweat, slowly crumpled on his head; making his hairdo appear like a wet rat ready to scatter down the nearest sewer.

One of the angriest men in court was John Martorano, who, for several decades, had committed murders for Whitey and Flemmi. For weeks, Martorano sat stone-faced in court while he heard testimony saying Whitey and Flemmi were not prosecuted in the 1979 horse race-fixing scandal because they were protected by the F.B.I., while Martorano, indicted in the same case, was forced to lam it to Florida for the better part of two decades. The final straw broke the camel's back when Martorano learned he had

The First Rat Makes a Deal

been arrested in Florida because Whitey and Flemmi had told the F.B.I. the location of his Florida hideout.

On July 20, 1998, as Salemme, DeLuca, and Flemmi sat in their usual courtroom seats, they noticed Martorano had not joined them. All three men knew what that meant. John Martorano was fed up with Whitey and Flemmi's double-dealing and betrayals. Martorano had cut a deal to save himself, which put Flemmi in a very bad place. Martorano could link Flemmi to several slayings. And murder, no matter how much Flemmi tried to justify his F.B.I.-sanctioned actions, would never be condoned by the feds.

But that was for another trial at another time.

The deal for Martorano was that he pled guilty to more than 20 murders for a sentence of 12½ to15 years. He was released from prison in 2007 with a $20,000 stipend from the government to start a new life.

When Steve Flemmi took the stand, he parroted what his lawyer, Fishman, had been peddling to the court for the entire trial. Flemmi said it was impossible to be guilty of racketeering under the RICO act because the F.B.I. had given him immunity for all his crimes.

As Fishman led him through a series of softball questions, Flemmi held his hand over his heart and he proudly proclaimed, "I believe I was performing a service for the United States government in my role as an informant."

All through Flemmi's testimony, his former paisan, Frank Salemme, sat there steaming. Salemme was a made-man in the LCN, and Flemmi, because he had turned down his button, was not. It rankled Salemme that his inferior in the Italian mob had been living a sweet life over the last three decades, all because Flemmi was gulping cheese like franks in a Nathan's Hot Dog Eating Contest.

During a recess, while Flemmi, Salemme and Deluca were sitting in the same holding cell, Salemme blew a gasket.

Salemme, a strapping six-footer, grabbed the five-foot-six-inch Flemmi by the collar, and he lifted him six inches off the ground.

Salemme spat out, "You piece of shit! You've fucked me all my life! Now you're screwing everyone around you! You scum! Now you're gonna die!"

That said, Salemme started choking Flemmi until his face turned a dark purple. The amused guards outside the holding cell just watched, knowing Flemmi was a rat, and he was getting what rats deserved. Incidents like this happen all the time in prison, and guards can be a willing audience if someone with a penchant for squealing is getting beaten like a raw egg.

However, before Salemme gagged Flemmi into the hereafter, DeLuca, to the chagrin of the guard spectators, jumped in between the two men and extricated Salemme's hands from around Flemmi's throat. From that point on, Salemme and Flemmi were separated in court and never spoke to each other again.

It took Judge Wolf several months to write his decision on this case; and when he did, it was a dilly.

In September 1999, Wolf delivered a 661-page dissertation. He maintained Steve Flemmi was full of bull when he claimed he had committed crimes with the tacit approval of the Boston F.B.I. Even if Flemmi's claim was partially true, no law enforcement agency had authority to look the other way when its informants were committing crimes. It just wasn't Kosher, no matter which way you spread the mustard.

Judge Wolf wrote, "In Boston, Flemmi and Bulger uniquely shared an apathy for La Cosa Nostra, a desire to profit criminally from its destruction, and, most notably, the promised protection of the F.B.I. I also do not view this case as a problem of what the government has at times referred to as a few 'bad apples.'"

In other words, besides John Connolly and John

The First Rat Makes a Deal

Morris, there were several other federal agents and federal prosecutors who, in the words of Ricky Ricardo, "Had some 'splain' to do."

Judge Wolf named Paul Rico, John Connolly, and John Morris as the most culpable, but he also cited eighteen other federal agents as fellow wrongdoers. These men included supervisor, Jim Ring, and F.B.I. agent, Nick Gianturco; men who had thrown out the F.B.I. playbook and created their own. The feds' actions benefited Whitey and Flemmi, and satisfied the Boston F.B.I.'s undying quest to smash the Boston LCN. They wrongfully let the end justify the means.

Judge Wolf didn't let Billy Bulger off the hook either.

Judge Wolf wrote, "William Bulger, who was the President of the Massachusetts State Senate and lived next door to the Flemmis (Steve Flemmi's parents), came to visit (the Flemmis) while F.B.I. agents Jim Ring and John Connolly were there."

Judge Wolf's decision started a domino effect that precipitated the total collapse of Boston's organized crime structure.

Frank Salemme saw the writing on the wall, and he figured a plea deal would be the right move. Salemme's lawyers huddled with the federal prosecutors, and they came up with 11 years in the can as their magic number.

On February 21, 2000, Salemme stood before Judge Wolf.

The 66-year-old Salemme told the judge, "I learned my lesson. Shame on me if I didn't know after what happened to me in the last 35 years with my best friend (Flemmi), and shame on me if it happens again. I know what the government has in place. I know what they're capable of. I want no part of anything ever again."

Before turning Salemme over to the federal prison system, Judge Wolf told Salemme, "I know the government will be watching you closely, and you'll never know if you can trust anyone who might engage in criminal activity with you. It would not be just wrong for you to engage in criminal conduct when you get out; it would be very dumb."

Outside the courtroom, Salemme's wife, Donna, said her husband was presently writing a book about his life in the Boston mob; especially his interactions with Flemmi and Whitey, as well as several other F.B.I. miscreants.

"There are many people that are evil out there," Donna Salemme told the *Boston Globe*. "I just want the truth out."

However, Frank Salemme forgot to confess to one little crime. It involved his son, Frank Salemme Jr.

In 1993, Salemme Jr. had a problem with his partner, Steve DiSarro, in The Channel nightclub in South Boston. One thing led to another and soon Salemme's Jr.'s hands were around DiSarro's throat, resulting in DiSarro's untimely demise.

According to federal prosecutors, there were two witnesses to DiSarro's murder: Frank Salemme Sr. and his old mate, Steve Flemmi. However, in 1995 when Salemme Sr. was questioned under oath about DiSarro's murder, he said he hadn't the foggiest notion about what happened to DiSarro, whose body was never found.

In 1995, Salemme Jr. died of AID's-related cancer. However, in 2008 when Flemmi spilled the beans about every crime he was aware of, Salemme Sr. was indicted for perjury in relation to his testimony about DiSarro's murder. Figuring a plea was his best move again, Salemme Sr. pled guilty to perjury and obstruction of justice.

However, due to clever maneuvering by Salemme's lawyer, Anthony Cardinale, Salemme was sentenced to only five years in prison, but was credited with the four years he had already served in the can.

Consequently, in 2009, Frank "Cadillac" Salemme became a free man, and he disappeared into the Witness Protection Program.

The First Rat Makes a Deal

*****

Although Steve Flemmi admitted in court that he and Whitey were informants for the F.B.I., Kevin Weeks continued to operate as his "main man on the outside." Weeks reasoned he had committed so many crimes, including murders, with Whitey and Flemmi that he had no choice but to stay a team player. This was not a particularly intelligent decision on Weeks's part, but then again, Kevin Weeks was a street thug, not a nuclear physicist.

Still, you have to give Weeks credit for one thing. Until his back was against the wall and he faced a life sentence in prison, Weeks never squealed (the same with John Martorano). Weeks laid back and played the cards as they were dealt to him. But he wasn't holding a very good hand.

On November 17, 1999, Weeks's house of cards crumbled. D.E.A. and the state police arrested Weeks and brought him to D.E.A. headquarters in Boston. There they hit Weeks with a 29-count indictment, which included charges for racketeering (the dreaded Rico Act), money laundering, extortion, conspiracy to distribute drugs, and two counts of using a firearm in the commission of a crime. One charge not included in the list of indictments was murder, and Weeks knew he had been involved in five murders with Whitey and Flemmi. So maybe Weeks thought this was his lucky day.

However, Weeks's luck didn't last for long. He consulted with two attorneys, and they both told Weeks the same thing. The government is pissed at Whitey and Flemmi, and they're going to throw the book at you. And the kicker was: even to get a minimum of 15 years in the slammer, Weeks would have to cough up at least six hundred thousand dollars for attorney's fees. That was a lot of cabbage for a rabbit, who was definitely going to the clink for a good portion, if not the rest of his life.

So, Weeks started thinking. He had crossed paths with a wiseguy in court who advised him "you can't rat on a rat."

The mobster also told Weeks he'd be a fool to take the heat for two slime-buckets, who had been singing like sparrows for the better part of two decades.

Then Weeks thought about John Martorano, at least as tough a man as either Whitey or Flemmi. After finding out in court that Whitey and Flemmi were Team America men, Martorano carefully weighed his options and figured "you can't rat on a rat." So, Martorano turned state's evidence in order to get a better deal for himself.

Weeks mulled over his options, but he wouldn't make a final decision until he knew for sure what would be in store for him once he started blabbing about the murders he had been involved with.

In January 2000, Weeks met with his court appointed attorney, Dennis Kelly. Kelly advised Weeks to sign an agreement with the government mutually beneficial to both parties. Kelly told Weeks the government was extremely interested in uncovering dead bodies, so a corpus delicti could be used in murder indictments against Weeks's former bosses.

Weeks told Kelly, "If I give them these bodies and they use them against me, I have nothing to sign now."

Kelly told Weeks not to worry.

"They have dealt with people who have lied and double-crossed them," Kelly said. "They want to make sure you can deliver what you are telling them before they make a deal with you."

Weeks figured the dead bodies were his ticket to a better life. So, on January 13, 2000, Kevin Weeks led authorities to the mass tomb of Debbie Hussey, John McIntyre, and Bucky Barrett, all of whom Weeks helped to exhume from the death basement at 799 East Third Street. The project to move the three bodies was necessary because Pat Nee's brother was selling the house, and he didn't want the new owners to find three unwanted presents hidden in the basement.

The First Rat Makes a Deal

Weeks directed authorities to the location of the second burial in a marsh near the Southeast Expressway in South Boston. After a few hours of digging with backhoes, the feds uncovered the remains of Barrett, McIntyre, and Hussey. These admissions put Kevin Weeks in a better place as far as the United States government was concerned.

In short order, Weeks also told the feds where to find the bodies of Tommy King, Paulie McGonagle, and Flemmi's other dead girlfriend, Debra Davis. Weeks wasn't present when these people were buried, but Whitey, prone to bragging about his accomplishments, told Week on several occasions where his victims had been planted.

Although some in the Boston underworld had dubbed him "Kevin Squeaks," Weeks's cooperation with the government reduced his prison term to only five years.

After his release in 2005, Weeks collaborated on his bio, "Brutal," with Phyllis Karas, now an adjunct professor at the Boston University School of Journalism. At a book signing at Barnes and Noble in Boston, Weeks told his audience he had originally intended to get back into a life of crime after he got out of the can.

"But now I can't. Everybody knows my face," Weeks said.

We can only assume Kevin Weeks was kidding.

*****

The man, who took the brunt of Judge Wolf's wrath in his 661-page exposition, was former F.B.I. agent John Connolly.

Judge Wolf put the kibosh on John Connolly, when he wrote, "John Morris solicited and received, through John Connolly, $1,000 (bribe money) from Bulger and Flemmi."

Wolf also wrote there was also sufficient evidence Connolly had received tens of thousands of dollars, maybe even hundreds of thousands of dollars in bribes, from Whitey and Flemmi, which explained Connolly's extravagant lifestyle, which could not be justified by his F.B.I. pay alone.

Wolf said there was proof Connolly had warned Whitey and Flemmi about Brian Halloran's cooperation with the government, which led to Halloran's murder and the murder of Michael Donahue, who was just giving Halloran a ride.

And then there was the case of John Callahan.

When it was clear John Callahan was knee-deep in the murder of Roger Wheeler, Connolly advised Whitey and Flemmi that Callahan loved the good life too much, and would not stand up if arrested. Because of Connolly's advice and intervention, John Callahan was murdered too.

Wolf also ruled Connolly had purged F.B.I. files of any indication of wrongdoings by Whitey and Flemmi, in addition to notifying the two gangsters when indictments were coming down.

John Morris had committed some of these crimes with Connolly. But since Morris had cut a deal for himself giving him complete immunity, Connolly was the only F.B.I. agent left standing who could be prosecuted for his and Morris's crimes.

On December 21, 1999, Connolly heard a knock on the door of his lavish home in the Boston suburb of Lynnfield. When he answered the door, Connolly, home alone with the flu, came face-to-face with a horde of F.B.I. agents, and they weren't there to throw him a surprise party. The feds read Connolly his rights, cuffed him, and hauled him off to the courthouse.

Gone were Connolly's fancy suits and his brilliantly coiffed hair. In court, Connolly donned a sloppy sweat suit; a getup Italian mobsters had made popular in the 1980's. Connolly's stringy hair ran down across his forehead and mingled with beads of sweat, presumably from the flu. Connolly was charged with racketeering and obstruction of justice. Connolly pled not guilty to all charges and was

The First Rat Makes a Deal

released on $200,000 bail.

United States Attorney Donald K. Stern said the indictment included Connolly's failure to investigate Steve Rakes's claim that Whitey and Flemmi had forced Rakes to sell them his liquor store. The charges also accused Connolly of "taking a series of gifts and cash from Mr. Bulger and Mr. Flemmi for his superior, John Morris, between 1981 and 1987. Mr. Morris has already admitted in court that he had accepted these gifts."

The obstruction of justice charge included Connolly tipping off Whitey and Flemmi about an F.B.I. wiretap in 1988, and warning both gangsters about the 1995 indictments that were about to put them in the clink.

Also, included in the indictment was Steve Flemmi's claim Connolly had told him, "You can do what you want; just don't clip anybody."

Outside the courtroom, Prosecutor Stern told the press, "These charges are serious and reflect a corrupt and long-term relationship between persons in the business of extortion, bribery, and loan sharking, and an F.B.I. agent who protected them from prosecution."

However, Connolly's attorney, Robert Popeo had a different take. Popeo said Connolly was being prosecuted for doing what he was told to do by his superiors.

"I characterize this indictment as outrageous," Popeo said. "Mr. Connolly did his job, and he did it well. The Justice Department has been embarrassed by the Bulger case. That's fine, but don't change the rules of the road retroactively."

On May 28, 2002, John Connolly was convicted by a federal jury of racketeering and obstruction of justice connected to his unholy alliance with Whitey (still at large) and Flemmi (stewing in prison awaiting his own trial). The jury found Connolly guilty of slipping Whitey and Flemmi the news that a secret grand jury indictment was ready to put the cuffs on them, which enabled Whitey to flee. The jury also found Connolly guilty of receiving a case of wine and $1,000 from Whitey and Flemmi, and giving it to his then-boss John Morris.

However, the jury could not conclude Connolly himself had ever taken any bribes from Whitey and Flemmi.

The obstruction of justice conviction was related to Connolly sending an anonymous letter, on Boston police stationery, to Judge Wolf, accusing Boston detective, Frank Dewan, of inventing evidence to implicate Flemmi in a series of crimes.

Inexplicably, Connolly was acquitted of the most serious charges; including disclosing information to Whitey and Flemmi, which led to the murders of Brian Halloran, Michael Donahue, and John Callahan.

Because of the verdict, Connolly was facing a maximum of ten years in the can.

Outside the courtroom after the verdict was announced, United States Attorney Michael Sullivan told the press Connolly's conduct "was appalling, and unfortunately the evidence showed that Connolly was not alone in being corrupted."

Sullivan was referring to the fact John Morris, Connolly's former supervisor, testified at Connolly's trial that he had been bribed to the tune of $7,000, in exchange for providing Whitey and Flemmi confidential F.B.I. information throughout the 1980's.

Sullivan added, "John Connolly became a Winter Hill gang operative masquerading as an F.B.I. agent."

When the media surrounded Connolly outside the courtroom, the usually verbose Connolly stormed past them, and mumbled an uncustomary "No comment."

But his lawyer, Tracy Milner, faced the music, and put a happy-face on the proceedings.

"We are obviously pleased that the most serious charges were not proven," Milner told the press. "It feels as

The First Rat Makes a Deal

if the jury was inconsistent in its verdicts."

Due to various delays, the sentencing finally took place on September 16th. In the interim, hundreds of people wrote letters requesting leniency in Connolly's sentencing. The usual liberal Hollywood buffoons, including Billy Friedkin (who directed *The Brink's Job*, a flick about a real-life Boston Bank robbery) penned missives of mercy to Judge Joseph Tauro. And not surprisingly, several present and former F.B.I. agents of some note, including Joe Pistone aka Donnie Brasco, also chipped in with dispatches suggesting tolerance for their former comrade-in-arms.

One especially alarming letter was written by federal judge Edward Harrington, who held court in the same building as Judge Tauro, and who had who once worked with Connolly as a United States attorney in Boston.

Judge Harrington wrote, "I always held Mr. Connolly in the highest regard and considered him to be a man of the highest character and ability."

Somehow, the Boston press got wind of this letter, and they put Judge Harrington's feet to the fire, accusing him of "violating the canon of federal judicial ethics by trying to influence another judge."

Judge Harrington quickly had second thoughts and decided to withdraw his letter. Judge Harrington also apologized profusely to Judge Tauro.

However, Judge Tauro was not swayed by all the pro-Connolly affirmations.

After Connolly refused to speak on his own behalf, and after Judge Tauro refused a request of bail for Connolly while he was awaiting an appeal on his trial, Judge Tauro hit Connolly with a ten-year sentence, the maximum allowed under federal guidelines.

Judge Tauro said, "It is important to send a message of deterrence."

Judge Tauro was particularly appalled by Connolly's

efforts to "subvert the trial of one of his mob informants (Flemmi)."

"Mr. Connolly's actions attacked the very heart of what we attempt to do every day in this building: administer justice fairly," Judge Tauro said.

Tears in his eyes and emptiness in his soul, Connolly, then 62-years-old, blew a half-hearted kiss to his wife, 19 years his junior, as he was hauled from the courtroom by federal marshals.

After Connolly's sentencing, United States attorney Michael Sullivan said, "The conduct of John Connolly was appalling; an affront to every decent law enforcement officer. The cost of Connolly's criminal misconduct has been grave."

Sullivan then added, "There was some skepticism that we would ever bring to justice one of our own. But this day had to come."

Boston police officer Frank Dewan, who was wrongly accused by Connolly, also spoke in his own defense.

"In those days, it was literally a situation where law enforcement was out of control," Dewan said. "John Connolly could do anything he wanted in the city of Boston."

*****

In 1999, after Judge Wolf's 661-word ruling was made public, Steve Flemmi decided to make a deal. Flemmi pled guilty to extortion and money laundering, and was sentenced to ten years in prison. But in 2003, with Kevin Weeks and John Martorano now in the government's camp, the 69-year-old Flemmi was indicted on a slew of murder charges. If Flemmi was convicted, the government made it clear they would try to convince the jury Flemmi deserved the death penalty. And with the ammunition the government had in its arsenal, the odds were heavily in favor of Flemmi sitting in that chair connected to the electrodes.

The First Rat Makes a Deal

Flemmi liked to gamble, but not with his life.

Consequently, Flemmi decided it was time for him to play his second government edition of "Let's Make a Deal." This time the only alternatives the feds gave Flemmi was life in prison or death in the electric chair.

Flemmi chose life.

As a result, Flemmi pled guilty to ten murders; including the murders of Roger Wheeler in Oklahoma and John Callahan in Florida. By this time, former F.B.I. agent Paul Rico had also been indicted in Wheeler's murder.

In 2003, Rico appeared at the U. S. House Judiciary Committee hearings into the 1965 murder of mobster Eddie Deegan, who was killed by the Winter Hill Mob. Rico knew in advance of the plans to kill Deegan. Since he was on the Winter Hill Mob's pad, Rico did nothing to stop Deegan's murder. Then, to add insult to injury, Rico testified in court at the 1966 trial of four innocent men who were convicted of Deegan's slaying. All four men were sentenced to 25-years-to-life. One of these men, Louis Greco, died in prison in 2001.

When one of the U. S. House Judiciary Committee members asked Rico how he felt about the innocent men's fate, Rico blurted out, "What do you want, tears?'

On January 13, 2004, Rico dropped dead from cancer before his trial for the murder of Wheeler commenced.

Some guys have all the luck.

As part of his plea deal for life imprisonment, Flemmi admitted he and Whitey had paid John Connolly more than $200,000 in bribe money. In addition, Flemmi said he and Whitey had bribed other F.B.I. agents, Boston police officers, and members of the Massachusetts State Police.

Flemmi's cooperation with the law led to John Connolly's indictment in Florida for the murder of John Callahan.

On May 4, 2005, John Connolly, now a scruffy 64-year-old shell of his former self, was charged in Miami with the first-degree murder of Callahan. Also charged were Steve Flemmi and John Martorano. However, both Flemmi and Martorano had already pled guilty to Callahan's murder and would testify at Connolly's trial.

After Connolly's arraignment, his lawyer, Edward J. Lonergan, said, "I've known John since 1961. John is a good, good man, and this is a sad, sad process. It's just very disappointing."

On the other hand, the state attorney for Miami-Dade County, Katherine Fernandez Rundle, gave the press the facts, not feelings.

"John Connolly assisted the criminal activities of the Winter Hill gang by supplying information and intelligence to Whitey Bulger, Steve Flemmi, and John Martorano that led directly to the murder of several individuals," Rundle said. "But for the actions of John Connolly, these murders could not and would not have happened."

With Flemmi and Martorano spilling their guts, Connolly's murder trial was a slam-dunk for the prosecution.

The only intrigue in Connolly's murder trial was when former F.B.I. agent Joe Pistone refused to take the stand in Connolly's defense because the judge would not grant Pistone his request to testify anonymously. Exactly what Pistone, who infiltrated the New York City Bonanno Crime family as Donny Brasco, knew about Connolly's actions in Boston is problematic. The most Pistone could have offered in Connolly's defense was that working inside the mob was big-boy work and fraught with dangers. Pistone did not work directly with Connolly in the Whitey/Flemmi informant debacle so how could Pistone have known for sure Connolly had done everything by the book?

(However, earlier in the trial, Pistone was said to have met Whitey and Flemmi during a mid-1980's dinner with Connolly at the home of another F.B.I. agent.)

The First Rat Makes a Deal

In November 2008, a jury of his peers found Connolly guilty of second-degree murder. Everyday hard-working individuals handed down their verdict, unsullied by F.B.I. officials intent on minimizing the negative effects on the F.B.I's reputation.

Immediately after the guilty verdict, the prosecutor, Michael Van Zamft, asked the judge to administer Connolly a life sentence, saying the 30-year minimum sentence was too little because, "Mr. Connolly abused his badge."

Before his sentencing, which was set for early December 2008, Connolly told the *Boston Globe*, "I did not commit these crimes I was charged with. I never sold my badge. I never took anybody's money. I never caused anybody to be hurt, at least not knowingly, and I never would."

In December of 2008, Connolly stood before Miami-Dade Circuit Court Judge Stanford Blake awaiting his sentencing. Before Judge Blake's decision, Callahan's son, Patrick, read letters that he, his sister, and his mother had written. Patrick Callahan said his mother considered his father "the love of my life" for 23 years.

After the Callahan family spoke from their heart, Connolly, who didn't testify at his own murder trial, finally took the stand, trying to get the lowest possible sentence.

His snow-speckled hair neatly brushed into his favored pompadour, Connolly turned to Callahan's family, and said, "It's heartbreaking to hear what happened to your father, and to your husband. My heart is broken when I hear what you say."

Judge Blake was not impressed by Connolly's spiel. To the delight of the Callahan family, Judge Blake sentenced Connolly to 40 years in prison, saying, "John Connolly had crossed over to the dark side."

And that's putting it mildly.

Chapter 18
A Cat and a Canary

The F.B.I. finally arrested Whitey Bulger and Catherine Greig because of a cat and a canary.

Before their life on the run, Greig had been an animal lover. She still loved animals, but because Whitey knew he had to be mobile at a moment's notice, having a permanent pet was out of the question. But that didn't mean Catherine couldn't take care of a stray cat or two, she encountered near the Princess Eugenia complex in Santa Monica, California.

Enter stage right - the former Miss Iceland - Anna Bjornsdottir.

Bjornsdottir, 52, was an actress who had been crowned Miss Iceland in 1974. Her acting credits included stints on *Remington Steele* and *Diff'rent Strokes*. Bjornsdottir was also famous as the lovely young lady with the immaculate skin who appeared in the 1970's Noxzema television commercials.

Bjornsdottir and her husband, Halldor Gudmundson, split their time between living in Iceland and at the Princess Eugenia complex in Santa Monica. Bjornsdottir worked as a yoga instructor in America and as a graphic designer in Iceland. Bjornsdottir, like Greig, was also fond of cats. In fact, she and her husband had published a book about a stray cat they had adopted named Mosa.

One day, Greig was fussing over a stray cat in front of the Princess Eugenia complex when Bjornsdottir joined her.

A Cat and a Canary

The ladies formed a friendship of sorts As a result, Bjornsdottir became acquainted with Carol and Charlie Gasko, Whitey and Greig's longtime aliases.

For almost 16 years, the feds had been trying to track down Whitey, even going as far as featuring him in Fox's TV's *Americas Most Wanted*. But they had always come up with bupkes.

Suddenly, someone in the F.B.I. got a rare brainstorm.

The feds' new approach was, "We can't get Whitey because Whitey is probably in a shell somewhere, and, most likely, rarely ventures out where he can be seen and identified. But Catherine Greig is a different story."

The feds knew that Greig frequented beauty parlors to get her hair done and pamper herself with a manicure. Greig was also a proponent of plastic surgery, and she had several lifts of this-and-that at times to please her man, Whitey. The feds also knew women sometimes saw things that didn't register with men. As a result, the feds launched a worldwide ad campaign that featured 30-second ads during daytime television with Catherine Greig, instead of Whitey, as the main attraction.

Bjornsdottir was sitting in her Icelandic living room when she spotted a woman in a CNN television ad identified as Catherine Greig, but who Bjornsdottir knew as Carol Gasko. The ad said there was a $2 million reward for the capture of Greig's traveling companion: the infamous killer, James "Whitey" Bulger.

Bjornsdottir took out her currency converter, and calculated 2 million clams was approximately 238,974,188 Icelandic Kronas, a nice haul in any language. Bjornsdottir then picked up the phone and dialed the number provided in the television ad.

Forty-eight hours later, Whitey and Greig were safely in federal custody inside a Santa Monica clink. On June 29,

2011, Whitey arrived in a federal helicopter at Boston's Logan Airport. His next stop was a trip to The United States District Court for the District of Massachusetts in Boston.

The fun was just starting.

Chapter 19
Boston's Trial of the Century

After Whitey Bulger's June 22, 2011 arrest, the circus came to town.

Flashed across every television set in America was Whitey, in shackles and wearing an orange jump suit, shuffling out of a helicopter and into a waiting federal vehicle. He was then whisked away to the John Joseph Moakley Federal Courthouse in South Boston for his arraignment.

Waiting for Whitey in the first row of courthouse seats were his brother Billy, now retired and out of the public eye, and his brother Jackie, who had been previously arrested for helping Whitey while Whitey was on the lam. Before his trial, Jackie Bulger pled guilty to perjury and obstruction of justice. He was facing four years, but the judge only gave him six months.

Also present at Whitey's arraignment were several other representatives of the Bulger clan, including Billy's two sons. Billy and Whitey mouthed silent hellos to each other, as if love was in the air and all was right with the world.

The comedy show began when Federal Judge Marianne Bowler asked Whitey if he had enough money to pay for a proper attorney. Whitey, mindful the feds had found $822,000 in the walls of his Santa Monica condo, along with a stash of weapons that could start a small war, just smiled.

"Well, I could afford a lawyer if you could give me my

money back," Whitey said.

The judge said fat chance, and then she told Whitey the government would provide him with the legal assistance a man of his notoriety deserved.

And the legal system did just that in spades. And we had to pay for it.

First, the prosecution tried to have the Bulger family, meaning Billy Bulger, who had made a few bucks in his time, pay for Whitey's defense. But Judge Marianne Bowler - playing a few pins short - said nix on that.

Judge Bowler said there was "no legal precedent which required a sibling to pay for a defense."

Then Bowler picked a fine rabbit out of her hat when she appointed the grizzled J.W. (Jay) Carney, a respected graduate of Boston College Law School, as Whitey's mouthpiece.

Carney, tall, bald, and bespectacled, told the press, "This is just the latest case when I have a client in a jam, and I'm going to be the person to try to get him out of it."

Then, trying to show his new client was no big deal, Carney said. "It's the thousandth time I've shaken hands with a new client and said, 'Hello, I'm Jay Carney.'"

Carney, having a firm grasp of the obvious, then said, "Our constitution guarantees every defendant the right to a fair trial, and we're going to see that he gets it."

Carney said he planned to engage a roster of attorneys, private investigators, and paralegals to help defend Whitey, all on the public's dime.

In the past, Carney had defended a man, John Salvi, who shot two people to death in an abortion clinic. Carney had also represented child killers, and men who killed their wives either by bashing their heads in or by poisoning them.

Someone once christened Carney "The Patron Saint of the Hopeless." Others remarked he should be called "The Patron Saint of the Wicked."

With Whitey as his client, Jay Carney got two for the price of one.

When Carney and Whitey came face to face for the first time, there was a broad grin on each man's face. Carney extended his hand. Whitey took it and squeezed hard.

"Hello, I'm Jay Carney," the lawyer said.

Each of Whitey's 32 pearly-whites was clearly visible.

Whitey replied, "Jay Carney, my pleasure."

Considering men of financial means would have had to pay hundreds of thousands of dollars for a lawyer with Jay Carney's guile and experience, Whitey's pleasure was certainly justified.

Standing on a podium outside the courthouse, Carney regaled the press with a tall tale. He said the average man on the street, and even members of law enforcement, didn't view Whitey as such a bad guy.

Carney told the press, as he was rushing to the courthouse, he was pulled over for speeding. The state trooper asked Carney why he was in such a big rush. Carney told the cop he was hurrying to defend his new client, Whitey Bulger.

Carney said the trooper smiled, refused to write Carney a ticket, and dismissed Carney with, "Congratulations. Good luck and Godspeed."

Again, I was born in the day, but not yesterday.

Then there was the little problem of what to do about Catherine Grieg.

As Whitey sat in his lonely cell, with a prison guard watching him 24 hours a day, he got to thinking. Grieg had been a wonderful companion during his 16 years on the run, and she was a good sport about it to boot. It would be a shame if Greig had to spend time in prison for Whitey's crimes.

As was reported in *Whitey Bulger* by Cullen and Murphy,

"Whitey claimed that he was willing to plead guilty to all of the charges against him, even if it meant facing execution in Florida for John Callahan's murder, or in Oklahoma for Roger Wheeler's, in exchange for Greig's release. But he said the government refused to make a deal with him."

The government not only refused Whitey's offer for Greig's freedom, but they doubled-down on her prosecution, seeking considerable jail time for a woman who, her defense attorney said, was "just supporting her man."

Greig's lawyer, Kevin Reddington, pleaded to the court at Greig's indictment, "She's in love with the guy. If she could be with the guy right now, she'd be with him."

Both Reddington and Greig knew her case was a piece of cake for the prosecution, as did the prosecution and anyone else with knowledge of the details.

However, in March 2012, in a move straight out of the *Twilight Zone*, federal prosecutors decided to let Whitey's moll, Catherine Grieg, plead guilty to three charges: conspiracy to harbor a fugitive, conspiracy to commit identity fraud, and identity fraud. Greig did so without an agreed-upon recommendation for sentencing negotiated by the government with her attorney.

To make this deal all the more ridiculous, the government also agreed not to force Greig to testify against Whitey in court.

Is America great, or what?

Kevin Reddington argued to the judge that Catherine Greig's only crime was falling in love with Whitey, and that she had no knowledge of any of Whitey's numerous and heinous crimes.

If anyone believes that, there's a bridge in Brooklyn waiting for a buyer just like you.

Despite what Reddington said it court, Catherine Grieg wasn't on the run for 16 years with someone she thought was a traveling salesman.

And what about the hidden fortune of $822,000 in their Santa Monica condominium walls and the arsenal of guns? It's not reasonable to believe Greig wasn't aware of the hidden cash or the guns.

And then there was the rumor Whitey had secreted millions of dollars in safe deposit boxes throughout the world? Does anyone really think the 822 grand found in his Santa Monica condo was all the money Whitey possessed in this world?

Did Grieg know the locations of these safe deposit boxes and the amounts of money in each location?

We'll never know because the feds never asked.

The feds could have pressed Grieg harder on this issue. If so, perhaps the families of Whitey's murder victims could have gotten a few bucks for their miseries - anything is better than nothing, which is what most of them got.

Although the families of four of Whitey's murder victims were at the meeting when the prosecutors agreed to Greig's plea-deal, they weren't exactly ecstatic about the outcome.

Steve Davis's sister, Debra, was allegedly strangled by Whitey in 1981, and Frank Donahue's father, Michael, was shot and killed by Whitey in 1982 on the South Boston waterfront. Both men said the prosecutors did not tell them what sentence they would recommend for Greig.

Donahue told the press, "She (Greig) helped that guy on the run. We could have had these answers 16 years ago. She's a criminal, she's not a victim. She's a criminal!"

Davis said he understood Greig was not a murderer, but he was disappointed by "the fact the government has not put a tight enough grip on everything."

"What they wanted out of this was a conviction," Davis said. "That's it."

On Tuesday, June 12, 2012, Catherine Greig was

sentenced to eight years in prison. Greig was also fined $150,000, which she immediately paid. Where she got that kind of money is up for conjecture. After all, her previous work experience was as a low-paying "dental hygienist."

The government had earlier tried to seize her $343,700 home in Quincy, which Greig owned with her twin sister Margaret. But due to the state's Homestead Act, the Greig sisters were allowed to keep their home.

Before Greig's sentencing, her lawyer, Reddington, told the court, "Why people fall in love has been debated since before Shakespeare's sonnets. Many times people fall in love and their family or loved ones do not approve or condone the relationship. The truth of the matter is that she was and remains in love with Mr. Bulger."

Please pass the hankies along with the barf bags.

In explaining his decision, U.S. District Court Judge Douglas Woodlock said Greig's role in helping Whitey stay on the run for 16 years involved "more than mere harboring."

Judge Woodlock also said, "The defendant is capable of making her own choices and had a long time to make her own choices."

The prosecution had asked for 10 years for Greig, but Judge Woodlock cut that down by 20 per cent. Counting the year she has already spent in prison, the 61-year-old Greig could spend as little as five more years in prison.

After Greig's sentencing, the press asked Reddington if Greig had any regrets about the 16 years she spent on the run with Whitey.

Reddington simply said, "No."

However, for some strange reason the federal prosecutors didn't feel Judge Woodlock was too light on Greig.

"Eight years is a very significant sentence," U.S. Attorney Carmen Ortiz told reporters.

"This was not a romantic saga. We believe the sentence imposed addressed the severity of the crimes. Now she's paying the price for the choices that she made."

Not surprisingly, the relatives of Whitey's victims did not share the same view as the judge and the prosecution.

In a statement to the judge before Greig's sentencing, Steven Davis, the brother of murder victim Debra Davis, wanted Greg to get the maximum penalty allowed by law.

Davis told the judge, "She never had the heart to look any of us in the eye."

Then Davis stared a laser beam straight into Grieg's forehead, and said, "Catherine, you dirty bitch!"

Catherine Greig showed no emotion at Davis's outburst.

Tim Connors, 37, whose father, Edward, was shot to death by Whitey, addressed a stone-faced Greig in court, saying, "You are as much a criminal as Whitey, and you ought to be handled as such. You are a cold-hearted criminal!"

To put Greig's sentence in perspective, on July 17, 2013, just before this book was set to be published, Hamilton County Court Judge Robert Ruehlman of Ohio sentenced Melowese Richardson, a local poll worker, to five years in prison for "voter fraud." It seemed that Richardson had the audacity to vote illegally eight times from 2008 to 2012. Most of those illegal votes were cast for Barack Obama.

Considering the severity of Greig's crimes, she got off easy; compared to Melowese Richardson, who was rigorously punished for a middling case of voter fraud.

Go figure.

*****

Whitey Bulger's trial began on June 4, 2013. More than 600 people were called for jury duty, and they all filled out questionnaires, which the prosecution and the defense used to eliminate potential jurors each felt was opposed to their positions. U.S. District Court Judge Denise Caspar, an African-American, was selected to be the judge in the most sensational trial in Boston court since the 1967 prosecution of the Boston Strangler, Albert DeSalvo.

People who knew Whitey snickered about the selection of Judge Caspar, since it was no secret that Whitey wasn't exactly fond of African-Americans. In fact, Whitey was vocal and physical in opposing the 1974 court-ordered busing of black students from nearby Roxbury into South Boston High. Billy Bulger, then a State Senator, was also strongly against the busing of blacks into his beloved Southie, and this caused a confrontation between Billy and Boston Police Commissioner Robert diGrazia.

After diGrazia ordered his police to arrest violent white, and mostly Irish, demonstrators outside South Boston High School, Billy, hot under the collar, rushed up to diGrazia and got right into diGrazia's face.

"You don't have to get this excited!" Billy screamed.

Then Billy, obviously out of line, told diGrazia his Boston police officers were acting like the "Nazi Gestapo."

However, the hulking diGrazia would not be cowered by a diminutive banty rooster named Billy Bulger.

"If you had any guts," diGrazia told Billy, "you'd tell those people to get their kids into school."

Billy's voice raised two octaves higher.

"The Community has a message for you, Commissioner," Billy said. "Go fuck yourself!"

There was also concern Whitey and his exploits were so well known in Boston, that finding an unbiased jury of Whitey's peers would be challenging, if not impossible. Journalist Dick Lehr, who had co-authored two books on Whitey, did not share this feeling.

"That element of worry and fear that could make the jury selection process difficult doesn't exist here," Lehr told the *Associated Press*. "His most important cohorts have turned into government witnesses. Once they learned Whitey was a rat, they all turned on him; having felt betrayed by their boss. So there's no loyalty there. In terms of public fear of gang retaliation, there's nothing there."

Tom Duffy, a retired state police major who had tracked Whitey throughout the years, agreed with Lehr's assessment.

"Nobody is going to step up to the plate for this guy," Duffy told the *Associated Press*. "He's betrayed so many people."

After two days of scrutinizing people of diverse ages, genders, and nationalities, the prosecution and the defense settled on 18 jurors, six of whom were to be alternates. Of the 12 primary jurors, eight were men and three were women. Of the alternates, the gender was equally divided at three and three. Their age was described in the media as "middle aged." There was no mention of the juror's race or their nationalities.

When Judge Casper swore in the jurors, she told them, "Do not make up your mind of what the verdict will be. Keep an open mind."

Judge Casper decided the jurors in Whitey's trial would not be sequestered. The judge also decreed the jurors would be referred to by numbers, and their identities wouldn't be released until after a verdict was rendered.

As soon as jury selection was complete, Jay Carney blew a gasket in court. He accused the prosecution of a "cover up" for failing to give Carney and his defense team important documents concerning John Martorano, who was scheduled to testify for the prosecution. Carney claimed Martorano, because of his cooperation with the government, was not being prosecuted himself for "ongoing crimes."

This caused Assistant US Attorney Fred Wyshak to blow his own gasket.

"Mr. Carney continues to impugn the integrity of the prosecution team," Wyshak said. "And I take great umbrage to it. Mr. Carney's courtroom manner is both unlawyerly and unprofessional. I hope this conduct doesn't continue."

Carney, his bald head glistening and his eyeglasses stained with sweat, yelled at Wyshak. "But it will continue!"

Judge Caspar told both lawyers to take a chill pill. Then she called them to the bench.

"Seriously, gentlemen?" Judge Caspar said.

Judge Caspar scolded both lawyers before shooing them back to their respective positions in the courtroom.

After Carney and Wyshak sat in their seats, Judge Casper said, "I think we have all taken a deep breath and are ready to proceed in this matter."

Assistant U.S. Attorney Brian T. Kelly was up to bat first and presented the prosecution's opening statement.

Kelly, who had a face like your neighborhood bartender, was dressed in a light summer suit with a garish solid red tie. Kelly was an old pro, having spent 26 years as a member of the Massachusetts State Bar.

With his receding forehead glistening with perspiration, Kelly addressed the court in his heavy "Bahston" accent.

"This is my chance to give you an overview of the case," Kelly said. "It's a case about organized crime, public corruption, and all sorts of illegal activities, ranging from extortion to drug dealing to money laundering to possession of machine guns to murder, 19 murders. It's about a criminal enterprise, which is a group of criminals, who ran amok in the city of Boston for almost 30 years. So you'll hear about crimes in the '70s, the '80s, and the '90s. And at the center of all this murder and mayhem is one man, the defendant in this case, James Bulger."

Just in case one of the jurors never heard about Whitey and his exploits (and in the city of "Bahston" that was almost impossible), Kelly explained to the court Whitey's modus operandi.

"This criminal enterprise headed by Bulger made millions of dollars extorting money," Kelly said. "And part of their success was due to their fearsome reputation; that is, other criminals were afraid of them, other criminals would rather pay them off than argue with them or fight with them."

Kelly proceeded to list some of the defendants who would be called to testify for the prosecution; most of them, some people might say, were just as bad as Whitey.

"Now, you will hear from several drug dealers who dealt directly with Bulger," Kelly said. "You will hear that Bulger liked to promote the myth that he had nothing to do with drugs. But you will hear from these drug dealers that in the 1980's Bulger was deeply involved in the distribution of drugs in the South Boston area, especially cocaine. And he and his gang made millions at it.

"You will also hear from Steve Flemmi. After several of the murders that Bulger and Steven Flemmi committed together, Flemmi pulled the teeth out of the victims in the mistaken belief that that would somehow prevent the bodies from being identified, not anticipating DNA testing years later. So, clearly, Flemmi is a vicious killer, but just as clearly, the evidence in this case will show that he was James Bulger's partner for many years.

"Now, Kevin Weeks is also going to testify in this case; he received a reduced sentence from a federal judge based upon his cooperation. He will tell you he testified at several trials. And he also took investigators directly to the bodies of 'Bucky' Barrett, John McIntyre, and Debra Davis."

Then Kelly got to the crux of his case. Kelly said Whitey and Flemmi could never have been as successful criminals as they had become if it were not for the explicit help of law enforcement; i.e., the local Boston cops, state troopers, and yes, the Federal Bureau of Investigation – the glorified F.B.I

"But there was another part to their success, and the other part to their success was public corruption," Kelly said. "Because you will hear that Bulger and his friends made a point of paying off members of law enforcement. They did that so they could get tipped off to investigations and stay one step ahead of the honest cops who were actually trying to make a case against them. So, it was part of a strategy they had, and it worked.

"You will also hear about FBI agents taking money and compromising investigations on behalf of Bulger, tipping him off to investigations that legitimate, honest cops were trying to make against Bulger and his colleagues."

By this time, Whitey was slouching in his seat at the defense table and sweating up a storm. Whitey's face was twisted into a half snarl, and it appeared, if he had the chance, he'd jump from his chair and sink his teeth into Kelly's neck.

Kelly completed his opening argument with, "And that, ladies and gentlemen, is what this case is about, a defendant, James Bulger, who was part of a criminal gang which extorted people, paid off cops, earned a fortune dealing drugs, laundered money, possessed all sorts of guns, and murdered 19 people."

Satisfied with his opening statement, Kelly strode back to the prosecution table and took a seat. He had a self-satisfied smirk on his face.

Now it was Jay Carney's turn at the plate with the defense's opening statement. However, instead of refuting Kelly's opening statement concerning Whitey's criminality, Carney was intent on proving Whitey was never a rat, which, according to all of the evidence available and common sense, was like saying the world is flat.

Carney puffed out his chest, and he swaggered back and forth in front of the jury, flaunting his brand new gray three-piece pinstripe suit.

"Now, James Bulger never ever, the evidence will show, was an informant for John Connolly," Carney said. "There were two reasons for this. Number one, James Bulger is of Irish descent, and the worst thing that an Irish person could consider doing was becoming an informant because of the history of 'The Troubles in Ireland.' And that was the first and foremost reason why James Bulger was never an informant against people."

Carney readily admitted Whitey had law enforcement in his back pocket, but not because Whitey was feeding the feds information.

"Sure, Bulger also gave money to state police, local police, and he did that consistently," Carney said. "Why would Jim Bulger pay this? *Because he wanted information.*

"James Bulger was involved in criminal activities in Boston. He was involved in illegal gaming, meaning selling football cards or other betting games and collecting the proceeds, which is illegal. It's called, in the business, bookmaking. He also lent money to people at very high rates. It's called loan-sharking. He was involved in drug dealing. These crimes, that's what he did. And in order to protect this business, he wanted to pay for information and receive it from corrupt law enforcement officers.

"Ladies and gentlemen, I tell you this history from the early '70s until the mid-'90s, so you will know the depth of corruption in federal law enforcement that existed during this period. Because it puts in context what happened after 1994. And this was how James Bulger was able to do illegal gambling, make illegal loans, be involved in drug trafficking and extortion of people, and never, ever be charged, and on top of that, make millions, upon millions, upon millions of dollars doing so."

Then Jay Carney left the world of improbability and entered the realm of the absurd.

Carney said, "Bulger settled in California, not hiding, living openly in plain sight for the next 16 years, while those former FBI agents, I submit, pretended to look for him."

Carney did not explain to the jury how a man who was being searched for by every law enforcement agent in the country, if not in the world, and who had *changed his name several times*, could "not be in hiding," and, in fact, "living openly in plain sight for 16 years."

But that's what defense lawyers do.

For the uninformed, it is not against the law for a lawyer, protecting his client, to stretch the truth in court. In fact, an outright lie spewing from a defense lawyer's mouth is not out of the ordinary. In America, it's up to the jury to separate the bull from the bullshit, and Jay Carney was flinging around plenty of both.

Carney then made another bad guy the real bad guy in this sordid situation.

"At this point, so many years had gone by that it's fair to say that Stevie Flemmi thought he'd never see Bulger again," Carney said. "And what Stevie Flemmi decided to do, I submit, was start blaming Bulger, Jim Bulger, for crimes that Stevie Flemmi himself had carried out."

By this time, Carney had shoveled so much shit in the courtroom, people were soiled above the shoe-tops. Carney increased this mess to knee level when he summed up his opening statement.

Carney summarized, "At the end of this case, I'll be asking you the question I asked at the beginning of my opening: Given these three individuals (Steve Flemmi, Kevin Weeks, and John Martorano), given their backgrounds, given their character, if that was all you knew, would you believe them beyond a reasonable doubt? But when you add to the recipe the unbelievable incentives the prosecution has given these three men so that they will testify in the manner that the government wants, do you believe them beyond a reasonable doubt? This process may be a pretty good recipe to get testimony, but it's an unreliable recipe to get the truth."

That said; Jay Carney returned to his seat at the defense table.

Whitey beamed. His defense lawyer turned out to be almost as duplicitous as Whitey on his most deceitful day, and many of those days were tied for first place.

Assistant U.S. Attorney Brian T. Kelly grilled his prosecution witnesses like a pit bull ripping into a juicy piece of meat. When Kelly had rested the prosecution side, he had called 63 witnesses to the stand.

Kelly's first order of business was to instill in the mind of the jury that Whitey was nothing but a lowly drug dealer, a charge Whitey had previously denied. To do so, Kelly brought to the stand Joseph Tower, 59, a drug dealer who said he had paid tribute to Whitey in order to operate unimpeded in the city of Boston.

Tower, who received immunity from prosecution, told the jury he ran to Whitey in 1980 because Tommy Nee was shaking down drug dealers in Boston, including Tower. Tower testified he cruised around Southie in Whitey's blue Malibu, while Whitey peppered him with questions about how lucrative Tower's drug operation was. Whitey solution to Tower's problem was to hook Tower up with John Shea, one of Whitey's top drug dealers.

Tower said Whitey told him, "If you're with Shea, there will be no problems. Nobody will bother you."

Tower took the deal and his drug business increased exponentially.

Tower said he bought upwards of a kilo of cocaine a week from Columbian suppliers, which cost anywhere from $28,000 to $34,000. After cutting the coke with quinine and other substances, Tower was able to double his money by selling his blow retail on the streets of South Boston. Tower estimated he made $200,000 a year in drug profits under Whitey's umbrella. Of course, Tower had to kick back to Whitey a substantial share of his income.

When the prosecutor asked Tower to explain the reasoning for his weekly donations to Whitey, Tower said. "I did it because he's the one who set me up with Mr. Shea. He was the protection."

While Tower was regaling the court with his exploits concerning Whitey, Whitey seemed amused, and then he started giggling like a girl. At one point, Whitey was chuckling so hard, his shoulders visibly shook up and down.

When Tower was asked to identify Whitey in court, Tower pointed at Whitey, sitting just a few feet away, smiled and said, "Hello Jim."

Whitey, a broad smile spread across his white-bearded face, nodded politely, and simply said, "Joe."

Whitey's mood was decidedly gloomier, when on the twelfth day of the trial, ex-F.B.I. supervisor John Morris took the stand. Morris's sparse brown hair was now entirely white, and he slumped in his chair as if he had a broken back. Morris, 67, was also testifying under a grant of total immunity.

Morris told the court he had been introduced to Whitey and his partner Steve Flemmi by John Connolly. Soon, Morris was taking bribes from Whitey, totaling $7,000 and several cases of fine wine, the exact number of cases Morris couldn't recall.

Morris said the first time Whitey tried to bribe him with wine, Morris was skeptical. In the early 1980s, Connolly called Morris to the F.B.I. garage under their office and handed him a case of wine from Whitey and Flemmi. Connolly told Morris he had to accept it or, "These guys will think you don't trust them."

Morris also admitted on the stand he had leaked information to Whitey and Flemmi, through John Connolly, which likely led to several men being killed. Morris said he gave Whitey and Flemmi F.B.I. information about Mafia leaders, Charlestown drug dealers, and other Boston-based gangsters.

But what really got under Whitey's skin was when Morris detailed a dinner party Morris said he attended with Connolly and Whitey at Steve Flemmi's parents' house, where Morris said Billy Bulger walked in unexpectedly.

"He (Billy Bulger) looked very uncomfortable," Morris said.

Whitey half-rose in his seat, and he snarled at Morris, "You're a fucking liar!"

Judge Caspar glared at Whitey. She told Whitey there were to be no more outbursts in her courtroom. Whitey nodded to the judge, and he sat back down in his seat.

Morris told the court, after Tulsa businessman Roger Wheeler was murdered in 1981, "I used bad judgment when I told Connolly that Brian Halloran was cooperating with the F.B.I. and had implicated both Bulger and Flemmi in Wheeler's murder."

Morris said he allowed Connolly to file a false F B.I. report that insisted Whitey and Flemmi didn't know Halloran was an informant. That false report took them off the hook for Halloran's murder and that of the innocent bystander, Michael Donahue.

Morris also fessed up about the $1,000 he requested Connolly ask Whitey for, so Morris could romance his girlfriend while he was attending an F.B.I. training camp at the Federal Law Enforcement Training Center in Glynco, Georgia.

Assistant US Attorney Fred Wyshak asked Morris why he had requested such a favor.

Morris said he did so because Connolly had once told him, "These guys really like you, and if there's anything you want or need, just ask."

Morris said, "After I received that money, I knew I was clearly compromised."

Morris admitted that, in 1984, he had accepted another case of wine from Whitey, only this case of wine had a thousand bucks stuffed between the bottles.

Soon after the thousand-dollar bribe, Morris said he dined with Whitey, Flemmi, and Connolly. During dinner, Whitey handed Morris an envelope containing five thousand simoleons.

Morris said Whitey told him, "This is to help you out."

When Wyshak asked Morris why, in 1988, he had told the *Boston Globe* both Whitey and Flemmi had been working with the feds for years, Morris said, "The only way I thought these informants would be closed is if their identities were compromised. I did it so what happened to me wouldn't happen to other agents."

Again, Whitey cursed out Morris loudly in court.

Quite annoyed at Whitey's outbursts, Assistant U.S. Attorney Brian T. Kelly told Judge Caspar, "I know James Bulger spent his whole life trying to intimidate people, but he should not be doing that here in federal court in the midst of a trial."

Kelly urged Judge Caspar to tell Whitey, "To keep his little remarks to himself when the witness is testifying."

Judge Caspar told Whitey, "You are well served by your lawyers. They are to speak for you in the courtroom. Do you understand that, sir?"

Whitey, his head down and still seething, responded to the female judge with a bizarre, "Yes, sir."

*****

The procession of cooperating witnesses began when hitman John Martorano took the stand.

Martorano, 72, wore a solid navy-blue suit, a light blue shirt, and a striped blue tie with matching pocket square. He also appeared much thinner than when he was on the streets whacking people.

Responding to questions put forth by Assistant U.S. Attorney Fred Wyshak, the jury sat spellbound as

Martorano recounted 20 murders he personally committed, including 11 he had done with Whitey. Martorano said Whitey was one of his best friends, and he even named his son James after him.

Martorano said, when he found out Whitey was eating cheese with the government, "I was beside myself. It nearly broke my heart."

Whitey's assistant defense attorney, Henry Brennan, tore into Martorano's testimony. But no matter how piercing Brennan's questions, and no matter how hard Brennan tried to show the jury Martorano was a cold-blooded killer and nothing more, Martorano still came off as someone's old, eccentric uncle.

Brennan first established the fact that Martorano, before he made his deal with the government, had been facing the death penalty for the murder of Martorano's best friend, John Callahan in Florida and that of Roger Wheeler in Oklahoma.

"So you sat there thinking before accepting a plea agreement about the death penalty in Florida and Oklahoma?" Brennan asked him.

"Correct," Martorano said. "I did think of it, but not all day long."

Brennan then asked Martorano how he was able to walk out of court a free man, after serving only 12 years in prison, despite the fact Martorano admitted to killing 20 people.

"I had a good lawyer, I guess," Martorano said.

Brennan asked Martorano if Whitey was his boss.

Martorano said, "He was older than me, but he was not my boss."

"Then why did you listen to him when he asked you to kill all those people?" Brennan asked.

"I listened to him because he knew how to press all the right buttons, I guess," Martorano replied.

Brennan then attacked Martorano's credibility, detailing a litany of times Martorano had lied.

"You even lied to your friend John Callahan before you murdered him," Brennan said.

Martorano looked at Brennan like he had an extra eye in the middle of his forehead.

"I couldn't tell John I wanted to *shoot* him," Martorano replied.

Even though, he admitted he had lied many times in the past, Martorano insisted this time he was telling the truth about Whitey and Flemmi, and himself being "murder machines."

"I was told by federal prosecutors if I ever told another lie, I would go to jail for the rest of my life," Martorano said.

Brennan insisted one of the reasons Martorano became a rat was because he wanted to write a book about himself, despite the fact writing such a book would inflict psychological damage to the families of his victims. The title of Martorano's book, which he co-authored with *Boston Herald* columnist Howie Carr, is *Hitman: The Untold Story of Johnny Martorano, Whitey's Enforcer and the Most Feared Gangster in the Underworld*.

"I didn't want to hurt anybody with the book," Martorano said. "I needed the money to support my family when I got out of prison."

When Brennan asked why Martorano had picked such a sensational title for his bio, Martorano replied, "That wasn't my idea; it was Howie Carr's. I went along with it because Howie thought the book would sell better."

Brennan asked Martorano how much money he had made so far from the sales of the book.

"Only about $70,000," Martorano said.

Brennan got Martorano to admit a film company had paid him $250,000 for the rights to his life story, and that Martorano could get another $250,000 if the company brought a movie based on his life to production.

When Martorano left the witness stand after three days of testimony, Whitey just sat there and shook his head.

John Martorano's testimony inserted nail No. 1 into Whitey's coffin.

*****

On July 9, 2013, Whitey's former protégé, Kevin Weeks, hate and contempt in his eyes, took the witness stand against his former boss. The 57-year-old Weeks and Bulger were once so tight, they spoke nearly every day for more than a decade

Since Weeks had served only five years in prison for aiding and abetting five of Whitey's murders, Whitey's lawyer, J.W. Carney, after the prosecution had elicited damaging evidence against Whitey from Weeks, tried to portray Weeks as a con artist who knew how to manipulate the court system.

"You won against the system," Carney told Weeks.

"What did I win? What did I win?" Weeks yelled. "Five people are dead!"

Carney asked Weeks if the killings bothered him.

Weeks shot back, "We killed people that were rats. And I had THE BIGGEST RAT right next to me."

Scant feet away, Whitey yelled at Weeks, "You suck!"

Weeks snapped back, "Fuck you, okay!"

As the jury sat stunned, Whitey barked at Weeks, "Fuck you, too!"

Weeks leaned forward in the witness chair, his eyes staring straight into Whitey's.

Weeks spat out the words, "What do you want to do?"

"*What do you want to do?*" is threatening street parlance, usually followed by the swinging of fists.

Judge Caspar was outraged. She yelled, "Hey!" at both

men.

Suddenly, Weeks and Jay Carney started cursing at each other. U.S. Marshals jumped from their chairs and created a blockade between Weeks and Carney, which probably saved Carney a trip to the hospital, if not to the morgue.

Judge Caspar told everyone involved she would tolerate no further outbursts in her courtroom.

When Carney resumed his cross-examination of Weeks, he asked, "What would you do if anyone accused you of being a rat?"

Weeks, still seething at both Carney and Whitey, shot back, "Well, why don't you call me a rat outside when it's just me and you and see what I do?"

When Weeks was questioned by the prosecution earlier in the day, he told the court that, in 2000, after he had become an informant, he led the feds to the graves of Bucky Barrett, John McIntyre, and Debra Davis.

"I knew where the bodies were buried because Jim Bulger, Steve Flemmi, and myself put them there," Weeks said.

Weeks explained the bodies were originally buried in the basement of 799 East Third Street, where the three murders had taken place. But in 1985, the house, which belonged to Pat Nee's brother, was sold and the bodies had to be moved; which they were on Halloween night 1985.

Weeks told the court Barrett and McIntyre were involved "in the life," and he was not shocked when they were both killed. Yet the murder of Debbie Hussy, who was Flemmi's girlfriend at the time, had been different.

"When Stevie brought Debbie to the house I didn't think anything of it," Weeks said. "She wasn't a criminal; she wasn't involved with us. I didn't think anything was going to happen to her."

Weeks also told the court throughout the years Whitey

had bragged to him about several of Whitey's past killings, including the murder of Debra Davis, another one of Steve Flemmi's girlfriends.

"Whitey told me about the killing of Debra Davis, but he never told me who did the killing; him or Stevie," Weeks said. "He just told me she was strangled, and that they had buried her body in the marshes near the Neponset River."

There's no doubt, Weeks's testimony hammered nail No. 2 into Whitey's coffin.

*****

The prosecution witness who was potentially the most damaging to Whitey was his former partner, the 79-year-old Steve Flemmi. Not only did Flemmi know who was killed and why, and where the bodies were buried, he also knew Whitey was a rat for the feds for years, because Flemmi ate from the same federal chunk of cheese.

For nearly 20 years, Flemmi and Whitey had tag-teamed with John Connolly and John Morris, feeding them information about the Italian mob - as well as hundreds of thousands of dollars in bribes - for information about fellow informers and a heads-up when indictments were set to come down.

When Flemmi took the stand, there was a look of disgust on Whitey's face. It was as if Whitey was saying, "The nerve of this guy ratting on me; we were both rats together."

Under questioning by prosecutor Fred Wyshak, Flemmi told the court he and Whitey had been informants together for the feds since 1975. Flemmi said they frequently paid John Connolly and other F.B.I. agents for tipping them about ongoing investigations concerning members of the Winter Hill Mob. Flemmi said they gave Connolly approximately $230,000 in hard cash during a 15-year period. Flemmi said he also greased the palms of five other F.B.I. agents.

In 1983, Flemmi testified they gave Connolly two separate payments of $25,000 each. When Connolly scooped up the second twenty-five grand, Flemmi said Connolly told him, "Now I'm one of the gang."

Flemmi said, beside the bribes, he had also given Connolly numerous tidbits on the Italian mob, which the F.B.I. was intent on decimating. Whitey didn't give Connolly much, Flemmi said, because the Italian mob didn't trust Whitey, and they never told Whitey anything that could incriminate them.

During Wyshak's questioning, Flemmi spit out murders committed by him and Whitey, which had been already divulged in court by John Martorano and Kevin Weeks. Then, in one rapid burst after another, Flemmi listed eight more killings, not previously mentioned in court, that he and Whitey had committed together in the 1970's and 1980's, while they were the kingpins of the Winter Hill Mob.

When Flemmi got to the murder of Debra Davis, who was 26 at the time, he got teary-eyed.

"Why did you and Bulger kill Debra Davis?" Wyshak asked.

"He wanted her dead, not me," Flemmi said. "I made a mistake when I told Debra that Whitey and I were meeting with the FBI. I had to tell her that because I used to disappear, and she thought I was seeing another woman. I told this to Whitey, and he said she was a danger to us, so she had to go."

Flemmi said Whitey gave him a list of reasons Debra had to die. Besides her knowledge of Whitey and Flemmi being F.B.I. informants, Debra was constantly showing off around town the gifts Flemmi had given her, including expensive diamonds and her always-new Mercedes. In addition, Whitey was told Debra was bragging in the Triple O that her boyfriend was the "biggest gangster in town."

"Whitey said all that was drawing attention to me and him," Flemmi said.

"What did you do while Whitey was strangling Debra," Wyshak asked.

"I was there, but I didn't do anything," Flemmi said.

"Why not?" Wyshak asked.

"Because that was the plan," Flemmi replied.

"What happened when you brought Debra to the house where she was killed?" Wyshak asked.

"As soon as we walked in, Jim Bulger stepped out from behind the top of the basement stairs, and he started strangling Debra," Flemmi said. "He lost his balance, and they both fell to the floor, and he continued strangling her. It didn't take long; she was a fragile woman. Then he carried her downstairs, and he laid her on a tarp. Then Whitey went upstairs and took a nap."

Flemmi also told the court when Whitey was sawing wood, two of their associates came by, wrapped Debra up in a tarp, and buried her in the marshes near the Neponset River in Quincy.

"Do you have any remorse for the death of Debra Davis?" Wyshak asked.

Flemmi put his head down and sniffled. "It's affected me, and it's going to affect me the rest of my life," he said.

Then, Flemmi accused Whitey of being, especially in jail, the vilest kind of criminal: a pervert and a child molester.

While under cross-examination by Whitey's mouthpiece, Brennan, Flemmi said he and Whitey used to hang out in front of a Catholic girls' high school on West Broadway, next to the old Triple O "Bucket of Blood" Bar. Flemmi said they enjoyed checking out the "local talent."

Flemmi said, "Whitey liked the uniforms the girls used to wear."

Flemmi said Whitey had several underage girlfriends, but Whitey's favorite was a 15-year-old named Tammy.

"Bulger and myself, we all had our weaknesses," Flemmi said.

For the third time in court, Whitey started mumbling obscenities at one of the witnesses. The word "motherfucker" could be clearly heard by court spectators flying from Whitey's mouth. However, neither the judge nor the prosecution heard the remark, so Whitey was not cautioned again.

Brennan then questioned Flemmi about his role in the death of Flemmi's stepdaughter, whom Brennan referred to as "Little Debbie Hussy."

"Did you ever sit her on your knee and read her stories?" Brennan asked.

"Of course not!" Flemmi said, angrily. "I never did that to my *own* children."

"Is it hard for you to accept the fact that you strangled somebody who sat on your knee as a little girl?" Brennan asked.

It was obvious Flemmi was trying to control his anger. He said slowly, and succinctly, "Mr. Brennan, I didn't strangle her."

Then Brennan asked Flemmi about the night "Little Debbie Hussy" died.

"When you drove the girl who once called you 'Daddy' to the house where she was killed, did you walk her to the front door?" Brennan asked.

"Yes," Flemmi answered.

"Did you fight for her in that house, Mr. Flemmi?" Brennan asked.

Instead of answering Brennan's direct question, Flemmi pointed at Whitey, who was staring bullets at Flemmi.

"He could have stopped it and that would have been the end of it!" Flemmi yelled. "All Whitey had to say was 'pass,' that's four letters – P-A-S-S. That's all he had to do."

"Didn't you put your stepdaughter into an unmarked grave?" Brennan asked.

"It didn't make sense to mark her grave," Flemmi said.

Brennan said, point blank to Flemmi, that Flemmi obviously had a proclivity for molesting young girls too. Flemmi just stared angrily at Brennan, but he said nothing.

Brennan walked back and forth in front of the jury, as if he were directing the next question to them.

"Isn't it true, Mr. Flemmi that in prison pedophiles are called 'diddlers,' or 'skinners,'" Brennan asked.

Flemmi half rose from his chair, and he pointed right at Whitey. "You want to talk about pedophilia, right over there at that table!" Flemmi said. "Jim Bulger took a 16-year-old girl to Mexico once!"

When Flemmi was finished with his six days of testimony, he stalked off the witness stand, staring at Whitey. Then Flemmi stopped in his tracks, and he said to Whitey, "Motherfucker!"

Whitey shot back, "Fuck you!"

Make no mistake, when Steve Flemmi exited the courtroom, he had sealed Whitey's coffin airtight.

*****

Whereas, the prosecution called 63 witnesses to the stand, the defense only needed nine witnesses to prove nothing. In fact, even though Whitey was accused of almost every crime known to man, the only thing Whitey's legal eagles seemed to be interested in proving was:

No. 1 – Whitey had never been, even for one day in his life, a federal informer. Sure, he paid the law, but he did so only to garner information favorable to his criminal cause.

And No. 2 – Whitey Bulger did not strangle women. That was beneath a man of Whitey's criminal stature, and yes – beneath his dignity. Whitey did not strangle Debra Davis, and he did not strangle "Little Debbie Hussey." That was all Steve Flemmi's doing.

The only defense witness who seemed to make an impression in the courtroom was former F.B.I. agent Robert Fitzpatrick, who had written a book about his exploits chasing Whitey throughout the years entitled, *Betrayal: Whitey Bulger and the FBI Agent Who Fought to Bring Him Down*.

Fitzpatrick said he had advised his superiors to close out Whitey as an informant; a move that would have allowed the bureau to begin investigating Whitey's crimes.

"They disagreed, they didn't do it, it was not done," Fitzpatrick said. "I didn't like it; there was nothing I could do about it. The F.B.I. wanted to keep Bulger open."

Although he told the jury he didn't believe Whitey had been as dynamic F.B.I. informant as the prosecutors claimed, Fitzpatrick seemed distracted on the stand.

To make matters worse for the defense, when U.S. Attorney Brian Kelly started grilling Fitzpatrick, it became obvious Fitzpatrick had a loose relationship with the truth.

"You claimed in your book that you were present on the morning in January 2000 when several of the bodies of the 19 people Bulger is accused of murdering were exhumed," Kelly said. "Is that correct?"

The 73-year-old Fitzpatrick started fidgeting and his eyes scanned the courtroom's ceiling, as if he were trying to remember something.

"I have no recollection that I was actually there for the exhumation," Fitzpatrick finally said. "But the event is firmly etched in my memory. This book, as a memoir, is a recitation of many things."

Kelly then moved in for the kill.

"Is the medication you're taking affecting your memory?" Kelly asked.

The court heard all it needed to know about Fitzpatrick's credibility, when Fitzpatrick blurted out, "Not that I can recall."

Priceless.

*****

The time had come for the jury, and especially the relatives of Whitey's victims, to hear from the Big Kahuna himself: Whitey Bulger.

All throughout the trial the defense intimated Whitey would take the stand in his defense to clear the record; i.e., he was never a federal informer, and he never strangled the life out of poor defenseless women.

But when it was time to put up or shut up, the court, the attending press, and the relatives of Whitey's murder victims, were aghast when Whitey told the court he was clamming up.

Whitey stood tall, put his head back, and looked Judge Caspar in the eye. He spoke in his distinct "Bahstan" street lingo.

"I involuntarily decided not to testify on the same day the defense rested its case," Whitey said. "I feel that I've been choked off from having an opportunity to give an adequate defense. My thing is, as far as I'm concerned, I didn't get a fair trial. This is a sham, and youse can do what ya want with me. That's it. That's my final word."

Whitey was referring to the fact Judge Caspar had refused to allow Whitey's defense team to use the argument that any crimes Whitey had committed while he was a federal informant should be erased because he had been given immunity from the feds. Whitey did not explain how this so-called "immunity" would allow him to sell drugs, beat up people, and murder 19 victims. But in Whitey's world up is down and down is up, and never the twain shall meet, unless it's on Whitey's terms.

As soon as it sunk in that Whitey was never going to

tell his side of the story, several relatives of Whitey's victims stood up in court and screamed at Whitey, "You're a coward!"

Another screamed, "You're a rat and a coward!"

*****

At 9 a.m. on Monday, August 5th, U.S. Attorney Fred Wyshak strode up to the podium and addressed the jury with his closing arguments. Sounding like Abe Lincoln giving the Gettysburg Address but not as briefly, Wyshak presented his closing argument for three-and-a-half hours, regaling the jury with Whitey's litany of crimes, and explaining why Whitey must be found guilty on all counts. These counts included murder, extortion, money laundering, illegal firearms possession (the feds found a small arsenal in the walls of Whitey's Santa Monica condo), and the one myth Whitey had always tried to dispel in the streets of Southie – drug distribution.

"This is no Robin Hood story about a man who keeps angel dust and heroin out of the streets of Boston," Wyshak said. "This is about James 'Whitey' Bulger, who is one of the most vicious, violent, and calculating criminals ever to walk the streets of Boston.

"The reason Bulger's racketeering organization was so successful was because these men were survivors of a gang war in the 1960's during which 60 people died. These men were the victors. They were feared. They were armed to the teeth. They were like a paramilitary organization. They had stolen vehicles and back-up cars to crash into police. They used walkie-talkies. They hunted their prey. They hunted people. They were the scariest people walking the streets of Boston."

Then Wyshak dispelled another myth that Whitey had the imprimatur of the federal government to do whatever Whitey pleased, as long as Whitey and Flemmi gave the feds the goods on Boston's Italian mob, the dreaded La Cosa Nostra.

"It does not matter that Mr. Bulger was an F.B.I. informant when he put a gun to Arthur 'Bucky' Barrett's head and pulled the trigger," Wyshak said. "Whether he was an informant or not, he was guilty of murder."

When Wyshak had finished, Whitey's assistant attorney, Henry Brennan, took the podium to present the defense's closing argument. Brennan sang a decidedly different tune than Wyshak, a melody that tried to put the government itself on trial.

Referring to John Martorano and Kevin Weeks, who had cut a deal for themselves in exchange for their testimony against Whitey, Brennan said, "If these men who testified are so bad why are they walking around - walking our streets? Is our federal government protecting us? What have they done? There has to be more to this story. There has been victim after victim who suffered at the hands of these men. The prosecution stands before you and almost brags about tearing down this criminal structure. So why did they let almost all of them go?

"You got to ask yourself - what's going on? Is there something as citizens we're not entitled to know about? There's got to be more to the story."

Between Brennan and Jay Carney, the defense's closing argument lasted two-and-a-half hours. And not once did either lawyer explain why their best defense witness, Whitey himself, did not take the stand to give his side of the story.

It was as if Whitey's statement to the judge - "This is a sham" - was all the explanation the defense needed.

In prosecutor Wyshak's rebuttal to the defense's closing argument, which took thirty minutes, Wyshak said about Kevin Weeks, "Yes, he is a thug, but he never strangled anybody; he never shot anybody."

After the defense and the prosecution had finished their closing arguments, Judge Caspar addressed the jury.

"You must decide which evidence to believe and which

witnesses have been truthful. You can believe some, or all, or none," Judge Casper said.

As for the testimony of killers like Flemmi and Martorano, or thugs like Kevin Weeks, Judge Caspar said, "You must weigh the potential that these witnesses may have had a motive to make up stories. Simultaneously, jurors are advised not to draw inferences from a witness's guilty plea."

Chapter 20
Guilty as Charged

The jury received the case at 11 a.m., Tuesday, August 6th. They were confronted with the task of sifting through mountains of evidence in the 111-page indictment, in which Whitey was charged with 32 counts. In one count alone, Whitey was accused of 33 separate criminal acts.

The jury had heard testimony from 72 witnesses, and they saw 840 exhibits during the two-month trial.

After the jury convened for 5½ hours, the first day of deliberations was over at 4:30 p.m. Since they were not being sequestered, the jurors left for the comfort of their homes.

On the second day of deliberations, the jury started submitting questions to Judge Caspar. One dealt with the statutes of limitations and whether they applied on conspiracy to commit murder.

Judge Caspar told the jury, "All of the charges before you were brought within the applicable statute of limitations."

In other words – no.

Judge Caspar then provided a copy of her written instructions to each of the jurors. She told the jury, "You must go through each of the 33 acts of the one charge, and try to reach a unanimous verdict of 'proved,' or 'not proved.'"

Concerning the racketeering charge (RICO Act), Caspar told the jury they needed to only find the government had proved Whitey had committed two of the criminal acts within a 10-year period.

"You have a duty to attempt to reach agreement on each of the racketeering acts, if you can do so conscientiously." Judge Caspar said.

During the third day of deliberation, the jury asked to see one of the machine guns used as evidence in the case. The gun was a German MP40 submachine gun, which was listed in "possession of firearms", the last charge itemized in Bulger's 32-count indictment. This led some observers to believe the jury was nearing the end of its deliberations.

However, it was not clear if the jury was reviewing the charges in the order they were listed in the indictment or if they had skipped over some charges because they could not come to a unanimous agreement.

Outside the courtroom, Whitey's legal eagle Jay Carney gushed kudos at the jury.

"All Americans can be proud of this jury," Carney told the assembled members of the media. "They have taken their constitutional role with great seriousness and are clearly looking closely at the evidence, evaluating the credibility of witnesses, and applying the instructions given to them by Judge Casper."

Carney said the most he had ever seen a jury deliberate was seven days.

"We've invested at this point more than two years of work getting this case ready for trial," Carney said. "But the longer the jury stays out, the more it shows us that they are as conscientious a jury as I've ever seen."

Patricia Donahue, whose husband Michael was innocently gunned down by Whitey in the Halloran hit, was sitting on pins and needles waiting for the verdict.

"This is probably the worst part of the case - the waiting, the anticipation," Patricia Donahue said. "It's the not knowing."

Guilty as Charged

The fourth day of deliberations was on Friday, August 9th, and by 4:30 p.m. the jury had still not reached a verdict. After emitting a sigh of resignation, Judge Caspar sent the jury home to enjoy the weekend with their families. Judge Caspar did not explain why she did not insist the jury stay the weekend to try to hash out their differences.

On Friday, the only interesting action was when Prosecutor Kelly beseeched the judge to admonish Jay Carney for telling the press the previous day what a great jury he had deciding the fate of his client.

"Your honor, what Mr. Carney told the press yesterday concerning the jury was an obvious attempt to influence them," Kelly said.

Carney had the look of a young innocent on his face.

"But your honor," Carney said. "I was just making a neutral comment, and in no way did I try to influence the jury."

Judge Caspar mulled it over for about the second, and then she decided not to take any action against Carney, not even a slap on the wrist, or an admonishment like, "please don't do that again, counselor."

It was clear Judge Caspar needed the weekend off as much as the jury did.

On Monday, August 12, 2013, the 41st day of the trial and the fifth day of deliberations, the jury finally reached its verdict. Whitey was found guilty of 31 of the 32 counts and guilty of 11 of the 19 murders in the indictment. The only count Whitey was not found guilty of was the alleged extortion of Kevin Hayes, a legitimate ticket broker, who had said he was warned in 1994 he had to pay off Whitey in order to make a living selling legitimate event tickets in Boston.

CNN legal analyst Sunny Hostin said of the verdict, "It's a complete victory for the government."

Whitey was "proved guilty" in the murders of Paulie

McGonagle, Edward Connors, Tommy King, Richard Castucci, Roger Wheeler, Brian Halloran, Michael Donahue, John Callahan, Arthur "Bucky" Barrett, and Deborah Hussey.

The seven murders that were "not proved" were those of Michael Milano, Al Plummer, William O'Brien, James O'Toole, Al Notorangeli, James Sousa, and Francis "Buddy" Leonard.

Inexplicably, there was "no finding" in the death of Debra Davis.

Steve Davis, Debra Davis's brother, was at the trial every day, praying for a guilty verdict in his sister's death. Davis left the court shaking his head.

"It is what it is, but I had to control my anger," Davis said. "I don't believe he hands-on himself killed my sister. But I do know he was guilty of conspiring or taking part in the whole thing. But the 'no finding' is still better than 'not guilty.'"

While tears flowed down both sides of his face, Davis said, "It's not over till I'm in the ground. She knows I'm a fighter."

Davis indicated he will implore the Massachusetts state authorities to reopen the case and charge Whitey with the murder of his sister, Debra. But it's not likely the state will take any action against Whitey because of the numerous guilty verdicts, and also because a new trial would be costly to taxpayers, totaling millions, and maybe even tens of millions of dollars.

Besides, Whitey isn't going anywhere soon; so what's the point?

In stark contrast to Davis's disappointment with the verdicts, Patricia Donahue's tears were ones of joy and satisfaction. Her husband, Michael, was an innocent bystander when Whitey gunned down Brian Halloran in 1982, and Michael was caught in the crossfire.

Guilty as Charged

"It's been a long time coming," Donahue said. "That's a lot of emotions I've been holding in for a long time."

Donahue's son, Thomas, was only a little boy when his father died, and he has spent the rest of his life praying for the day his father's murderer would be brought to justice. Yet, Thomas Donahue said other families were unfairly "robbed of closure."

"He should have been found guilty of everything," Thomas Donahue said. "He's just a sick, psycho individual."

In a separate action, just before the verdicts were announced, Whitey agreed to forfeit the $822,000 in cash and the arsenal of weapons found in his Santa Monica condo when he was arrested in June of 2011. But Whitey was adamant he be allowed to keep the Stanley Cup Championship ring that was given to him by an "unnamed party" - most likely his old fighting hockey friend, Chris Nilan.

Incredibly, the government agreed to Whitey's request.

Whitey's sentencing was set for November 13, 2013, but there is no doubt he will never see life again as a free man outside prison walls.

"There are no sentencing guidelines needed here. He will be in for life," said federal prosecutor Brian Kelly.

U.S. Attorney Carmen Ortiz told the press outside the courtroom, "He will spend the rest of his life in prison, far away from the beaches of Santa Monica and far away from the streets of Boston."

As for people like Steve Davis, who were not satisfied with the verdicts, Ortiz said, "I hope all the families find some degree of comfort in the fact that Bulger is being held accountable for his horrific crimes, even if he were not found guilty of killing their own loved ones."

After the verdict, Jay Carney took the podium outside the courtroom, and he sounded like a lawyer who had just won his high-profile case.

"Jim Bulger was very pleased with how the trial went and even by the outcome," Carney said."

When asked how Whitey, facing life in prison, could be pleased about anything, Carney replied, "Mr. Bulger is pleased because the government corruption was exposed. Mr. Bulger knew as soon as he was arrested that he was going to die behind the walls of a prison, or on a gurney and injected with chemicals. This trial has never been about Jim Bulger being set free."

Carney's assistant Hank Brennan chimed in with, "James Bulger wanted to tell his story from the moment he was arrested. I don't think you've heard the last word from James Bulger."

Those, in themselves, are chilling words.

The statements of Whitey's lawyers began to make a little sense, however, when Carney said Whitey was going to appeal the verdict, on the basis that Judge Caspar did not let Carney use the argument that Whitey had received immunity for his crimes by former federal prosecutor, Jeremiah T. O'Sullivan, who is presently quite dead, and, therefore, quite incapable of testifying in court.

Good luck with that.

As for Whitey's future life behind prison bars, Whitey's former drug dealer, John Shea, who did 12 years for his crimes, told *Fox News*, "Oh God, they cannot let this guy into general population. If he's let loose among the other prisoners, he won't last an hour. They will have to guard him for the rest of his life."

The most satisfying aspect of Whitey's trial, and subsequent convictions, is Whitey will spend the rest of his rotten life, either in a small cell by his lonesome, or in a segregated section of the prison set aside for the lowest of the low, child molesters and other rats like Whitey.

The least satisfying aspect of this debacle is that we, the people of the United States of America, will have our tax dollars shuffled along to the federal prison system to provide Whitey with food and shelter as long as he breathes a rancid breath.

If there were true justice in this case, Whitey would be forced to sit in the federal electric chair. Then, a relative of one of the victims Whitey was found guilty of murdering, could have pulled down the lethal lever, surrounded by the family members of the rest of Whitey's murder victims.

That would have been a proper ending to the life of one of the vilest individuals ever to haunt the earth: James "Whitey" Bulger –The Biggest Rat.

The End

Addendum

The 64-thousand dollar question people have been asking for decades is exactly what culpability does Billy Bulger have in the sad saga of his brother, Whitey.

When Whitey was in prison the first time, Billy surely used his Southie political influence, and his connection to House Speaker John McCormack, to get Whitey more favorable prison conditions, transfers to prisons closer to home, and an earlier release than Whitey merited.

But that's what good brothers do.

In 2002, Billy appeared before the House Committee on Government Reform. When asked if he had any contact with Whitey since Whitey went on the lam seven years earlier, Billy exercised his Fifth Amendment rights against self-incrimination. As a result, Billy lost his well-paying job as the President of the University of Massachusetts.

Again, that's what good brothers do.

Throughout the years, there has been absolutely no proof Billy Bulger did anything illegal concerning his brother. If there had been any evidence indicating criminal activity on Billy's part, he certainly would have been arrested and indicted by now.

So in this humble author's opinion, Billy Bulger is guilty of nothing more than being Whitey Bulger's brother.

Like they say - you can pick your friends, but you can't pick your relatives.

Postscript
What Makes a Rat, a Rat?

Mathew J. Mari – New York City Criminal Attorney for 36 years.

http://www.mathewmarilaw.com/

"The one thing that makes it so hard to believe Whitey was a rat is that his general character and background doesn't fit the bill. Contrary to popular opinion, rats are born and not made.

People think law enforcement 'turns' people into rats by persuading them to 'turn state's evidence,' as the old saying goes. There is a difference between the verb 'rat,' which is what a lot of people do, and the noun 'rat,' which is what a lot of people are.

Real men don't rat because they still have to look at themselves in the mirror. The reason they don't rat is not because of some oath of silence (omerta), or because they are afraid of being killed, but because they simply ARE NOT RATS. The people who rat (the verb) do it because they ARE RATS (the noun). The people who rat were born rats and simply do what they were born to do when the circumstances benefit them.

It's really that simple."

****

Sonny Gerard - *Mob author and former member of organized crime.*

Sonny served seven years in federal prison after being

convicted of racketeering under the RICO statute.

http://sonnysmobsocialclub.com/index.html

"To some degree I agree with Mr. Mari, but not entirely, as it does not explain the large number of rats today compared to the past heyday of the mob.

First, there was a past loyalty based on shared experiences. Guys grew up together in neighborhoods, saved each other from harm, dated each other's sisters, and ate in each other's houses. Today, wannabes grow up in the suburbs. The only person they ever needed to survive was their mothers.

Second, the term 'wiseguys' was coined; not 'stupidguys.' When mob guys see rats are getting book deals, sitting under palm trees with bikini-clad girls next to them, and no one takes them out, the mob guys question their own intelligence.

Yes, there are men who look in the mirror and like what they see: Junior & Allie Boy Persico, John Gotti, and many others who were not bosses. They grew up in a neighborhood where everyone knew everything they did, and everyone despised rats; even while some of them were dry snitches (Lucky Luciano and Meyer Lansky were rats who sent Jake Lansky - Meyer's brother - to the IRS with Waxey Gordon's books to get Gordon out of their hair). Today, society encourages snitching, even on one's parents.

Whitey had the opportunity, through his politician brother, to have the best of both worlds, and he took it. Yes, Whitey probably would have ratted anyway when the opportunity presented itself, as Mr. Mari says. Who knows?

All I know is - I have no problem looking in the mirror while I shave every morning."

I hope you enjoyed reading this book as much as I enjoyed writing it. If you want to be added to my email list, email me at jbruno999@aol.com.

I would also appreciate it if you wrote a short review on Amazon.com at: http://www.amazon.com/Mobsters-Gangs-Crooks-Creeps-Volume-ebook/product-reviews/B0058J44QO/ref=dp_top_cm_cr_acr_txt?ie=UTF8&showViewpoints=1

Just click the button that says "Create Your Own Review," and fire away!

All reviews, positive and negative, will be greatly appreciated. Sometimes I learn more from the negative reviews than I do from the positive reviews, so don't be bashful.

Joe Bruno's *Mobsters, Gangs, Crooks, and Other Creeps* was the runner up in the 2013 eFestival of Words Best of the Independent Book Awards in the category "General Nonfiction."

http://www.efestivalofwords.com/2013-efestival-of-words-winners-t473.html

The complete list of Joe Bruno's true crime books contains:

Mobsters, Gangs, Crooks, and Other Creeps - Volume 1 - New York City (June 2011)

Mobsters, Gangs, Crooks, and Other Creeps - Volume 2 - New York City (December 2011)

Mobsters, Gangs, Crooks, and Other Creeps - Volume 3 - New York City (March 2012)

Mobsters, Gangs, Crooks and Other Creeps - Volume 4 (December 2012)

Mobsters, Gangs, Crooks and Other Creeps - Volume 5 – Girlfriends and Wives (April 2013)

Murder and Mayhem in the Big Apple - From the Black Hand to Murder Incorporated (March 2012)

The Wrong Man: Who Ordered the Murder of Gambler Herman Rosenthal & Why (May 2012)

Mob Wives - Fuhgeddaboudit! (August 2012)

Boxed sets written by Joe Bruno are:

Joe Bruno's Mobsters - Three Volume Set (March 2013)

Joe Bruno's Mobsters - Five Volume Set (April 2013)

Joe Bruno's Mobsters - Six Volume Set (September 2012)

Joe Bruno's Mobsters - Eight Volume Set (April 2013)

Joe Bruno's fiction books include:

Snakeheads: Chinese Illegal Immigrant Smugglers - A Screenplay (June 2013)

Big Fat Fanny: The Biggest Mafia Killer Ever (June 2010)

Both books are available in the two-book boxed-set: **Snakeheads: Chinese Illegal Immigrant Smugglers - A Screenplay and Big Fat Fanny: The Biggest Mafia Killer Ever - A Novel** (2013)

Angel of Death (2000) is available only in the print version.

Bibliography

ABC News.

Associated Press International

Boston Globe.

Boston Herald.

Bulger, William. *While the Music Lasts: My Life in Politics.* Houghton Mifflin. 1996

CBS News.

CNN.com.

Chinlund, Christine, Cullen, Kevin; Lehr, Dick; O'Neill, Gerard. *The Bulger Mystique.* The Boston Globe. 2011.

Cullen, Kevin; Murphy, Shelly. *Whitey Bulger: America's Most Wanted Gangster and the Manhunt That Brought Him to Justice.* W. W. Norton & Company. 2013.

English, TJ. *Paddy Whacked.* Harper Collins. 2005.

Foley, Thomas J., Sedgwick. *Most Wanted, Pursuing Whitey Bulger. The Murderous Mob Chief the F.B.I. Secretly Protected.* Simon & Schuster. 2012

Fox News.

Huffington Post.

Lehr, Dick; O'Neill, Gerard. *Black Mass.* Harper Collins. 2000

Lehr, Dick; O'Neill, Gerard. *Whitey: The Life of America's Most Notorious Mob Boss.* Crown Publishers. 2013

NBC News.

Nee, Patrick; Farrell, Richard. *A Criminal and an*

Irishman. Steerfort. 2007.

New Hampshire Junior Leader.

New York Times.

Weeks, Kevin and Karas, Phyllis. *Brutal*. Harper Collins Publishers. 2006.

Salon Magazine.

Shea, John. *Rat Bastards*. Harper Collins. 2009.

Slate Magazine.

Sun Journal.

The Telegram.

Made in the USA
Charleston, SC
09 October 2013